CYCLONE TAYLOR
A Hockey Legend

CYCLONE TAYLOR

A Hockey Legend

Eric Whitehead

Doubleday Canada Limited, Toronto, Ontario
Doubleday & Company, Inc., Garden City, New York   1977

Library of Congress Cataloging in Publication Data

Whitehead, Eric.
Cyclone Taylor: a hockey legend.

1. Taylor, Fred, 1884–   2. Hockey players—
Canada—Biography.   I. Title.
GV848.5.T39W48   796.9′62′0924   [B]
ISBN 0-385-13063-5
Library of Congress Catalog Card Number 77–70902

1

To my good friend, the subject of this book, without whom the narrative would hardly have been possible; and to my wife, who helped so much with her patience and understanding.

CONTENTS

PROLOGUE

An unseasonably cool dusk had settled over suburban Moscow, and the grounds outside the Lenin Palace of Sports were deserted except for a platoon of Red Army soldiers on the asphalt perimeter.

Attired in their drab gray uniforms with the red lapel tabs, they slouched at-ease in ranks three-deep, on call for what in the Soviet Union is euphemistically termed crowd-control duty. Restive in the autumn chill, the soldiers shifted with the muffled swell of the crowd noises that thrummed through the walls of the arena. Inside, where 14,000 hockey fans were jammed around the brightly lit rink, the din was at an edgy, raucous pitch, and the place reeked with tension.

"*Da da,* Canada . . . *Nyet nyet,* Soviet! . . . *Da da,* Canada . . . *Nyet nyet,* Soviet! . . ."

The roar from the 3,000-strong contingent of Canadians at the North end was more of a challenge than a chant. The answering Russian roar of "Shei-bu . . . Shei-bu!" was angry, defensive.

The hockey fans in Moscow had never before seen anything quite like this aggressive, uninhibited show of Western-style emotion. It puzzled them. They neither understood nor liked it.

It was the same and a lot more so down on the ice, where the passions were rooted in a bitter and sometimes ugly East-West confrontation. There at this moment, Esposito, the Canadian, and Ragulin, the Russian, came crashing together in a corner, players of both teams converged on the scene with sticks high and elbows slashing, and the stands were bedlam.

In his seat midway up the east center section, Frederick Wellington Taylor, O.B.E., otherwise known to millions of Canadians as just plain "Cyclone," showed no signs of emotion other than a tightening of his grip on the black Homburg that lay in his lap. His face gaunt, high-boned, deeply etched with the lines of his eighty-eight years, was expressionless.

A few rows below, in the heavily guarded equivalent of the Western-style royal box, Alexei Kosygin was equally inscrutable.

Yet both the visitor from Canada and the Premier of the USSR were uneasily aware of the tension, which had a strange, brooding, unsettling quality. Certainly, Taylor had experienced nothing quite like it in his own lifetime in hockey as a pioneer and patriarch. He could look down at the Canadian bench and see that the raw nerve ends, frayed by weeks of bitter, gnawing frustration, were at the snapping point.

Harry Sinden had quit the traditional coach's beat behind the bench and was up at the wooden barrier with his players, slamming his fist against the side and screaming epithets at the West German referee, Franz Baader, who slid by, tight-lipped and unheeding.

Sinden's fiery aide, John Ferguson, was up on the emptied bench, arms akimbo, cursing volubly to himself as Phil Esposito lumbered sullenly toward the penalty box. Baader had seen Esposito high-stick Ragulin and bring blood trickling down from a cut under the Russian winger's right eye. Sinden was screaming that Baader had not seen or had chosen not to see Ragulin's holding and elbowing, or the subtly applied Russian kicks that had bruised and lacerated the ankles of his players.

As the gate of the penalty box slammed shut on the glowering, outraged Esposito, the invective increased, now led by a furious John Ferguson, who was up at the barrier with Sinden.

"You chicken-livered Kraut!" he screamed. "You gutless bastard!" He thumped at the boards, and towels came flying onto the ice from the Canadian bench.

The West German official skated up, white-faced, jabbed a finger at Ferguson, indicating a bench penalty, then skated off again. Moments later, Baader's whistle shrilled through the pandemonium that rocked the arena and play was restarted. Deep in trouble, as they had been so many times during this extraordinary series, the Canadians were trying desperately to hang onto a 3–2 lead that just minutes before had been 3–1, and the relentless Russians were again turning it on.

This was Moscow, September 23, 1972, game six of the first historic Team Canada vs. USSR duel.

The blistering eighth game that was destined to cap the most dramatic comeback in hockey history would get the ultimate raves and would always be best remembered, but it was this sixth confrontation, the second game in Moscow after four in Canada that had turned the tide. Lose this one, and the Russians had the series. The two remaining contests would be a meaningless exercise in futility, with the Canadian humiliation complete. The USSR, the new kid on the block, would be No. 1.

Cyclone Taylor had his own private thoughts about these turbulent nights in the Lenin Palace of Sports, and they were mixed.

He admired the swift, fluid style of the Russians and their marvelously disciplined pattern play, graced as it was with all the basic skills of skating and puckhandling. Much of what he saw in them, especially in the electrifying Valeri Kharlamov, was what the fans saw in Taylor himself as he had been seventy—or, Lord, was it a hundred—years ago, when the excitement he generated packed arenas in Ottawa, Montreal, Pittsburgh, Vancouver, and yes, in New York and Boston, long before the birth of the National Hockey League.

He greatly admired the Canadian players for their spirit and fearlessness and free-wheeling abandon, other qualities he could recall firsthand from a long time ago. But he was openly disturbed by the Canadian style's growing accent on unnecessary roughness and disregard for personal discipline, to the detriment of the skills.

It wasn't that he had anything against rough, bruising, bone-rattling hockey, with which he was personally very familiar. His quarrel was with the "chippy" stuff, the elbowing and butting and spearing and the fighting that could become tactical suicide against an able opponent. As he saw it, it demeaned the natural beauty of the sport as it destroyed the effective rhythm of play. In practical terms, as here and now against the cagey Russians, its inevitable by-product of dumb penalties could kill you.

Alexander Yakushev wheeled in, flew down the boards, and then flicked a picture pass to Kharlamov right at the crease. A quick whip of Kharlamov's wrist and the Canadian goalie, Ken Dryden, flat on the ice, looked around for the red light. But it didn't go on.

Wherever the puck may have been a split second before—in

the back of the goal or slipping back off a post—it was now suddenly, somehow, in Dryden's glove, and there was no goal. At full strength now, Team Canada had miraculously survived the double-penalty, and the north end of the arena was again bedlam.

"*Da da,* Canada . . . *Nyet nyet,* Soviet! . . ."

Taylor marveled at the thrill of it all as he surveyed the scene around him, the like of which even he had not seen before and would not likely see again. You could look out there and see where the East ended and the West began—right there in that line in the stands where the drab grays, browns, and blacks of the Russian fans suddenly gave way to the brilliant hues—the reds, blues, greens, and the wild checkerboard patterns—of the Infidels.

It was a sight to see, this scene from a whole new world of hockey, and he marveled too at the stroke of fortune that had brought him here.

It had been just after ten o'clock on that morning, little more than a week ago when the phone rang in his Vancouver apartment. On the line was his old friend Arthur Laing, a former Cabinet Minister who had just that month been appointed to the Senate.

"Cyc," said the Senator, "I'm heading a small informal diplomatic delegation to Moscow for the Team Canada series. I'd like to have you as our guest. Will you come?"

There was a slight pause from the Vancouver end of the line— maybe all of a split second—and then: "Will I come? Arthur, you know I'm no diplomat and I don't own a silk hat, but you bet I'll come. My goodness, yes."

Four days later, Taylor was one of the Laing party of seven who were met at the Moscow Airport by a welcoming party headed by the Canadian Ambassador to the USSR, Robert Ford, and several Soviet dignitaries.

The quarters provided for the Canadian party's stay in Moscow were in two of a settlement of fifteen luxury residences known in the English translation as The Mansions. Tucked into a lovely suburban area in the Lenin Hills, The Mansions had been built by Nikita Khrushchev for his favorite ministers. It was an opulent retreat, the hospitality was lavish, and the service magnificent. And Taylor, as usual in his travels, was accorded a special respect by the Russian hosts.

It was evident here that part of the man's appeal as an enduring celebrity was the general fascination with his age, framed as it was with a sparkling vitality and wry humor. This probably accounted for the rare social note that had appeared in the Communist Party newspaper, *Pravda*, hailing his arrival in Moscow, The note expressed "sincere welcome to the great hockey hero, Mr. Cyclone Taylor, who is 98 years old. . . ."

This was perhaps just an innocent exaggeration born of the quaint Russian obsession with longevity. There are recurrent reports of some humble woodcutter or farmer in some obscure Soviet province who is claimed to have just celebrated his 130th or maybe 140th birthday. Taylor, although certainly a senior citizen, is hard-pressed to match that sort of thing even in myth. He himself had some understanding of the Russians, as he had been here before.

It had been fourteen years earlier that Taylor first visited Russia with a British Columbia Senior A team called the Kelowna Packers. On his return he had penned these prophetic words: "If Canadians don't accept the Russian challenge and put new life in their game, from the junior ranks up, then I would say this: with its intense desire to 'beat the West,' Russia will eventually match and perhaps outclass the best in Canada, and that includes the National Hockey League." How soon would this happen? "Within perhaps a decade—the next ten- or twelve-year span."

Had he been anyone but the patriarch of hockey, widely revered as the game's first superstar, and had he been perhaps twenty years younger, he might well have been stoned in the streets. Instead the reaction of his countrymen ranged from outrage to amused tolerance. Now, before his eyes, the gloomy prophecy was fulfilled.

Down on the ice, the Soviets were boring in on Sinden's embattled penalty killers, sending wave after wave over the blue line, taking crackling hits from Serge Savard and Gary Bergman.

The scoreboard that hung high over the drama of this second game in Moscow still read Kanada, 3; URSS, 2; and the north end of the arena was bedlam as the fans there were up and roaring at a sudden swing of the tide. The Russians had missed their chance to put it away—both the game and the series.

Having miraculously survived the penalties, Team Canada was now forcing the play, and the aroused Canadians were swarming furiously around the Soviet goal as the whistle blew to end the second period.

The game officials were off the ice in a flash, scurrying through the gate at the north end of the rink with Baader out in front, fleeing for the safety of their dressing room.

Quick as they were, Sinden and Ferguson were close behind, accompanied by the ailing star who was here only as a spectator, Bobby Orr. The Canadian fans gaped and cheered wildly as the trio flew up the runway that led under the stands, screaming to get at the retreating officials. Before they could, a swarm of Soviet police providentially closed in and halted the chase.

Taylor sat watching this little drama until it disappeared from his view, and the grim-faced Team Canada players, followed by the stoic Russians also exited up the ramp.

He stayed in his seat a few moments longer, pondering the night's remarkable events. It was like nothing he had ever before seen, or felt. Then as Senator Laing and his party rose to leave, he followed them into the aisle and through a concourse toward the private room provided for the between-periods use of dignitaries.

Premier Kosygin had already left with his party, convoyed by plain-clothesmen of the NKV, the state police.

Enroute to the VIP room, Taylor gazed around the crowded rotunda and recalled his previous visit here in 1958, with the Kelowna Packers. He vividly remembered his amazement and delight in finding that 1907 photo of himself in Ottawa Senators strip hung on a Hall of Fame wall otherwise decorated with the USSR's own hockey heroes. He wondered now if the photo was still there, or if the display had just been a temporary courtesy to mark his first visit.

Around him as he moved past the drably attired Russian fans thronged around the concession stands munching on their fat, steaming sausages, were so many echoes of his thoughts of fourteen years ago, when he had foreseen the Soviet challenge that had surfaced here in 1972.

Arriving at the door of the VIP room, he was met and deferentially ushered inside by a Soviet official. The sparsely furnished area was dominated by a long table laden with a buffet featuring the Russian snack staples of caviar and smoked salmon. There and at smaller tables scattered around the room were generous supplies of that other Soviet staple, vodka.

The president of the Soviet Ice Hockey Association and lesser dignitaries and officials were already there, cocked and ready for any toast that might be proposed. Toasts were and always have been a little awkward for Fred Taylor, a lifetime teetotaler who will go no farther than a glass of ginger ale.

However, there was really nothing to toast, at least not yet, what with the result of this edgy confrontation still in uneasy limbo.

Midway during the rather strained and tentative soiree, the door opened and in came Alexei Kosygin and his party for a surprise visit. Deference immediately became the order of the day, especially among the cluster of Soviet officials. There were introductions, polite small talk, and then there was the top man being introduced to Taylor.

Although Kosygin does speak some stilted English and understands more, he prefers to converse through an interpreter, and to Taylor he said, "You are enjoying the game?"

"To be honest, Mr. Premier," said Taylor, "I'm not quite sure. I hope you'll ask me again later on."

The heavy black brows arched a little and the eyes, usually so somber and calculating, twinkled.

"Why," asked Kosygin, "are you not playing tonight?"

"Mr. Premier," said Taylor, "I'll tell you this: it's not because I don't want to."

Kosygin chuckled appreciatively.

"I'm told that you were a great hockey star in your country."

"Well, Mr. Premier," replied Taylor impishly, "I'm certainly not going to quarrel with you about that."

The Russian chief liked that, and he laughed again.

"But I think," he said, "that was a long time ago."

"Yes," said Taylor softly, "it was. A long time ago."

Chapter One
TARA AND LISTOWEL

The second son and fourth child of Archie and Mary Taylor was born in Tara, Ontario, June 24, 1884. A week later at a family ceremony in the Methodist Church, he was christened "Frederick Wellington."

Although the names do have a lofty ring to them, there is no historic connotation. The ghosts of Frederick the Great and the Duke of Wellington can rest easy. These eminent gentlemen were not the source. Although Taylor didn't discover this himself until sixty years after the fact, the truth is that he was named after the town vet.

"It was a humbling discovery," he smiles, "but as it should be. The names really didn't suit me. The only time they ever seemed to fit was when they appeared one day shortly after the end of World War Two in the King's Honors List, followed in print by 'Member of the Order of the British Empire.' I liked that."

This isn't much of a thing really, this business about the names, but the yarn has remained one of Fred Taylor's favorite bits of trivia because it offers a rare warm glimpse of a father with whom he was never close.

Tara is a small, friendly community tucked cozily between the East shores of Lake Huron and the gentle waters of Georgian Bay. It is a proud, introspective town, and sentimental, especially when it comes to the matter of favorite sons.

Listowel, fifty miles to the south, has occasionally laid claim to Cyclone Taylor because of his boyhood there, but Tara is fond of setting the record straight. It has done so periodically through the years by inviting Taylor back to take part in civic celebrations hailing his birth there.

The Diamond Anniversary party marking his sixtieth year was a very special affair, and Taylor remembers it well, especially his arrival in town.

"I was met at the station and was walking along Main Street with one of the welcoming committee, and there coming slowly toward us on the other side of the street was an old gentleman who seemed vaguely familiar. Perhaps I'd seen him around on other visits.

"I said, 'Don't I know that man?' and my companion said, 'Well, I believe you used to. He certainly knows you, and is always telling us about watching you grow up.' 'Well,' I said, 'I'd sure like to speak with him.' So we crossed the street and as the old fellow drew close, the name came back to me. Doc Thomas. Of course. He was a great friend of my father. The two of them were practically inseparable. They did a lot of fishing together. And drinking. Maybe too much drinking, folks used to say.

"Oh yes. It was a long time ago and I wasn't old enough to remember much, but I remembered.

"Then we were standing together shaking hands, and he just looked at me, all smiles, wagging his head. 'Yes sir,' he said, 'it's been a year or two since I went to Listowel to watch your last game there before you went West and absconded with my name.'

"I must have looked a bit quizzical because he laughed and said, 'Yep, that's me. Frederick Wellington Thomas. Doctor of Veterinary Medicine. Best damn vet in Tara. The only one.'

"Then he told me about this day when he'd gone fishing with my father, and he said he remembered two things in particular: it was blistering hot, and they weren't having any luck. However, they had brought along some liquid refreshment and were about to liven things up when up dashed some fellow with the news that I'd just been born. As Doc put it: 'Well, Archie just dropped his rod, let out a whoop, and headed for home. Just as he set course, I hooked into a fish and I yelled out, "Hey, Arch, I've got me a beauty!" He looked back over his shoulder and shouted something like, 'Okay, Doc, and in honor of the only time you ever beat me to the first fish I'm going to call the kid Frederick Wellington. Whether he likes it or not.'"

Apparently, there had been no serious objection, and the town vet had his place in the hockey history books, courtesy of his fishing and drinking buddy.

Archie Taylor had been born in Clinton, Ontario, of Scotch

parents. He worked as a traveling salesman for the Cockshutt Company of Brantford, manufacturers of farm equipment. Among other lesser items, he sold plows, and he was very good at it, but his job kept him on the road a lot, away from a family that eventually numbered five children.

Fred and the others remembered their father as basically a kind and thoughtful person, but more of a loner than a family man. He was headstrong and moody, and could quickly withdraw into himself and become belligerent.

Fred says, not unkindly, "Unfortunately, he had weakness for drink. That caused trouble at home, and there were times when he was a severe strain on my mother. This always disturbed me, but then he'd be appealingly contrite and we'd try to forget his other moods. He was really a good man at heart. I think the problem was that his job kept him on the road too much, too long away from his family."

Never close to his father, Fred enjoyed a strong bond of affection with his mother, Mary, a slender, handsome woman of gentle nature and deceptively strong will. She was the strong one of the family, the leader. "My mother had a great serenity about her, and a very special understanding of young people. She was deeply religious, yet never preached to us. She just taught us the basic good rules of living by example, and hoped we'd follow them. Within the family, and sometimes it was a troubled one, my mother was just a saint."

Neither Fred's father nor his brother, Russell, older by eight years, were athletically inclined. Two of his three sisters, Harriet and Rosella (the third, Elizabeth) were. Harriet became an outstanding skater, and Rose, the baby of the family, played hockey well enough to organize and star on her own team during the years in Listowel.

In Tara, the Taylors lived in a white frame four-bedroom house just three blocks from the Methodist Church. Fred shared one of the bedrooms with his brother. The whole family, except for Archie when he was off selling plows or fishing with the town vet, attended church regularly. That meant three times each Sunday, including Sunday school. Mary Taylor saw to that. In her mind, the church and the home were inseparable, and there was constant involvement in church activities, especially in the church concerts and Christmas plays.

Fred recalls that he once played a cowboy, another time an angel. He remembers once being late for a Christmas play—hadn't dressed properly and was the only angel without a halo. "I'm sure," he says, "the minister was convinced this was a sign that I was headed for damnation."

Of all the Taylor children, none more than Fred grew and lived in her image. Bound to his mother's beliefs and perhaps influenced by the problems that grew out of his father's drinking, he has himself never smoked or drank, or even so much as cussed—give or take the odd "dammit." To his fellow tradesmen along the notoriously indelicate hockey trail, this would become not only a thing of wonder but also at times a matter of acute frustration and aggravation.

There is an account of a 1906 hockey game in Houghton, Michigan, down in the rough-and-rowdy International League (the sport's first professional circuit) that illustrates this point. After what Taylor considered a rather dubious call by an official, he skated alongside the fellow, engaged him in a long, malevolent glare, and then just glided silently away. The referee was plainly nettled by the maneuver and stood there for a moment just scratching his head. He then chased aimlessly after the retreating figure, wagging his finger. He was still fuming at Taylor's heels when Fred coolly popped in the winning goal.

As the poor chap explained afterward to a reporter: "That bleeping Taylor gave me that bleeping glare of his and didn't open his bleeping mouth. I knew what he was bleeping thinking, but I couldn't bleeping prove it."

It was just before Fred's seventh birthday when Archie Taylor pulled up roots and resettled the family in nearby Listowel, to be a little closer to the Cockshutt headquarters. Still, there had been time in Tara for a unique and uniquely warm adult-child friendship with a young man named Jack Riggs, the town barber. Riggs, then just into his twenties, operated a little shop on Main Street and was famed throughout the region as an outstanding speed skater. He used to spend the winter evenings on the pond down near the river, watched by the village youngsters.

One of these was Fred Taylor, barely past five years old when he first sat wide-eyed in the snow, entranced by the smooth sweep of the barber's long, gliding strides.

There came an evening, late in young Fred's fifth winter, when he himself ventured out onto the pond, wearing an outsize pair of his sister Harriet's clamp skates. This, in its wobbly way, in the comic fashion of earnest, floundering five-year-olds, was the beginning of Cyclone Taylor, hockey superstar. He remembers it well.

"I just had to get out there and try it, and one day I pinched my sister's skates and ran out with them. I got the dickens for it afterward, but it was worth it. I'd had my first great adventure. It was a marvelous feeling."

From that first clandestine outing on the pond, Fred and the barber became warm friends. Thereafter, thanks to a generous loan arrangement with Harriet, Fred joined Riggs for evening sessions that included a strict teaching program based on the fundamentals of good skating, an art that he himself had so well mastered. Unconcerned with the wide gap in their ages, the village barber was a marvel of patience that seemed born of a sincere affection for his young pupil. Taylor has never forgotten.

"My, that man was kind to me. He taught me to skate there on the pond and then later took me out on the river where he'd pace me. He'd get ahead and make me stretch out just enough to give me confidence."

The barber and his sturdy little friend became a familiar sight on the ice during the long, cold Tara winter evenings when the shop was shut and supper at the Taylor house was over.

It was Riggs who gave Taylor the first skates he ever owned. They were a late present for this sixth birthday. Like those of his sister, they were clamp skates. Fred had seen them on display in the hardware store. They cost $2.50, and in those days, that was a lot of money for a Tara barber. It was at least a couple of days' wages.

Riggs had brought the skates from his shop and was waiting with them when his protégé arrived after an early supper. Fred put aside his sister's skates, sat in the snow to put on the new ones and then slid out onto the pond "feeling like a young millionaire." There was never, not even during the halcyon days when he fashioned whole evenings of thrills for both himself and his fans, a feeling quite like that.

A bond was struck that was to stay with him all his life. As Taylor was to say a full eighty-six years after that marvelous evening: "Jack Riggs was a very important person in my life. I have never forgotten him and his patience and his kindness. Although I didn't know what a hero was in those days, I guess he was my first."

Taylor's next skating was done on another river, the Maitland, a stream that skirted the downtown area of Listowel.

When the Taylors arrived in Listowel in late 1891, the stream was frozen over, offering a fine sixteen-mile stretch of ice along its snow-girt banks to the town of Wingham. This was a route that was to become well known to Taylor as he built up his legs and his wind and developed the speed that was to be his trademark throughout his eighteen years in top class hockey.

In those days, the Maitland often overflowed its banks during the spring rainy season, flooding the downtown streets. The stream was subsequently rerouted to stop the damage, and although it continued to dry to a trickle in the heat of summer it was always back up the banks in time for the first freeze and the long, lusty skating season.

Just off the banks of the Maitland was a pond that was used as a skating rink. It was called the Piggery because it was situated next to the town *abattoir*. It was never considered the choicest of Listowel properties, especially when the wind blew in from the direction of the slaughterhouse.

The Piggery was not the only skating rink in town. There was another one. The big, fancy one, named, logically enough, the Listowel Arena. This was the home of the area's top hockey club, the Listowel Mintos. The team, of junior class, competed in informal league made up of neighboring clubs before eventually moving up under the banner of the prestigious Ontario Amateur Hockey League.

The arena was the haunt of Listowel's more affluent youth, a group that did not include Fred Taylor. "We were a poor family. My father earned no more than maybe fifty or sixty dollars a month, and with five kids to keep, it was a tight squeeze. Listowel certainly wasn't a snobbish town, but some folks were better off than others, and there were social distinctions. I suppose you'd have to say that the Taylor family was from the wrong side of the tracks."

For the town's young hockey players, the wrong side of the tracks meant the Piggery, and that's where young Fred and his friends learned the game. "It wasn't much, but it was all we had, and it looked beautiful to us on a crisp winter's day with a good firm freeze and a light fall of snow on the ice. It wasn't much bigger than a rink, although it daren't call itself that. It was just a small, shallow body of water formed by a dam that had been built alongside the river bank, and it retained just enough water for us to skate on.

"I've played on a few rinks since that one, and been on a few others, but there was nothing grander than the Piggery in its time and place. I can still feel that tingle in the nostrils and that sweet bite in the air as we stepped out onto the ice and just cruised around a while with our sticks, like lords of the manor. With all their fancy trappings today in their million-dollar arenas, I swear that today's kids don't have it as good. At least, they can't have it any better."

There were, of course, occasional visits to the Listowel Arena, but only for an awed look at the roofed elegance that accommodated 1,200 fans for the Mintos games. This was a world that seemed far beyond the reach of the gang from the Piggery.

There were other diversions for a healthy youngster like Taylor, who from the beginning had an insatiable lust for competition of any kind. In the spring and summer there was soccer and lacrosse and baseball, and even a little cricket. He played all four, and well, with a special talent for baseball that he never quite had time to develop. He settled for an avid scrutiny of reports from the National League down to the south, where the stars of that period just before the turn of the century were budding legends like Wee Willie Keeler, Honus Wagner (known as "The Dutchman"), and the boisterous third-baseman of the Baltimore Orioles, John J. McGraw.

Throughout his teens, Taylor did find time to excel at both soccer and lacrosse, and led Listowel teams to Ontario championships in both sports.

For other recreation, there was also that wonder of the age, the nickelodeon movie machine. In the 1890s, Listowel got its first, in an establishment then known as a Kinetescope Parlor. It was situated in a remodeled store in the downtown area. For a nickel a fellow could be entertained and uplifted by such spicy epics as, "The Gayety Girls," "Lady Fencers," and "Madame Rita."

Another modern delight available to the young swingers of Listowel in the nineties was the Tonophone, an ornate contraption that could be decently described as the granddaddy of the jukebox. It was an automatic player piano, also activated by a nickel-in-the-slot. There was no Top Fifty then, but had there been, stirring ballads like, "Won't You Fondle Me?" "Shame on You," and "Moonlight on the Watermelon Vine" would surely have made the list.

Such were the sin spots of early Listowel, which Taylor claims he rarely patronized, although not altogether because he was unappreciative of the arts. Nickels were hard to come by in the Taylor household.

"Anyway, we kids had our own amusements. Our favorite hangout was Livingstone's Drugstore on Main Street. There, you could buy hokey-pokey (that's ice cream in cups; there were no cones then) and ice-cream sodas. They were two for a nickel, and the girls bought their own. But it was outside the store, on the corner, where the action was.

"Almost everything that happened in downtown Listowel—and the business section was only a couple of blocks long—happened on that corner. I suppose we were the first of the drugstore cowboys, and we'd gather there in the evenings and just wait for the world to go by. Traveling men used to set up their stands there to sell their patent medicines and fancy gadgets, and when the minstrel show came through once a year they'd put on a couple of acts there before setting up in McDonald's Music Hall just down the street. The touring Chatauqua shows did the same before putting up their big tent in the park on Mill Street."

"Then, too, on the warm summer evenings—and, come to think of it, on the cold winter ones—there were the Salvation Army Band concerts, with the band playing and people singing. The kids used to join in the singing, and sometimes I'd help pass the hat. But I guess we mostly got fun out of just hanging around together, enjoying each other the way teen-agers do. Once in a while there'd be a good fight, usually over a girl, but nobody ever got hurt much.

"We never had any trouble with the police, or vice versa. Not much anyway, and none that comes to mind now. There was never any real mischief, maybe because there wasn't time for any. We were always home by nine and in bed very shortly after.

"There were just two policemen in town, and they were respected. One was on night duty, and the other was on patrol during the day. We knew him just as Mr. Osborne, and he was well liked. We played baseball and football on a vacant lot next to the Baptist Church, and he'd often stop during his rounds to watch.

"His busiest time was in the evening, when he had to tend the street lights. They were carbon lamps, and each light had a cluster of two electric globes. He had to check them all every evening and change them as they burned out.

"I suppose there was juvenile delinquency of a kind, but what there was was pretty mild stuff by modern standards. But then it was a pretty mild way of life by modern standards. There were very few temptations and diversions—of course, not even television or radio—and our taste was for the simple things because it had to be. It made things a lot easier for the parents. Discipline then was no great problem."

"We had two weekly newspapers in town, the *Standard*, and the *Banner*—the latter is still going strong. And two Toronto papers, *The Globe* and *The Mail & Empire* arrived each day around noon, and you would buy them for two cents each at Livingstone's Drugstore. If we wanted news faster than that, there were always the two telegraph offices, the one downtown and the one at the railroad station. People preferred to go to the one downtown on any special news because the bulletins called out by the telegraph operator didn't run the risk of being drowned out by the arrival or departure of a train.

"It was a great place to be during things like the Stanley Cup games, when hundreds would gather there to get the latest bulletins. The mobs would hang around at night in sub-zero weather just waiting for the operator to leave his key and come dashing out with an announcement. He'd appear in his shirt and arm-bands and celluloid eye-visor and there'd be a sudden hush as he'd clear his throat and cry out something like: 'Ottawa has just scored, and the game is now tied . . .' and there'd be loud cheering. He'd chalk up the score on a blackboard, and then go back into his office, and we'd just stand there and talk hockey and wait for the next bulletin."

"I was there with a huge crowd on an evening in 1901, and that was one of the sad times outside the downtown telegraph office. On that night, the operator came out slowly with his visor in his hand and told us that Queen Victoria had died. People cried, and for minutes after the announcement they just stood there, silent. Then one by one and in little groups they left and went quietly home.

"Oh yes, we were very empire conscious, and we had a great affection of the Royal Family. I remember in 1897, when Queen Victoria celebrated her fiftieth year on the throne, we were all called together at school and presented with a commemorative jackknife. I don't know why they—it was a gift of the Federal Government—picked a jackknife, but it was very nice. For the boys, anyway. They also gave us a half holiday, and there was no quarrel with that.

"I suppose the most exciting happening that I remember, apart from some of those hockey and lacrosse and soccer games, was the time the first automobile came to town.

"That was, I think, in the summer of 1896, when I was twelve. The car belonged to Mr. J. C. Scott, who was the manager of a private bank. There'd been no autos in Listowel up to then, although we knew of them being in Toronto and Ottawa and such places. All our local transportation was by horse and buggy, although you could easily walk anywhere and back.

"Mr. Scott's new car was an Oldsmobile, and it was quite a sensation. It arrived on a Sunday afternoon, and every kid in town and most of their parents turned out to see it. Mr. Scott was at the wheel of the contraption, which seemed all wheels and wheezes. He was dressed in the approved motoring style: floppy cap, goggles, a muffler around his neck, and a long, white dustcoat.

"There he came, snorting along Main Street with everybody waving and cheering, and of course, he stopped in front of Livingstone's Drugstore and we all crowded around, oohing and aahing and touching.

"Mr. Scott was proud as punch, and after a refreshment, he started off again for a run along Main Street, which was just a dirt road, and very dusty. He had a little trouble with the cranking, but he finally got it going and off it went with a great snort and a jerk, with us kids in pursuit. We wanted to see how long we could stay with the auto, and we'd gone nearly a mile before it pulled slowly away with Mr. Scott looking back and waving through huge thick clouds of dust. We walked back to town and then went home and had a bath."

In the wintertime, with the air chilled and the nights drawn in, there was no doubt as to the number one excitement in town—certainly for young Fred Taylor—and that was hockey at the Piggery. There, the game was played with crude clubs of ash or elm for sticks and any old object from a tin can to a stone for a puck. It was primitive, but it was rousing, heady stuff, and for the learners there was a very special art in mastering the rutted ice surface and caroming an old tomato can off a snowbank.

For the Taylor boy there was also—almost—boxing.

Knowing her son's constant need for venting his enormous energy, Fred's mother did a curious thing for a lady of such gentle qualities. She bought him a set of boxing gloves and a punching bag for his twelfth birthday. He was already well-muscled and sturdy, well on toward the eventual modest dimensions of 5'8", 165 pounds that so many big, tough head-hunting defensemen would find so stunningly deceptive.

Delighted with the surprise gift, he rigged up the bag in the attic and spent the odd hours pounding away with his new gloves. He went at it with typical abandon, and for a while it looked as though Archie and Mary Taylor had a budding pugilist on their hands. The prospect didn't bother his father, who at best took a very casual view of life.

Mary Taylor had different thoughts about the thudding noises from the attic. She began to have grave qualms about her choice of gifts, but said nothing about it. It was not until many years later that she confided to Fred that she had been worried sick that he might turn to pugilism for a living.

But the Listowel winters came too soon and stayed too long

for that to happen. They offered their sweet gift of hockey, and that was enough for young Taylor. Eventually, the punching bag came down and the boxing gloves were put away for good.

Curiously, although the young Taylor had summarily rejected the pugilistic arts as a means of making a living, he would the next summer meet up with a youth from nearby Hanover who was fated to become Canada's first and to this date only heavyweight boxing champion of the world. This meeting came in the summer of 1898, during a lacrosse game in Hanover between the home club and Taylor's team from Listowel.

It was a meeting in the most basic sense of the word. Taylor and the Hanover youth, Noah Brusso, collided in a race for the ball and collapsed to the turf at mid-field. Brusso, then a stocky, thick-necked boy of seventeen, three years Taylor's senior, was the first one up, but slowly. Taylor followed him up, more slowly. There was a cool, tentative nod from each, and off they went again, back to the battle. They met again several times in subsequent games and developed a mutual respect for each other.

At the time of that first thumping hello in Hanover, neither boy dreamed that within two years Brusso would turn to prize fighting, change his name to Tommy Burns, win the world heavyweight title, and then lose it in a bloody brawl with a ferocious black man named Jack Johnston down in far-off Sydney, Australia.

Taylor's winters on the ice of the Piggery were numbered. In that rough-and-tumble world of hockey where science was a make-shift thing, the blossoming genius of the Taylor boy somehow shone through. With his swift, sure-footed style and the quick moves of a prairie jack rabbit, he was clearly the class of the neighborhood, and word got around.

The word was that Taylor was not only a player of unusual skills for one so young, but that he was also tough and resilient. In that company, in those conditions, with so many of the other players bigger and stronger, he had to be.

Taylor was thirteen when he received a visit from a Mr. Elwood Hacking, proprietor of the town drugstore. Hacking was also an official of the Listowel Mintos, who were in need of a good center. Somebody had told the druggist that the Taylor boy was it, and after one eye-filling scouting trip to the Piggery, he agreed.

He asked Fred to go with the Mintos on their next trip, for a game in Palmerston, twenty-six miles away.

The team traveled to Palmerston by train, and for the new center, two or three years younger than the others, it was like a trip to the moon. There were nearly a thousand people packed into the arena, and the entire game ritual, from start to finish, was a new experience for Taylor. This was his first venture in organized hockey, in an official league game.

Like the Piggery contests, the game lasted one hour, split into two thirty-minute periods. The eventual standard structure of three twenty-minute periods was still fourteen years away.

In this first contest under league conditions, the Listowel rookie made himself right at home. Although the Palmerston team had heard that the new kid was good, they didn't know how good until they watched him coolly shake off his checks for three goals in a 5–2 Listowel victory. In a sense, it was a curious display, as Taylor just simply went out and did it his way, on his own. Nor could his older, bigger teammates have kept with him stride for stride had he wanted them to. In that first game in a formal league, speed was his instant trade-mark.

His new teammates had been a little aloof on the train ride to the game, but they gave the new boy lots of attention on the ride back. The Taylor kid had made it to the other side of the tracks. He was on his way up.

In that Palmerston game, Taylor had played the full sixty minutes, as had all of the other players. That was the way of hockey then and for the next couple of decades, until the practice of frequent substitutions became the vogue and changed the whole early nature of the game.

A hockey squad then, and until the substitution rule began running amok, rarely consisted of more than eight players: one for each of the seven positions plus one spare. That system was perfect for Taylor, whose speed was matched only by his stamina, plus a couple of cute tricks he would learn to help him steal a breather when he needed one. Like flicking the puck into the crowd. Later on, they put a new rule in the books to stop that.

There is no record of game scores and goals scored during his five seasons with the Mintos. In the after years, Taylor had no reliable recollection of his statistical performance in that period, but newspaper accounts are unanimous in the judgment that by the time Fred was sixteen, he was the league's best player and its most prolific scorer.

What Taylor did long remember was the move into the new world of the Listowel Arena and the trappings of a sport that he lived and breathed, and knew to be without a doubt the world's most beautiful and most exhilarating pastime. He was awed by the Listowel crowds, by their enthusiasm, and their own unbounded love for the game.

"The fans then were an amazingly hardy lot, and they had to be. In those days of more than seventy-five years ago, it seemed that the winters were much colder and longer than they are now. The wind would howl and the temperature would get down way below zero, but out they'd come in the bitter cold, packing those draughty arenas, and loving every minute of it. They came on foot, by train, in sleighs and cutters, dressed in furs and mufflers, and sat huddled under blankets. And they'd stay right to the end. They rarely left before the final whistle. During the ten-minute break between periods they'd drink coffee at a nickel a cup and be all ready—just as we players were—for the last thirty minutes. We at least had the comfort of a pot-bellied stove in our dressing room, if little else.

"No, there were no showers, nor," he adds in wry reference to one of today's standard pieces of dressing-room equipment, "hair-dryers."

"And as to the enthusiasm of those fans, well, there is simply nothing like it now. Those crowds didn't need any organs or horns or flashing signs to whip up their fervor. They were just simply crazy about hockey, and were as much a part of every game as we players were.

"Whoop it up? Well, I'd say that when those Listowel crowds of twelve hundred let loose, the noise decibel level was every bit the equal to that of, say eighteen thousand fans in the Montreal Forum. And they can get pretty noisy."

This last bit may be a bit of an exaggeration, but Taylor in his recollections of so long ago is entitled to a little poetic license. And he stands by his point about the gut enthusiasm and the spontaneous response of those early fans as being above and beyond that of the game's later and more sophisticated era.

"Sometimes on those mean winter nights, I'd look at those packed stands and I'd say to myself, 'Why are they here? Why do they come out on a night like this?' But of course, I knew why. They simply loved hockey. And in those days there was a very close bond between the player and the fan. Maybe one of the reasons was that they shared the discomforts."

Taylor was sixteen and going strong with the Mintos when he met up with another man who was to have a great impact on his future. He was Norval Baptie, a muscular youth five years older than Taylor. Born in Bethany, Ontario, of Irish stock, he was raised in North Dakota, where he learned to skate. He learned well enough to whip world speed-skating champion Jack McCulloch in a match race in Winnipeg when he, Baptie, was just fifteen.

Between then and the time he first crossed paths with Taylor in Listowel in 1889, Baptie had become established as the world's foremost speed skater, and held world records at many distances. He was already well on his way to winning a remarkable career total of more than 3,000 races on courses measuring from 200 yards to five miles. Baptie was also a showman who eventually expanded his art of pure speed into such variations as figure skating, barrel jumping, stilt skating, and other stunts.

One of these stunt offerings was an exhibition of speed skating backward. It was part of the act he developed for his annual barnstorm tours of Ontario, Quebec, and the prairie provinces, and he brought it with him to Listowel on his first date there in 1899.

Acting as his own promoter, publicity man, ticket taker, and one-man cast, he set up his show in the Listowel Arena, charged $.15 admission, and played to his usual packed house.

The Listowel Mintos team, including Taylor, were in the stands, and when Baptie announced that he would give a pair of skates to anyone who could beat him over a quarter-mile skating forward while he, Baptie, skated backward, the Mintos boys pushed Taylor onto the ice.

The crowd roared its encouragement. He was the fastest skater in town, and if anyone could handle this Baptie fellow, Taylor could.

That was another night that stayed fresh in Taylor's mind throughout the years. "I was awed by Baptie. He was the first world champion of any kind we'd ever seen. But I was pretty fast, and I guess the people figured I should be able to go faster forward than he could backward. I certainly thought so, but then I always did think I could beat the other fellow, no matter what. It was my way. I don't think I'd have been worth a pinch of salt without it."

So the two of them lined up for the race. The starter was the promoter, Baptie.

In a sense, it was shades of those other winter nights in Tara a decade before with that other speed skater, Jack Riggs. But this time the tutor was a professional and a world champion, and his business was winning, not teaching. Especially with a six-dollar pair of boot skates at stake.

Baptie demanded a thirty-foot start, and that seemed fair enough. Taylor still figured to catch and pass him long before they'd completed a quarter-mile.

"We hadn't made two circuits of the rink before I tumbled to his strategy. Each time I'd get close enough to pass, he'd swing out just enough to block me off. Just a little shift and a subtle move of his hips, and he'd bump me off stride and I'd drop back a little. Right away I began to appreciate and comprehend the art of skating backward. The trick was not the speed but the balance and the maneuverability. Baptie was a master at it, and I was completely fascinated. Right then and there I told myself I was going to learn to become as good at it as he was. I could see its value to a hockey player."

Baptie won the race and kept the skates to offer again at the next stop. Afterward, he and Taylor talked about skating, and when the traveler pocketed his take and went on his way, Fred went to work mastering the business of skating backward.

Before that winter was out he, too, was issuing challenges, and beating all comers. When Baptie returned with his show the next year, he added a local attraction to his Listowel program: Fred Taylor, the Listowel Flash, in his backward-skating challenge

race. Baptie still took all the proceeds, but Taylor shared the
bows.

By now, the young entrepreneur had added barrel jumping
and stilt skating to his act. He was developing a new style of ice
entertainment from which would eventually become the spectacular ice revues of a later era. It was Baptie who in the thirties
directed the Madison Square Garden extravaganza starring the
glamorous Norwegian world figure-skating champion, Sonja
Henie. That was the start of a spectacular ice show and movie
career than would earn Sonja Henie more than $20 million, then
the greatest sum ever reaped by a sports figure.

In 1963, Sonja and the man who taught Fred Taylor to skate
backward became the first two to be named to the U. S. Skating
Hall of Fame.

Later, both Taylor and Baptie would enter the Canada Sports
Hall of Fame, and there is little doubt that the Baptie influence
helped Taylor get there.

With his mastery of the special art of skating backward—an
art he has always insisted is woefully overlooked by hockey
players who want to develop their maximum skills—Taylor
became the complete artisan. Quite apart from his Godgiven
speed, hockey has rarely if ever seen a more masterful skater.

Taylor seemed to have an affinity for athletes destined to become Hall of Famers. Baptie was one of these, and Noah Brusso,
alias Tommy Burns, the prize fighter, was another. Two others—
and all were from that fertile area within little more than a sixty-
mile radius of Listowel—were Fred's long-time Listowel school
chum, Cal Bricker, and the Indian lad named Tom Longboat.

Bricker, who was Taylor's age, excelled in track and field. He
left Listowel to win the All-Round Track and Field Championship of Toronto in 1905 (the year Taylor was to turn professional) while attending university. Before eventually turning to
his career in dentistry, Bricker earned his ticket into the Canada
Sports Hall of Fame as a competitor in the Olympic Games.

Even in his early teens when Tom and Taylor first met in track
competitions around Listowel, Longboat seemed destined for
greatness as a runner, and Fred had an athlete's special admiration for the marvelously fluid style that would eventually take
the Indian youth to the peaks of adulation, and down again.

They met for the first time in the deep summer of 1899, when Longboat traveled up from his home on the Onandaga Reserve near Brantford for a town festival. Fred was sixteen, Tom thirteen. These were the last months of the old century. The Governor-General of Canada then was Lord Minto, fated to be remembered less for his statesmanship than for his patronage of the Minto Cup, then the symbol of the Canadian lacrosse championship. The Premier was Sir Wilfrid Laurier, who had just recently hosted his United States counterpart, President William McKinley, in Ottawa.

In Britain, Queen Victoria lay gravely ill, shortly to bequeath her crown to that likeable royal rounder, Edward Albert, Prince of Wales, patron of England's last glorious fling at opulence, the Edwardian Age. In Russia, the Czar was Nicholas the Second, and the peasants were still a revolution and a few wars away from Hockey Night in Moscow.

None of this meant much to the young star of the Listowel Mintos and his friends. Hockey was the name of their game.

But there is one part of those turn-of-the-century days that Cyclone does remember well, and this, curiously, had to do with the Boer War in South Africa. It may have been the highly romanticized story of the capture and escape of the dashing young British officer, Winston Churchill, that had brought the distant conflict to the special attention of the youth of Listowel, but whatever it was they were certainly fascinated by it.

"We read all we could lay our hands on about the war in South Africa, and events like the relief of Mafeking were just like marvelous adventure stories. Then when we heard that Lord Strathcona was looking for recruits for his Strathcona Horse Brigade to go down there and fight the Boers, a whole group of us kids decided we wanted to enlist. I suppose the idea was just to get to South Africa for some of that wonderful adventure we'd been reading about. But the main recruiting was in Regina, and our big problem was how to get there.

"Then one day our mothers heard talk of what we were up to and they clamped down in a hurry. The war just had to go on without us."

One seventeen-year-old, whose name is long forgotten, did make it to the Listowel railway station with his suitcase packed, but got no farther. Upon learning that $2.00 wouldn't get him to Regina and that no amount of pleading would lower the prevailing rail rates, he went back home, arriving just in time for supper.

Another of the so-called romantic figures of that distant conflict was the British officer Lord Robert Baden-Powell, the hero of the battle for Mafeking. For some reason he didn't quite understand, the war adventures of Baden-Powell held a special fascination for Taylor.

"Maybe it was the ring of the name, or the almost make-believe quality of the stories we read about him in the papers that came in from Toronto, but I could never hear enough about the man. I never dreamed that he would have a very great influence on my future."

After the end of Boer War in 1901, Baden-Powell had stayed on to organize the South African Constabulary. He had later returned to England, and in 1907 he founded the Boy Scout movement that was to become world-wide. The sixteen-year-old Fred Taylor had no way of knowing back there at the turn of the century that eight years later, just one year after the birth of Baden-Powell's amazingly popular brain-child he would help organize and become scoutmaster of Ottawa Troop No. 7 and begin a life-time involvement in the Scout movement.

But how did a boy growing up in a little Ontario town view the approach of that epic event—after all, there had been but eighteen like it since the beginning of Christianity: the turn of a century? What indeed, went on in Listowel on the evening of December 31, 1899, there at the edge of a new era?

Queried about this three quarters of another century later, Fred Taylor scratched his brow, pondered, and then had to admit that he really didn't remember too much about it. And that maybe there really wasn't a great deal to remember. "Nobody seemed to think of it as something special, and it was the usual fun sort of New Year's Eve for us teen-agers. I know we were out on the streets, roaming around and ringing bells and blowing horns and such things that the kids did then on New Year's Eve.

"But at midnight? Where was I then? Well, I guess I was down at the rink, skating. The rink had lights, and people always gathered there at night. That's where the fun was. Yes, I'm sure that's where I was at midnight 1899."

Where else and what else for the young Taylor boy, even as the last tremulous stroke of twelve sent a wondering universe tumbling into another age? To each his own universe, and at that time his was the world of the ice rink, where hockey was played, by kids like himself.

In that winter of 1900–1, Taylor was in his fourth season with the Mintos. The team had now left its informal parochial circuit and entered the new Northern League to compete within the powerful structure of the Ontario Hockey Association.

With Taylor dominating the play at center, the Mintos won the championship of the league in its first season.

It was excellent schooling for players of ambition, as the quality of competition was just a step below that of the tough senior brand of hockey that was flourishing in Montreal, Toronto, Kenora, Ottawa, Portage la Prairie, and points west to Winnipeg.

The game was spreading and flourishing, but by later standards the rules and the equipment and the general trappings of the vigorous pastime were pretty crude. They were less so by the time Taylor quit Listowel and moved up to senior hockey in 1904. Along the way, he was credited with inspiring and spreading the newfangled fashion of padded uniforms to provide some protection against injuries.

The innovation was at first regarded with some disdain as sort of an affront to masculinity—much as the reaction to the plastic-helmet fad decades later—and it wasn't popular. But the idea obviously made common sense, and Taylor was then and always has been a common-sensical fellow. Also, as he was invariably the lightest player on the ice—and was just as invariably the faster—he was a marked man.

To at least muffle the bruising checks that slipped past his own natural armor of speed and guile, he had his mother sew layers of felt into his underclothes, particularly around the shoulders and the lower back. Then he went a step farther and had bone stays, as those used in lady's corsets, sewn into his canvas pants to protect the thigh muscles.

"My first fitting was in our parlor, and believe me I had the curtains drawn. Some of the so-called tough guys would have laughed had they then been able to look inside and see me tucking those stays into my pants, but it was I who had the laugh when I went out onto the ice."

The padding, with the bone stays as an extra refinement, offered excellent protection, and as it was very light it did nothing to detract from Taylor's speed. On the contrary, with the confidence of a little protection, he was flying faster than ever.

The other players took note, and in the ensuing weeks after Taylor's first bone stays fashion show there was a heavy run on felt padding in the Listowel area, and no lady's corsets were safe. It was, in fact, the beginning of the elaborate protective equipment now the vogue at all levels of hockey, most recently topped off by the plastic helmets that were first made widely familiar by the Russians.

The sticks of young Taylor's day were sturdy, broad-bladed clubs of elm. The best, as used by the Listowel Mintos, were made by McNeece and Orchard of Montreal. The sticks, varying only in length, were given free to the top players, with their names inscribed, as today.

By 1900 the skates were already mostly tubular, attached to boots lightly reinforced with steel toe plates. Taylor recalls the first of these skates coming out of Winnipeg, made by a fellow named Tom Hooper.

The rinks themselves were all of natural ice, most of them lit by clusters of carbon arc lamps. There were no line markings, not even at center ice. A mark at the side of the rink indicated approximately where the puck would be dropped for face-offs. There were boards on the perimeters of the rink, but they were squared at the corners, requiring a pretty cute technique for off-the-board passes.

Before 1900 there was no goal marking at the entrance to the net, which was at first simply a pair of horizontal pipes and then eventually a cage of iron pipe and chicken wire—placed unanchored on the ice.

With the arrival of the nets, and still no goal-line marking, a goal was called when the puck hit the back of the net.

This could be a pretty tricky call that lent itself to some pretty tricky use, especially by officials working before a hometown crowd that could occasionally be loosely classified as biased.

There were just two types of officials: the referee and the goal judge. The latter stationed himself just behind the net, wrapped in sweater or overcoat and wearing rubbers. During an attack on goal his was by far the most perilous perch in the house. There was just six feet of ice between the back of the net and the boards, and that area could get to be pretty violent territory, with the man in the rubbers caught in the middle. "I've often marveled," Taylor has mused, "how those goal judges escaped getting killed. Some of them almost were."

One of these was an heroic chap who was working a big game between Listowel and Maitland in the latter's outdoor rink. He was at his post behind the Maitland goal when Taylor came flying around on one of his patented moves to break out and across the goal mouth for a shot from close in. The trapped goal judge was just lightly dislodged by a fast-moving Taylor hip and was then caught full beam by a burly Maitland forward who was in mad pursuit of the Listowel Flash. There was a resounding thud and the official went tumbling clear over the boards and into a snowbank beyond.

He landed face down, and the poor man, obviously stunned, came close to suffocation before some fans raced up to pull him out. But not before they had watched in dismay as Taylor swept across the goal mouth to tuck in the go-ahead goal. Fortunately for the goal judge, who was in dire trouble with the fans for interfering with the local player, the Maitlands came back and won that game.

The survival rate of goal judges was no less remarkable than Taylor's own infirmary record. In all his years as a marked man —smaller, cockier, and certainly faster than most—Taylor never suffered any injuries other than cuts, strains, and bruises, although there were some bad ones.

There was another interesting first out of Listowel in the winter of 1900–1. It came on a visit to play a game in nearby Southampton. The Listowel rink at that time was the only one in the league equipped with goal nets. Other towns still had the iron posts stuck into the ice.

Sometimes a puck would whistle between the posts with no goal called, and at other times the puck would go just wide and a goal would be called. Depending on the local loyalty and in-

timidation factor, this situation led to some interesting inter-
pretations of a shot on goal. All of them, of course, thoroughly
honest.

As this particular Southampton game was important, the
Mintos decided to reduce the chances of (perish the evil
thought!) skulduggery by taking along their own nets.

This they did, transporting the folding contraptions of pipe
and chicken wire on a horse-drawn wagon and then setting them
up in the Southampton rink. There was some heavy opposition to
this curious gambit by the local team, but the novelty of the idea
prevailed, and the nets were allowed to stand.

There is no record of the outcome of that contest, and for the
life of him Taylor himself can't remember, but one thing is sure:
The Listowel Mintos, by Taylor's account, was the first hockey
team able to boast the slogan: "Have nets, will travel."

From that game on, as other league cities installed their own,
goal nets became a commonplace and then an official piece of
rink equipment.

What Taylor does remember with clarity from those days is
the general conduct of the sport and the style and manner of the
officiating. "It was very tough, hard hockey, but it wasn't dirty
hockey, which to my mind is today's worst evil. There was lots of
nasty play, including spearing, but things rarely got out of hand.
The officials were respected. The referee made far fewer penalty
calls than is common today, yet he was always in command of
the game.

"There was one little ritual then that I think would be a great
thing in today's game. It was common in those days for a referee
to come into the two dressing rooms before a game for a chat
with the players. He'd say something like this: 'Boys, there are a
lot of people out there waiting to see this game, and they've
come to watch a good one. We have rules. Let's observe them.
Let's just go out there and play hockey.' I am convinced that a
little communicating along that line would be a big help in
hockey today, especially in the amateur leagues where the habits
are formed. As those old referees used to say, and despite what
you might now hear otherwise, people come to watch hockey,
not mayhem."

At the age of seventeen, in the midst of leading the Listowel

Mintos to a second league championship, Taylor quit school and went to work in the local piano factory. His father was making no more than seventy-five dollars a month, and Fred was able to supplement the family income while keeping half of his five-dollar weekly wage for himself. He was still a few years away from making a lot more money that that.

It was at this point in Taylor's career that he first came into conflict with the Establishment that even then exerted autocratic control over the world of amateur hockey. Lavish reports of the Listowel star began getting wide circulation, and started to receive big play in the Toronto papers. Toronto was the bastion of the all-powerful Ontario Hockey Association.

In the early winter of 1902–3, Taylor, then eighteen, was invited to play in an exhibition series in Houghton, Michigan, a rising hotbed of hockey in the U.S. During the two previous years, three of Taylor's Listowel teammates had been attending a dental college in Detroit, and the college had been asked to play a Michigan team in Houghton.

His friends phoned Taylor from Detroit and invited him to join them for the two-week series over the post-Christmas holidays. He went, and was the outstanding star of the series. This was the first wide recognition of his status as a top-notch player. His play got raves in the Michigan papers, and the stories were picked up in Toronto.

The next autumn, October 1903, Taylor got a phone call from Toronto. It was from Billy Hewitt, then secretary of the OHA and an imposing figure in amateur hockey. (It was Billy's son, Foster, who was to become the "Voice of Hockey Night in Canada," and the nation's most popular and celebrated broadcaster.) Hewitt asked Taylor to come to Toronto to play for the famous senior team, the Marlboros. In Taylor's own recollection of many years later: "I was flattered and I wanted to go. After all, it was my chance to move up into big-time hockey, but then I had second thoughts. To a young fellow like me, born and raised in a small town, and I guess a homebody, Toronto suddenly seemed awfully big. I liked Listowel, my home was there and I had my job in the piano factory. I decided to stay put. I thanked Mr. Hewitt for asking me, but said I wouldn't come. He couldn't believe it. I insisted I meant what I said, and he insisted that I change my mind. I said no, I wouldn't change my mind. Then he told me straight out, 'All right, if you won't play for the Marlies, you won't play anywhere.'"

It was an early example of how the self-assumed guardians of amateur hockey used their power to club young players into line and establish control over their futures. This was just verbal intimidation, albeit effective enough. Later, there would be a Canadian Amateur Hockey Association law that gave professional teams the right to claim any youngster and sign him to a form that made him their property for life once he turned pro—until released, sold, or traded. The player, or if not old enough, his parent, signed that form or else the boy didn't play in any organized league anywhere. That system went on for more than sixty years before it was challenged in the courts and modified.

The strong-willed teen-ager knew that the OHA had complete control over hockey in the province and that Hewitt could make good his threat, but he stuck to his guns. "My parents were much more upset about it than I was. They damned Hewitt and the OHA when I guess they should have been damning me. I had provoked the situation, although I did get some help from Hewitt."

After declining that imperious bid from the Marlies, Taylor got another chance to widen his horizons when he received an invitation to play with the OHA team in nearby Thessalon, which was not fully aware of the situation. Knowing that the OHA would certainly refuse to sanction play that season in Listowel, he decided to test the ban with the Thessalon club.

He reported there, turned out for practice, and was then informed, with regret, that word had come from Toronto that he was barred from playing anywhere in Ontario, and that certainly included Thessalon. The Thessalon officials, who badly wanted Taylor on their team, were almost as upset as he was. "We're sorry," they said, "but we daren't touch you."

The blacklist was official.

Hoping that they might get the ban lifted, the Thessalon people paid Taylor to stay around town for a few weeks, but there was no change. He went home, glumly resigned to sitting out the whole season.

The memory of that enforced winter of inactivity, locked out of the game that had for all the years since those first tentative thrusts on the rough ice of the Piggery had been his whole life, rankled for a long time.

"I've never forgiven Billy Hewitt for that."

Chapter Two
HOUGHTON

The long arm of Billy Hewitt and the Ontario Hockey Association did not reach out behind the provincial boundaries, so in the summer of 1905 the Listowel outcast decided to go west.

He accepted an invitation to play for Portage la Prairie of the Manitoba Hockey League. This was a strong senior circuit, and the move was a big step up for a player who was fast becoming known as one of the game's outstanding and most exciting performers even though he had played only as a junior. He had one lost season behind him, and now, past his twentieth birthday, he was overdue for his test against the best players in the country.

The Portage la Prairie invitation came by letter. "I was offered board and room plus twenty-five dollars a month pocket money, but what attracted me most was the chance to play against established stars in a first-rate league. The memory of that lost year gnawed at me, and I was terribly anxious to get going and play again. I was a bit worried about how I would play after a winter's layoff, and I needed a real challenge to help me get my confidence back. I figured I'd find it in the Manitoba League.

"Apart from that lost winter in Thessalon, which really wasn't that far from Listowel, this Manitoba trip would be my first real break from my family and friends. As far as I was concerned, Manitoba was a foreign land, and going there represented quite an adventure. My father was on the road when the letter arrived, but I talked it over with the rest of the family, and my mother agreed that if this is what I wanted I should certainly go.

"I'd already quit my job at the piano factory to go to Thessalon, so I had no other ties. I wrote right back and said I'd come. That was in the late summer. In November they sent me my train ticket."

Portage la Prairie, then a town of about three thousand, and not a great deal bigger than Listowel, lay just beyond Winnipeg on the road to Brandon, home of the then Manitoba Champions.

Winnipeg itself, with its Victorias, was a member of the Canadian Amateur Hockey League six-team circuit, otherwise composed of teams from Ontario and Quebec.

These were times of flux for Canadian hockey, a game that was struggling for a true national identity and would eventually stretch westward beyond Winnipeg. It was racked by growing pains. There was no dominant league or association in the latter-day style of the National Hockey League and its president, Clarence Campbell, or any truly national governing body. The game's growth seemed aimless and confused.

Leagues were formed, shrank, were enlarged, revamped, folded, and reformed. Teams moved, changed names, and players drifted about the landscape like snowflakes in a lazy prairie breeze. It was difficult for even an expert observer like Taylor to know exactly what was going on, but he did know that there were some great players out there waiting to test him.

Scattered around the Manitoba League, the CAHA and the neighboring Federal League, were such stars as Russell Bowie and Blair Russell of the Winnipeg Victorias, Montreal's Ernie ("Moose") Johnson and Ernie Russell; the Ottawa Nationals' Newsy Lalonde and Harry Westwick; Westmount's Art Ross and the Patrick brothers, Lester and Frank; Kenora's Si Griffis and Tom Phillips.

It was in this same year of 1905 that another youth in another sport, fated like Taylor to scale the heights, also arrived for his test at the top. He was the eighteen-year-old baseball player from Narrows, Georgia, Ty Cobb.

After swamping Atlanta *Journal* columnist Grantland Rice with telegrams containing lavish reports of the exploits of "a sensational new player" on the Georgia sandlots, young Ty (who turned out to be the "sensational new player") got the look he wanted. On Rice's recommendation, the brash young hustler was signed by Detroit, and got his ticket to the Tigers' training camp.

That was the start of Cobb's twenty-three marvelous years in the big leagues, years that produced an unmatched lifetime batting average of .367, 4,191 hits, 892 stolen bases, and a popular judgment as the best ballplayer in history.

This coincidental inaugural down in Detroit is worth consider-

ing here because for years afterward, as both of these super athletes were rising to stardom, Taylor, especially during exhibition
trips to New York and Boston, was constantly hailed as "the Ty
Cobb of hockey."

Cobb could hardly have been displeased. Taylor certainly
wasn't.

In many ways they were alike, these two. Both were superbly
talented and were tremendous competitors with that little extra
bit of fire that represents the sometimes very fine difference between being good and being great. Both were fast, tricky, aggressive, and owned a world of confidence. Cobb, a ruthless
competitor who was famed for snarling into second base with his
razor-sharp spikes raised high, was meaner than his hockey
counterpart.

Although Taylor established a lifetime career reputation as a
clean player, he knew he was in a very rough trade and he was
quite willing to play it that way when he had to. The difference
was that Cobb would go out of his way to rough up an opponent
and dare him to respond. Taylor had to be goaded into retalia-
tion, at which time he'd give as good as he got, and more. That
master tactician, Lester Patrick, put it this way:

"Fred Taylor is a counterpuncher. He won't lead with his left
or come out swinging with a round house right, but hurt him
once, and look out. Once riled, he could be mean as a wounded
cobra. He was always pretty subtle about it, but he had sharp
elbows and was pretty handy with the butt end of a stick too. He
could hurt you if you'd asked for it, although, as often as not,
he'd just seem to ignore his tormentor, work him into a corner,
steal the puck and then go off and leave him standing there looking like a damn fool. That can be worse than mean."

In Portage la Prairie, Taylor was boarded in a hotel where he
shared a room with a young winger named Dick Hudson, fresh
from Brockville. Played at center, he was an instant hit on the
ice, scored a pair of classic goals in his first game against Winnipeg, and just took the local fans by storm. But in a stay that
was fated to be a short one, the game in Portage la Prairie
Taylor remembers best was the one against the Kenora Thistles,
reputed to be the fastest team in hockey.

The Thistles had two outstanding stars in Si Griffis and Tom

Phillips, and Taylor had never faced players quite of their caliber.

"I worked myself into a nervous state wondering how I'd stack up against these fellows, but I needn't have worried. It was one of those nights when I could do nothing wrong. Everything worked. I don't think I ever skated faster or moved better.

"Tom Phillips was my check, but he couldn't stay with me that night. He just couldn't get the puck away from me, and I sure got a kick out of that."

The personal pleasure was understandable. "Nibs" Phillips was then rated as the top left-winger in hockey, a superb checker and a prolific scorer. The year before, during the unsuccessful Kenora (then known as Rat Portage) Stanley Cup challenge series against Ottawa's famed Silver Seven, he had scored five goals in one game.

"Maybe it was because I'd heard that Kenora was the fastest team in hockey and because players like Phillips and Griffis were there. I suppose I just wanted to show them what I could do. It was my first chance against the very best, and I think I was testing myself as much as the Kenora boys. I scored two or three goals, I can't remember which. The crowd loved it, but what tickled me most was the grumbling comments of the Thistles as I skated by.

"When the first period ended, Griffis came dashing over toward me as we headed for the gate. I thought he was going to hit me, but he just pulled up alongside and said, 'Hey, where the hell did you come from?' I said, 'I come from Listowel, a town in Ontario. Is there anything wrong with that?' He just sort of wagged his head and skated away."

After the game, Griffis and Phillips were waiting outside the Portage Lake dressing room as the players emerged from the steamy, overheated quarters.

They lounged on the threshold and wrinkled their noses in mock distaste at the strong masculine aroma wafting from the long johns that hung near the pot-bellied stove. Players muscled by, emitting pleasant blasts of approved trade profanity as Griffis and Phillips just grinned and waited for their man.

When Taylor emerged, Griffis clutched his arm and said, "Let's go."

"Where to?" said Taylor, taken aback by this surprise visit.

"You're hungry aren't you?" said Phillips.

"I certainly am."

"Okay. Let's go."

The trio trudged through the frigid, wind-blown streets and into the warmth of a downtown cafe. They ordered ham-and-eggs, and over the ketchup Griffis said, "Taylor, we just want to say that we think you're great."

The rookie, luxuriating in a mug of steaming hot coffee, rose nicely to the occasion. "Thanks, Si," he said. "I hear you and Tom aren't too bad yourselves."

Griffis, who would get to know this cool customer a lot better as the years went by, grinned amiably. "Thanks. I appreciate that. Now. We were wondering if maybe you could shake this ham-bone outfit here in Portage la Prairie and come along with us to Montreal. It's a big series. You'd help us."

Phillips nodded. "How about it, Fred? We missed the Cup last year, but we're going to challenge again. With you with us, I know we could win it."

"There'd be no problem here," said Griffis. "You're out of the league race, and we'd just want you for a couple of weeks, on loan. At least for this season. I think it could be arranged."

Taylor pondered his coffee.

It was an intriguing proposition. Invitations to join a team about to challenge for the Stanley Cup don't come along every day of the week. As a matter of fact, since his arrival in Portage la Prairie he had often mused over what might have happened had he got into town just a few days earlier, when that crazy gang from Dawson City had passed through.

The Klondikers were the talk of the country with their precocious challenge to the defending Cup champion Ottawa Silver Seven.

Under the auspices of their angel, wealthy prospector Col. Joe Boyle, they had set out over their 4,400-mile Alice-in-Wonderland journey from Dawson City, traveling through blizzards by dog-sled to Skagway, by boat to Seattle and then to Vancouver, then off across the prairies by train.

To bolster the woefully inexperienced squad that was rolling inevitably to its doom in the Capital city, the Klondikers had picked up a player in Winnipeg and then two more as they passed through Portage la Prairie, where they had stopped for an exhibition game. In the few weeks since then, Taylor had often wondered what might have happened had he been here then, and been one of the chosen two.

Some later musing would have been just as intriguing, as the Klondikers were to be blasted into some sort of immortality by Cup scores of 9–2 and 23–2, with one Ottawa player, "One-Eyed" Frank McGee, scoring fourteen goals in the second game. But a Kenora challenge would, of course, be little different to that.

By the time Griffis laid down his dollar bill for the late snack, the decision had been made. Taylor had agreed to talk to the Portage la Prairie people and ask for permission to join the Thistles in Montreal.

There was a train due out in a couple of days time that would get him into Montreal in time for the weekend game with the Wanderers. As Griffis had suggested, there wasn't much trouble getting a release from his Portage la Prairie obligation, but Taylor never made the train. At least not that one.

The day before he was to leave for Montreal, he had a phone call from a Mr. John McNamara, in Houghton, Michigan, a member of the International Professional League that had been formed two years before, when Taylor had made his brief visit as a junior. The Portage Lake team of Houghton, explained McNamara, was in a battle with Pittsburgh for the league championship, and in dire need of a center. "In fact," said McNamara, "we need not just a center, but a player who can handle any position, except maybe goal. I'm told you're the man who could do the job."

McNamara had obtained his advice from some Canadians already with Portage Lake—Bruce Stuart, Grindy Forrester, and Riley Hern. All three had been outstanding players in the Quebec and Ontario leagues before signing up as hired guns in Houghton, and they'd all heard of the whiz from Listowel.

"You'd sign a professional contract," said McNamara.

"How much?" asked Taylor.

"Four hundred dollars for the rest of the season plus expenses."

This was the crossroads. A chance to turn professional and to get paid for what he'd been quite happy to do for no more than a cheap room, his meals, and the roar of the crowd. There were also complications. There was his agreement to join Kenora and the arrangement to return to Portage la Prairie after that.

Throughout a career of shrewd bargaining marked with offers, counteroffers, stubborn defiances, careful considerations and grave reconsiderations, Taylor became known as a very practical man. Very fair, but very practical.

This was a practical time. "My arrangement with Kenora was just for the one series, after which I was to return to Portage la Prairie. And by that time the season there would be almost over." The practical reasoning was that the way things were, he would be of very limited use to one party and then of even less use to the other. In which case a change of plan would really hurt nobody, and might help Fred Taylor.

"I talked it over on the phone with the Kenora people, then discussed it with Portage la Prairie. There were regrets in both places, but no great objections. They could see the possibility of a future for me with the Houghton offer, and it was agreed, reluctantly, that I should accept."

After having told McNamara that he'd think it over, he then called back and said he'd come. McNamara sent the train tickets plus ten dollars travel money, and Taylor, having missed the train east to Montreal, took the one south to Houghton.

Houghton, a community of about five thousand souls, sits beside Portage Lake in the middle of a slender finger of Michigan that just bleakly up into Lake Superior. It is in the state's northernmost area, and it is in the rugged heart of the copper mining country.

In the winter of 1905–6, it was a bustling, wide-open town known as a great Saturday night fun place for miners who prefer to patronize something other than art museums or the opera house. Hockey was one of their favorite indulgences, and the town's Portage Lake team, already with a two-year history as a member of hockey's first pro league, gave them the tough, rough action they wanted.

As Taylor left for the Portage la Prairie railway station, he was headed for a whole new kind of hockey country and a whole new experience.

The station was no more than a block and half from the hotel, and Dick Hudson walked there with him to see him off. "I was flattered that anybody would go along at that unearthly hour to meet a 6 A.M. train, and in that weather." It was bitterly cold, and a Manitoba snow blizzard whitened the landscape.

"All I had was one small club bag and a funny feeling in my stomach. Fortunately, the train left right on time, or else Dick would have frozen to death standing there on the platform. Even the station master seemed a little surly when he had to come out of his office to see me aboard. It was a CPR train to Emerson, a border town about fifty miles below Winnipeg, where we had to go through immigration before changing to the Chicago-Milwaukee-St. Paul line.

"I had a telegram from Houghton confirming that I was going to a job there, and I had no trouble with the U. S. Immigration people. One of them was a hockey fan who said he'd seen me play in Winnipeg, and he even brought me a cup of coffee. He said he was very impressed with meeting me, and I thought that was a pretty fine introduction to a foreign country. It made me feel a lot better.

"It was an overnight ride to Houghton, and I had an upper berth, although I don't know why. I never slept. I guess I just wasn't used to all that shaking and rattling, or to traveling abroad. I was out of the bunk at dawn for another look at the countryside. It was pretty forbidding. I guess I must have felt something like that astronaut fellow did when he peered out of the capsule and looked out across the moon for the first time."

The train pulled into the Houghton station at 10 A.M. on that morning of January 30, 1906. The temperature was below zero and a cutting wind whistled in off the lake. "When I stood with my bag waiting for the porter to open the door of the coach, I was scared stiff. I'd never felt so lonely in my life. Then I looked out and there were these three fellows walking up to greet me, all smiles."

The three fellows were Bruce Stuart, the captain of the Portage Lake team, the goalie, Riley Hern, and another of his new teammates, Harry Bright.

"Suddenly, as I stepped down on the platform, I felt great. I'd never felt better. The only thing was I'd forgotten to tip the porter. I guess he was glaring over my shoulder because Bruce went up to him and slipped him a coin. When he came back he grinned and said, 'You owe me a quarter.' You know, come to think of it, I don't think I ever did pay that man back. They took me straight to a hotel, where they had a room waiting for me. Practice was at noon. They told me to be there. I said I'd be delighted to be there."

The rink, a handsome covered structure called the Amphidrome, was in the middle of town. It seated 3,000, which was just a touch under the urban population. The fact that it was almost always jammed to capacity for hockey games offers an idea of the sport's popularity in that part of the world.

When Taylor arrived for his first workout there were several hundred fans in the stands there with their lunch to watch the new boy just in from Canada. He was met by McNamara, a fine tall figure of a man with a big, drooping moustache. He was the Portage Lake manager.

There was a minor crisis when the new man announced that he had left his skates back in Portage la Prairie, but the manager quickly tapped the treasury for five dollars and sent into town for a pair. When Taylor skated out to join the workout, the others were already there and they paid little heed to the newcomer. Bruce Stuart waved him to take up a position as rover.

There was no question as to what line he was to support. There was only one: Joe Hall was on one wing, Grindy Forrester on the other, with Bruce Stuart at center; Barney Holden was at cover-point alongside Fred Lake; Riley Hern was in goal. Of that group, as a fair indication of their abilities, Stuart, Hern, and Hall would all eventually enter the Hockey Hall of Fame, joining Taylor there.

The lesson of the day and, as Taylor was to learn, every day, was combination play. Grindy Forrester was the coach, helped by Stuart.

"It was obvious right away that there was more accent here on skating and stickhandling than in the Canadian leagues. I didn't mind that at all. And right away Stuart noted something that I'd been doing habitually that he said was hurting my play. It was my old habit of getting ahead of my linemates. Grindy took over and gave me the devil every time I broke out ahead of the line pattern. He told me how that hurt both the line and myself. I started working on it, lagging back when I had to, and I found out Grindy was right on both counts.

"I think from that very first practice in Houghton, I was a better hockey player."

There is no doubt that the lunch-box crowd in the Amphidrome was pleased with the new recruit. "I could hear them talking as I skated along the boards, and they sounded impressed. They did a lot to balance the devil I was catching from Forrester."

The evening of that same day, Taylor got his first notice in the columns of the Houghton *Mining Gazette*.

"Fred Taylor, the new rover for the Portage Lake hockey team, arrived in the city this morning. Taylor is one of the fastest and most effective if not the very best player that Western Canada has ever produced, and now takes up professional hockey for the first time in his life. He may not be played in the rover position only, as he is good for any position on the forward line, and can play just about anywhere. The Portage Lake boys are just glad that he is playing here."

The International League was composed of six teams: Houghton's Portage Lake, two teams in Pittsburgh, the American Soo, Calumet, and the Canadian Soo. When Taylor arrived the teams lay in that order in the standings. A peculiarity of that league was that the standings were noted in percentage points, as in baseball, and as in baseball the teams competed not for the "championship," but for the "pennant."

On the eve of Taylor's arrival, Portage Lake had beaten the Canadian Soo by a score of 4–2. That win gave them a record of eight wins against three losses, for a percentage of .727. Pittsburgh was next with nine wins and four defeats, at .694.

In that victory over the Soo in the Amphidrome, the outstanding star of the visiting club was none other than Edouard ("Newsy") Lalonde, the tough, happy-go-lucky little fireball who was to dog Taylor's footsteps for the next fifteen years.

Newsy had rapped in both of the Soo goals—after first rapping both Grindy Forrester and Barney Holden firmly on the snout in a free-for-all that had the local miners, many of them already high enough, up out of their seats. As was noted in the next day's *Mining Gazette*, Newsy adjourned to a saloon after the game to make peace with the locals.

A non-drinker himself, Newsy bought for the house, charmed the boys with a couple of French-Canadian folk songs highly suspect of being a little ribald, and then got into a fight with "a gentleman who described himself as a traveling salesman from Detroit."

Whatever the traveling salesman was peddling, little Newsy obviously didn't care for his line. However, Lalonde emerged relatively unscathed from the fracas, and his new-found friends saw him safely aboard the train headed back to the Soo.

Taylor's own first test in his new league was in a game against Calumet. The *Mining Gazette* reporter gave this account of his debut as a professional:

"Last night at the Amphidrome the Portage Lake hockey team toyed with Calumet in a slow game. The home team scored almost at will and finally ended the game playing on the defensive with the score at 8–2. With the new man Taylor in charge of the attack, Riley Hern, the Portage Lake backstop, had but little work to do in goal. Nicholson, goalie for the Calumets and their only star last night, was kept busy, especially with Taylor buzzing about him for most of the game. Portage Lake scored two goals that were not counted, both by Taylor, who didn't seem to mind. Harry Bright, the goal umpire, missed one goal and referee Elliott called an off side on another. As it was, Taylor did score two other goals that counted. He is a whirlwind, and has not a superior on any of the league teams."

A later piece noted that "The other teams are doing all they can to stop Taylor or at least slow him down, and they don't mind how they go about it. They are using elbows and sticks and going at him any way they can, but so far he is too slippery for them. It is a marvel that he remains unhurt."

It was a very tough league, and two of the toughest players were Taylor's teammate, Joe Hall, a rambunctious competitor who could use his fists like hatchets, and the Canadian Soo team's irrepressible Newsy Lalonde. Maybe it was because they were around the same size and of equally sparkling talents, but it seemed that Newsy always took Taylor as a personal challenge. Lalonde was invariably the hunter and Taylor the hunted, and this was a reflection of their contrasting natures.

"Newsy? Sure, he was a tough little guy, and he'd always try to intimidate you. He'd come at you with his fists, elbows, and skates, trying to incite. He was a rough, all right. But I don't want to dwell too much on those things. Newsy was a wonderful player, and later on he mellowed a lot."

Meanwhile, in the Houghton duels, Taylor never backed off, would give good as he got, and then, both players, equally content, went back to playing hockey.

There was a game one night at a return date over in Calumet when things got rough all over. With only three victories in eleven games, the Calumet boys were hungry for No. 4, and were getting a lot of help from the sympathetic officials. One of them, the referee, was later said to have received a lot of pregame help over the bar from an understanding tavernkeeper.

In the second period, with the home team ahead by a goal that the whole Portage Lake team swore on a miner's Bible never went close, let alone in, Joe Hall became visibly upset over what he considered a gross misinterpretation of a friendly action against a Calumet player who had gotten a little too jolly.

All Joe did was give the fellow a genial tap on the nose with his elbow and then send him joy-riding into the boards with a rousing cross-check. Joe got the gate, but declined to leave. He called on his teammates to support his argument to the effect that the whole town was a nest of thieves and scoundrels, or words to that effect, adding explicit instructions as to what they could do with their hockey rink.

A mass battle ensued, enjoined by several dozen interested spectators. The melee was eventually subdued, and the contest, if it were that, continued. A minute later the Calumets were awarded another mystery goal, and Captain Stuart summoned his enraged troops to mid-ice.

"Boys," he said, "that's enough. We're going home."

Along with the others, Taylor nodded, perfectly agreeable.

"We talked a bit, then walked toward the gate at the end of the rink, but when we arrived there, a huge mob of fans were waiting, waving clubs and sticks and chairs or whatever they could lay their hands on and yelling blue murder. They dared us to leave the ice."

Joe Hall moved forward and started to push through the crowd, then made a brilliant shift to avoid a descending two-by-four. Reconsidering, he beat a hasty retreat.

Captain Stuart eyed the assembled citizenry and said quietly, "Boys, maybe we were a little hasty. Let's go back and play a while longer."

They returned and finished the contest. There was no more scoring.

It was, as a Calumet reporter gravely noted, "a hard-earned triumph by the home team."

By late February, it was still a tight scrap between Portage Lake and Pittsburgh for the pennant, and a climactic three-game series was billed for the Pennsylvania city. The games there were played in commodious Duquesne Garden, an arena that boasted one of the only two artificial ice surfaces then extant. The other was in the new St. Nicholas Arena in New York City.

With a long tradition as a hockey town, Pittsburgh had no trouble filling the arena for the big series, with a sellout of more than 6,500 fans assured even before Portage Lake left Houghton.

The eight-man Houghton squad arrived by train just before midnight of the chill eve of February 26, two days before the first game date. It was too late to catch a trolley to the team hotel, so Stuart hailed a couple of hansom cabs and jammed players and luggage aboard. Just as the cab with Taylor, Joe Hall, Stuart, and Riley Hern aboard pulled away from the platform a shirt-sleeved chap sporting a green eye visor darted out of telegraph office waving a piece of paper. He hailed a guard who was walking off along the tracks.

"Burns!" he yelled. "The Canadian, Tommy Burns. Decision! In twenty rounds!"

The guard paused, turned and wagged his head. His response couldn't be heard, but it looked very much like, "Well, I'll be damned!"

The hansom cab was pulled to a halt while the Canadians aboard confirmed the report. It was true. The flash had just come in from Los Angeles, where Burns had whipped Marvin Hart for the heavyweight championship of the world. Taylor let out a whoop of delight for the fortunes of his one-time adversary on the playfields of Hanover and Listowel, and there were congratulations and back-slappings all round.

That wasn't quite enough for Joe Hall, a patriot who liked his life in large doses. Leaping from the cab, he jumped up into the driver's seat, pushed the startled cabbie aside, and took the reins. With a roar from Joe, the vehicle took off over the cobblestones, careening through the dark Pittsburgh streets like a stagecoach pursued by a band of Apaches.

Miraculously, the wild ride eventually led to the hotel, with all passengers safe and sound but plainly shaken. Having revived, the cabbie began shouting for the constabulary but was mollified when Joe grandly slipped him a dollar tip, bowed, and ambled happily off to the desk to check in. For a Staffordshire Englishman raised in Winnipeg and Brandon, he had cut a fine Western figure up there on the stagecoach.

Joe scored a goal in each of the first two games at Duquesne Garden as the pair were split, Pittsburgh taking the first game 4–3 and Portage Lake winning the second, 4–2.

Although he thrived on the arena's big ice surface and had the fans marveling at his dazzling skating and stickwork, Taylor was shut out in both contests, being stopped time and again by the inspired goaltending of Pittsburgh's Jack Winchester.

Then there was the third game. The big one.

The report of that contest as wired back to the *Mining Gazette* was unusually terse, frugal, and rambling, but it finally got to the point.

"The Portage Lake hockey team took care of the Pittsburgh team in a hard struggle last night in Duquesne Garden. Portage Lake won and thus took the pennant of the International League. The first half was exceedingly fast and exciting, Pittsburgh having the visitors down 2–1, but Portage Lake recovered strongly. It was the windup of the hockey season in Pittsburgh, and this combined with the fact that Pittsburgh had to beat the crack visitors to retain second place served once again to pack the Garden. Taylor shot all three goals for Portage Lake. The final score was 3–2."

A climactic affair like that deserved more of a story, and the Pittsburgh *Evening Journal,* not burdened by the telegraph charges to Houghton, obliged. That paper devoted almost an entire sports page to the event. Some passages are worth quoting because they show the sort of impact Taylor had on the fans and the writers, and are typical of the kind of rave response he was to receive throughout his entire career.

The story, here in minute part, also gives a good picture of the feel and the excitement of the game, so much of it generated by the Houghton player, Taylor.

"Pittsburgh's fine hockey team was defeated last night by Portage Lake in the final game of the season, the score being 3–2.

"There was considerable delay in getting the game started, occasioned by the fact that the Pittsburgh star, Hod Stuart, wanted to play despite his bad ankle, but it might have been better had he remained out, as the ankle was so sore and swollen he was of little use to his teammates. There was a crowd of 6,500 present and it shouted all sorts of encouraging words to the home team, but all the shouts, blowing of whistles and rattling of cowbells failed to bring the hoped-for hometown victory. The battle had only progressed a minute or two when Campbell shot the first goal for Pittsburgh midst the wild plaudits of the spectators . . . thereafter the pace of the game rose to a fever pitch.

"Taylor was the king bee for the visitors, and his amazing exhibition of fast skating and perfect dribbling of the puck has never been equalled in this city and perhaps in no other. The goal had hardly been scored for Pittsburgh when he got hold of the puck, and starting up the ice with it, aided by some magnificent interference on the part of his associates, he took the disk along and evened the game with an absolutely perfect shot. Winchester, who was playing wonderfully in goal, was utterly unable to stop the puck from registering.

"During the game, the only goals scored by the visitors were through the magnificent work of Taylor, and regardless of the fact that his work meant actually knocking the local team out of second place and into third, it was so thoroughly brilliant and beautiful to watch that the audience couldn't refrain from manifesting its approval. They did this by getting to their feet with loud and vociferous shouts, and the blowing of horns."

There were some other passages suggesting that the hockey of these days was hardly patty-cake stuff.

"While the players of both sides showed that they were in deadly earnest by their efforts to win, there was not the viciousness and slaughter shown that many of the crowd had looked for. It is true that Kent was struck by the stick carried by Houghton's Lake, and a lot of his blood was spilled on the ice, but the unprejudiced onlookers agreed that the knockout was accidental. Kent was carried from the rink but soon returned well bandaged and looking none the worse for wear for the little collision.

"Later on in the game, Hall kicked Pittsburgh's Hod Stuart in the stomach, but as Hod was unable to do very much to protect himself because of his ankle, he contented himself with simply retaliating by smashing Hall on the top of the head with his stick. Hall then skated out of the way of further possible danger, and the game resumed.

"Taylor made one grievous mistake when in his rushing he mistook one of his teammates, Bruce Stuart, for one of the Pittsburgh players, and ran plump into him with his stick out, catching Stuart in the pit of the stomach. Stuart was out cold for four or five minutes."

The *Evening Journal* reporter offered another interesting sidelight:

"There was a great cheer just after the start of the game when the star of the Pittsburgh Pirates, Honus Wagner, appeared, accompanied by the Pirates' manager-outfielder, Fred Clarke. They took seats a few rows behind the Portage Lake bench. Wagner, considered the finest shortstop in baseball history, had travelled from his home in nearby Plattsville to see the game. He is a real hockey fan, and he seemed to be greatly excited by last night's proceedings. He was on his feet many times, and afterwards said that he thought the Portage Lake player, Taylor, was as fine an athlete as he has ever seen."

That, from the Dutchman, one of Pittsburgh's summer heroes and a player who was to become one of baseball's immortals, was special praise indeed.

That paper's same edition listed the League's All Star Team. Taylor was listed No. 1, at cover-point. Three other Portage Lake players made the team: Barney Holden, Stuart, and Fred Lake.

Portage Lake had two more games back home, and that was it for Taylor's first season as a professional. Having made the All Star Team, he was also named as the loop's top scorer, although no total was recorded. As to assists, well, they were not even acknowledged then, and would not be recorded until the Patrick brothers began their revolutionary innovating out on the Pacific Coast a half dozen years later.

The eight Canadians left Houghton and headed home for the summer, Taylor going straight back to Listowel. There, he filled in the summer playing lacrosse with the Guelph Intermediates. It wasn't a great league, but as Taylor put it, it passed the time and "there was a few dollars in it."

There was great optimism when the players assembled again in the Copper Country the next December for another season, but it was to be the league's last.

There is no point in pursuing the course of that season in great detail as, especially for Taylor, it was much the same as the previous one. He was the top scorer, and the outstanding player, and Portage Lake again won the pennant. To win it, they again had to face Pittsburgh in a critical three-game series at the end of the season. The difference this time was that Portage Lake shocked the packed houses in Duquesne Garden by winning all three contests.

Back in Houghton, an elaborate homecoming party awaited the conquering heroes. With the exploits of Taylor and his mates before the packed houses in Pittsburgh already liberally reported, the *Mining Gazette* told of the reception that was being prepared:

"Arrangements have been made by hockey enthusiasts whereby the Quincy Band will meet the Portage Lake team at the depot when the Northwestern train pulls in at noon. The champions of the International League, and probably the world, will be shown better than words can express that the people of Houghton appreciate their heroic work in Pittsburgh, by which they have driven so many ten-penny spikes into the coveted pennant that hangs in the Amphidrome that it will now be impossible to remove it. . . ."

The players were to be escorted from their train in a triumphal parade through town, to a banquet at Douglass House. Appeals had gone out to all "factories, foundries, and other such establishments in the area" to blow their steam whistles at word of the approach of the steam train. There was an appeal to the entire community to turn out at the depot, and just about all those who could turn out did.

There are no records kept of such things, but the homecoming scene must surely be one of the most colorful and enthusiastic such occasions in the history of hockey. It was certainly a remarkable commentary on the honest enthusiasm for the game in that pioneer time and place.

The *Gazette* was to report that "more than half the town was at the depot yesterday to watch the heroes of Pittsburgh alight from their train . . ."

The Quincy Band was there waiting, and a battery of U. S. Army artillery under the command of a Captain Morton Haas was perched on the top of a boxcar with its cannon "covering the train's approach to the village." The word to the area's factories had been heeded, and as the train rounded the bend just outside town, the steam siren on Carroll's Foundry gave the first shrill warning cry. It was taken up "by a score of others."

When the locomotive finally huffed to a stop in the depot, the players were mobbed by a huge throng of townsfolk, and it was only after several minutes of joyous bedlam that the players were assembled for their parade through town. Forming behind the band and trailed by the welcoming crowd, they marched off through the green-and-white decorations of Sheldon Street to Douglass House, where a lavish spread had been prepared.

There had been nothing quite like this in hockey before, and perhaps, with its quaint overtones, nothing quite like it since. That day remained as one of Fred Taylor's fondest memories.

Only a couple of days later, as the town heroes packed for the long summer back home, there were reports that they might not be asked back. A recession had hit the U.S. economy, and tumbling copper prices had left northern Michigan the hardest hit area of all.

When in the next autumn it came time to make a decision on the future of the league, it was admitted that the teams just wouldn't be able to pay the salaries. They weren't much. The total payroll at Houghton was no more than $5,000, but even that was too much to handle.

On November 8, 1907, Houghton's John McNamara, the league secretary, announced: "With regret, that there will be no professional hockey this year in the Copper Country." A week later, it was announced that an amateur league would be formed. Hockey's first self-avowed professional league had died a sudden, unexpected, and improvident death after a lifespan of just four years, two of them shared by Fred Taylor.

They were boisterous, exciting, stimulating years, and they left their mark on the game and on the players who shared them: "That league was a wonderful testing and training ground, and I was a far better player for my experience there. It was good, scientific hockey, but robust enough to teach a young player how to take care of himself. When I first arrived as the new kid in town, I was a marked man, and I guess they were still trying to intimidate me two years later, but there's no quarrel with an honest school of hard knocks. After that league, I knew I could handle anybody, anywhere. It was a marvelous maturing process.

"The people too, were great. There was a different feeling there with the sport seemingly so far from its home and us all down from Canada as sort of paid mercenaries. But the people opened up their homes to us, and a player who was so inclined could walk into a tavern and walk out again a couple of hours later without it having cost him a nickel.

"The social life was a little limited, but I did get to know one girl there very well—Florence Knox was her name—and I used to go to her house for dinner and go skating with her and her sister. Nothing came of it, though. When I left town for good, she was there to see me off, and there were a few tears, but just for old-time's sake.

"I was very, very sorry to see it all end. It was a fine league, and there's no telling where it would have gone if it hadn't been for the recession. It may well have become what the National League is today."

But it was all over, and those who would not return to the Copper Country were marked elsewhere as hot property. The ink had hardly dried on McNamara's wistful edict before every

top club in Canada started jockeying for a piece of that sea-
soned, pro-toughened experience.

The battle was on to grab the best players, and at the very top
of the Wanted List was the illustrious namesake of a Tara veteri-
narian, Frederick Wellington Taylor.

Chapter Three
OTTAWA

It was springtime in Listowel.

The Maitland River was in gentle flood, the daffodils were up, the ladies were out along Main Street in their bright silks and ginghams, and the prodigal son had returned for another summer.

All was well with the world in that April of 1907.

As the star player of the team that had just won a second straight world professional hockey championship, Fred Taylor was firmly entrenched as the town's No. 1 celebrity and its proudest showpiece.

So what to do with a conquering hero?

The Toronto *World* had a reporter keeping an eye on the situation, and printed this on-the-spot report under the headline: "Taylor is Feasted":

"Fred Taylor, the sensational point man for the Portage Lake Hockey Team, who went to his home at Listowel at the close of the hockey season, was last Wednesday evening tendered a banquet in the Queens Hotel and presented with a handsome remembrance by a number of his friends.

"After partaking of a very dainty supper, all adjourned to the parlor. Mr. George Loree being called to the chair, a very enjoyable evening was spent at songs, instrumentals, recitations, and impromptu speeches, the musical part of the program being presented by the Messrs. Loree, Scott, Krotz, Daum, and Stewart. A very pleasant part of the program was the presentation of a gentleman's companion to Fred, accompanied by a laudatory address by Mr. George Stevenson."

Asked nearly seventy years later just exactly what was a "gentleman's companion" in the year of 1907, Taylor replied thoughtfully, "Well, I'd say a gentleman's companion then was about the same as a gentleman's companion now. Some nice young lady."

But when he was reminded that such was the gift made to him at that banquet in Listowel's Queens Hotel made possible by the generous hospitality of Mr. and Mrs. Boehmer, he remembered differently, "clear as if it was yesterday." After a good laugh, he said, "The 'gentleman's companion' was a leather shaving-kit. A beautiful thing. I still have it somewhere. And say, that young Loree fellow, he was quite a singer. He was a woodworker in a furniture factory, and he was in great demand around town for parties."

Did he recall what George Loree had sung? "I certainly do. 'Sweet Adeline.' It was the big thing then. We all joined in the chorus."

That mental picture of Fred Taylor seated in the parlor of the Queens Hotel joining in a chorus of "Sweet Adeline" after "partaking of a dainty supper" was a little at odds with the travails of the star of that rough, tough league in the Michigan Copper Country. It would not, as Taylor would agree, have been Joe Hall's or Newsy Lalonde's cup of tea.

At the time of that springtime soiree in the Queens Hotel, Newsy was back in Montreal, getting ready for another lacrosse season with the Nationales. Good as he was at hockey, this tough little son of a Cornwall, Ontario, shoemaker was even better at lacrosse, and he revelled in those rollicking summertimes on the turf. He was in no hurry to consider the hockey offers that would come flooding in when the demise of the International League was confirmed, thus making him, like the others, a free agent.

Joe Hall was also in Montreal and already listening to overtures from the Wanderers, the Eastern Canadian Hockey Association team he would ultimately join along with Bruce Stuart.

When Lalonde eventually did turn again to hockey, it would be to sign with Toronto of the Ontario Professional Hockey League, the first Canadian circuit to declare itself fully professional. Others, such as the Eastern Canada League, were amateur in name only, and would soon abandon that charade. Bigtime hockey in Michigan was finished, but it had pioneered a breakthrough and the game was about to become a whole new world.

Taylor, like Lalonde, was in no rush to talk hockey. The mountain, as he well knew, would eventually come to Mahomet.

Meanwhile, there was a summer and autumn to kill before the start of the next hockey season, so Taylor went back to his second love, lacrosse. Since there was no league team that year in Listowel he accepted an offer to play for nearby Hanover, of the Ontario Lacrosse Association.

Long missing from that team was Noah Brusso, now known as Tommy Burns. The new World Heavyweight Champion had gone a long way in the seven years since Taylor had last met him on the lacrosse field. But Burns's tenure at the top of the boxing world was to be brief and troubled. The U.S. press refused to accept him as a worthy successor to their retired champion, James J. Jeffries. They accused Burns of avoiding a confrontation with Jack Johnson, the big brooding black they called the "Galveston Giant."

Back home, Taylor's problems were lesser ones. In fact, there were really no problems at all. By mid-August 1907 the International League was pretty well known to be doomed, and the race was on to sign the top twenty or thirty players who were now available, although not yet declared free agents. Taylor was a prime target, and it was the Ottawa Senators of the Eastern Canadian Amateur Hockey Association who were the first to make an attractive offer. The term "amateur" was a whimsical misnomer that has persisted as a gentle fraud throughout the history of Canada's senior "amateur" circuits.

It was on a sunny Wednesday morning when the train from Ottawa pulled into the Listowel station bearing the well-known figure of Malcolm Brice, sports editor of the Ottawa *Free Press*. Disembarking, Brice inquired of the stationmaster as to the whereabouts of the Taylor residence. Upon being informed, he proceeded there on foot. He knew he would find Fred there since he commuted for his weekend games with the Hanover team and spent the rest of the time with his family.

Fred was at home all right, and not greatly surprised when the visitor introduced himself. He had heard that the Ottawa people were interested in him, and he was very pleased about it. The Senators were a big-league outfit with a strong following in that part of Ontario, and with fine veterans like goalie Percy LeSueur and forwards Harry Westwick, Alf Smith, and Harvey Pulford around, a Stanley Cup challenge was almost sure, and a Cup victory quite possible. Ottawa, then famed as the Silver Seven, had last won the Cup in 1905, and as Taylor had it figured, the team needed only his youthful spark to do it again this coming season. It appeared that the Ottawa team executives were inclined to agree.

Brice came right to the point, announcing that he was authorized to make Taylor an offer. It was for $500—a top wage for E.C.A.H.L. players—for the ten-game season, plus a job in the Civil Service, in the Immigration Department. That $500 was more than Taylor had made in Houghton, but he was in no rush to commit himself. He was already learning the bargaining game.

Playing it very cool, he informed Brice that it seemed to be an interesting sort of proposition, and that he would think it over and let him know. Privately, he was definitely intrigued with the pitch, especially the promise of a job with the Federal Government, in the Civil Service. There was the chance that it could turn into a permanent career job. He considered that this prospect was worth more to him than the $500 salary, which, in his rising personal assessment of his value, really wasn't much.

So he told Brice he'd sit on it for a while and then just maybe come up to Ottawa and talk it over with the club directors. Brice was taken aback by Taylor's reluctance to leap right up and sign on the dotted line, but on getting Taylor's promise that he would indeed come to Ottawa for a chat, he departed, reasonably content with his mission.

Early that same evening, another train huffed in from the East, and who should show up at the Taylor residence but Fred's onetime Houghton teammate, Riley Hern. He had come straight through from Montreal.

Hern had left the Houghton team midway during his second season there to take over in goal for the Montreal Wanderers, a powerhouse team led by a rising new star named Lester Patrick. Hern had been in the nets the previous March when the Wanderers, winners in 1906, had taken the Cup again in a rousing two-game challenge series with the Kenora Thistles.

Taylor was delighted to see his ex-teammate, and more delighted when Hern told him that he'd come with instructions from the Wanderers management to sign him up. Fred, by his own account, felt "like a bride with two handsome suitors," but he knew he could be true to but one.

"Riley," he said, "I'm sorry, but I'm already promised."

By this time, just a few hours after Malcolm Brice had left, Taylor was sure he would take the Ottawa offer. Before supper, he had walked the six blocks to the downtown post office to tell the postmaster about the Ottawa offer of a job with the Federal Government and get his reaction. The local ranking civil servant was very impressed.

"Why," he said, maybe overstating the case a little, "you'll be hob-nobbing with the Prime Minister and all those people. You might even get to meet the King and Queen!"

Many years later Taylor would meet the King and Queen. Twice, in fact, as a guest at Buckingham Palace garden parties. But here and now, he was quite happy thinking about what Canada's capital city had to offer an ambitious young gent from the boondocks.

What impressed him most about the general situation was that the world was now beating a path to his door. Apart from the Ottawa and Montreal overtures, there had been letters and calls from other clubs, including Quebec City and the Montreal Victorias, as well as from Cobalt of the Upper Ottawa Valley League. This last bid had strongly tempted him.

Cobalt was a silver town of about 3,000 people, and it was very prosperous. M. J. O'Brien, a multimillionaire who affected an extravagant beard and an imperious manner, owned a big piece of the Cobalt mine. He could well afford to pursue a burgeoning family ambition—strongly supported by his son, Ambrose—to own a first-class hockey club, and eventually a Stanley Cup Championship. Step one was to make Cobalt the power in the Valley League, and both M.J. and Ambrose coveted Taylor as their key player.

Strangely, maybe because the O'Briens as yet didn't fully realize that their man was dealing in such a competitive market, the pitch to Taylor never got much past the tentative stage. When it finally did, it was in the face of the very attractive bid from Ottawa.

"I guess," said Taylor, deep in the kind of retrospect he enjoys, "I could have gotten some pretty good money from M.J. at that time as he was a very wealthy man and crazy about hockey. But we never actually got to the point of talking terms, and that as it turned out, was all right with me."

The Cobalt money might well have been enough to swing a deal, but there was another factor of importance to Taylor at this stage of his career. The little Upper Ottawa Valley League was not of the best caliber and was simply not challenge enough for a top-notch player who would be out of place and miscast in anything but the best competition. He was now twenty-three, an established star but not yet bloodied in a major Eastern Canada league, where the recognized quality action was, especially now with the pending demise of the International League. A diversion at this juncture would be foolhardy and also very bad for the ego, a quality that is indispensible to a star performer in any enterprise.

Jilted this time around, the O'Briens would be back again waving their money bags, and with a proposition that Taylor would eventually be unable to resist. As it was, having been offered the chance to move from a copper town in Michigan to a silver town in Ontario, Taylor, a canny young man with a keen eye for the grades of metal in the coin of the realm, did not buck the trend.

It was all a very fascinating lesson in the economic principle of supply and demand, and he never forgot it. The game would henceforth know Taylor as a shrewd bargainer who always angled for the top dollar, and got it. Within two years of that Sunday seminar in the Taylor parlor, he would become by far the highest paid team athlete, per game, in the world.

The Taylor family was delighted with the Ottawa offer, and especially with the idea of the post in the Civil Service. The hard times that had struck the Michigan mining country had rippled up across the border, and jobs there were scare. To a hard-working if fun-loving citizen like Archie Taylor, who was finding the life of a traveling salesman an increasingly uncertain one, a government job with its promise of long-term security looked like a ticket to Shangri-La.

The head of the family was off on one of his sales trips when Fred left Listowel in the soft rain of an October morning and headed for Ottawa and his appointment with the bigwigs of the

Ottawa Senators hockey club. There was a lot to think about on that train ride, and all of it stimulating to a passenger with ambitions beyond just the next stop. In the weeks before leaving Listowel he had been well aware of a controversy that raged in the Ottawa press over the fact that the Senators were after him. Word had leaked out that negotiations were under way, and there was a lot of opposition to the idea.

Taylor hadn't even arrived in town yet, but he was already a subject of heated controversy. Some of the fans, some of the club directors, and certainly some of the players felt that it would be wrong to tamper with a lineup that had won the Stanley Cup in 1905 and seemed even stronger now, two years later.

There was a strong public affection for the squad that had been known as the Silver Seven, and it was theorized that Taylor, touted as a speedy and spectacular individualist, might not fit into Ottawa's highly disciplined and conservative team pattern. And there was the other faction that pointed out the fact that the Silver Seven veterans were beginning to get a little long in the tooth and that a dash of youth and speed as represented by the Listowel man was just what the team needed.

This latter view prevailed at the top.

Tom Phillips of the Kenora Thistles, the player who had wooed Taylor in Portage la Prairie and was himself no slouch, had already been signed as part of the contentious rebuilding process. So had Marty Walsh, a high-scoring forward who had played against Taylor in the International League. The way Taylor read all this as he speeded toward Ottawa was that team politics was none of his business. His business was playing hockey, which is what the Senators would pay him to do. The team had only to close the deal and he would see to it that they got full value for their money.

The Ottawa appointment was with a group of directors headed by the top man, Llewellyn Bate, who owned a chain of grocery stores in the city. Taylor had been directed to go straight from the station to Mr. Bate's main downtown establishment on Sparks Street. There, he found the proprietor and four other team officials waiting to meet him.

The group had been mustered there to proceed to the 11:00 A.M. meeting at the Immigration Department to settle the matter of the promised job in the Civil Service. After a polite discussion in the rear of Mr. Bate's establishment, the party boarded the gentleman's carriage for the short trip to the Parliament buildings.

The carriage was a smart one-horse rig that Bate used for his daily store rounds. It was quite handsome, and generally considered more reliable than the newfangled Oldsmobiles, Maxwells, Franklins, and Model T's that were now increasingly seen and heard coughing and spluttering along the downtown streets. In fact, one of these rambunctious contraptions—a Stanley Steamer —had that morning shuddered to a gasping halt at the corner of Sparks and Bank, where it had been swiftly and prudently abandoned by its owner.

With time to spare and a chance to impress the boy from the sticks, the driver, at Mr. Bate's suggestion, took a leisurely detour. The newcomer basked in the sunshine that had emerged from the overcast, spilling its brisk autumn warmth over the city. It certainly wasn't sleepy little Listowel nor was it Toronto with the big-city feel that had turned Taylor off a couple of years ago.

A pleasant, tree-shaded community of 85,000, Ottawa had both charm and substance and a fast-emerging tradition of style and grace that befitted the nation's capital. Remarkably, the tradition went back a mere eighty years, to when a wild cedar swamp had sprouted the village of Bytown, named after Colonel John By, the British officer who had developed the site to house gangs working on the construction of the Rideau Canal.

As Taylor could see, Colonel By had really started something, and he quickly decided he was going to like it here. All other things, such as the hockey and the money that went with it, being equal, that is.

After a pleasant ride, Mr. Bate's rig drew up outside the government building that housed the Immigration Department. Met by an aide, the delegation was ushered directly into the office of the Honorable Frank Oliver, Minister of the Interior.

Seated behind the huge oak desk, the Minister, a notoriously gruff, no-nonsense M.P. from Edmonton, presented a forbidding sight. He viewed Taylor in a manner from which it was difficult to tell if he approved, or otherwise, and just said brusquely, "Sit down." The scene that followed is one that has persisted in Taylor's memory.

"I'd heard about Mr. Oliver and his reputation as a very blunt customer. We also knew him in our house as a pretty powerful Liberal. This impressed us, although we were all staunch Conservatives. He'd been very well known in political circles out West before he came to Ottawa, and had quite a reputation as a cusser. My dad used to talk about that, and I think he was actually a little upset because he couldn't think of a Conservative politician who could match him at it. The story was that back in Edmonton when Oliver was a young man, his fiancée held up their marriage for a year until he promised never again to swear. He didn't keep the promise, but as far as I know, the marriage turned out all right. Maybe he cut down a little on his vocabulary.

"Oh yes, when I walked into his office I was impressed all right. And when he barked at me to sit down, I was a little scared. He had that way about him."

The Minister of the Interior, and thus the top man in the Immigration Department Taylor hoped to join, came right to the point.

"I suppose you have a letter from your M.P.?"

Taylor was nonplussed.

"What letter?"

"The letter supporting your request for entry into the department without the usual Civil Service examination."

Taylor had a problem.

"Mr. Minister," he said, "I didn't know anything about such a letter, but I couldn't have gotten one anyway. Our M.P. is Mr. Rankin. Now, he's probably a nice enough fellow, but, unfortunately, he's a Liberal. Our family wouldn't go anywhere near him."

There was what could be reliably described as a stunned silence.

Mr. Bate and his friends of the delegation were all good Liberals, which is how they had gotten this far with their protégé— about whom they were now beginning to wonder. The Honorable Minister finally broke the awkward spell, and what happened then has always been one of Taylor's favorite stories.

"He was very quick-tempered, and he had a habit of stuttering when he got excited. I guess he was excited then. He got half out of his chair, wagged his finger at Mr. Bate and shouted, as best as I can repeat it: 'I want you and these other gentlemen to know that as far as your request for this person's appointment is concerned, I am under no obligoddam . . . obligamdod . . . obligo . . . under no damn obligation . . . to approve it.'"

Nor did he approve it.

"I'm very busy," he said brusquely. "Go and talk to the Deputy Minister."

"Well, those Ottawa people hustled me out of there and I remember Bate taking me aside in the hall and saying, 'Taylor, from now on, don't open your mouth unless you absolutely have to. Just act as dumb as you look. We'll do the talking. Okay?'"

Fortunately, the Deputy Minister, a Mr. Carey, was a rabid hockey fan. He knew all about Taylor and what he might do for the Senators, and he quickly pronounced the words that earned him a pair of choice tickets for two for the coming season in the brand new arena rising on Laurier Avenue.

He said, "Okay, Mr. Taylor, you can start work on Monday."

He was to begin as a clerk, at thirty-five dollars a month. It looked like a pretty good job, although, as Taylor has observed, it was bound to be a little lonely: "I was the only Conservative in the whole department."

He managed to survive this indignity, and by December had settled nicely into his new position, on his way to a lifetime of distinguished service in the employ of the Federal Government.

Now it was hockey time again, and he turned out for his first workout with his new team. His reception wasn't exactly rude, but it was less then enthusiastic. The coach, Petie Green, wasn't himself sure that the brass were doing the right thing in bringing this hotshot newcomer into a team stocked with capable veterans who preferred the conservative style of hockey to the Taylor razzle-dazzle.

At one practice after watching the new center break out front twice on a line rush and take the puck in on his own, Alf Smith, a battle-scarred veteran of eight seasons with Ottawa, skated over to the coach and muttered, "Petie, this cocky little cuss isn't going to do us any good. He plays his own game out there."

Two days later, during another workout, Smith sought Green out again and said, "I take back what I said about Taylor. He's better than any of us. It's just that he's so goddam fast it's impossible to stay with him."

Still, a feeling of resentment persisted, at least in Taylor's view, and it was an uneasy December. Then, less than two weeks before the opening game at Quebec on January 4, a storm broke, and Taylor was right in the eye.

It broke publicly with a *Free Press* story headlined: "Has Taylor Jumped?" The story read, in part:

"Has Fred Taylor left the Ottawa team? Has he gone temporarily, or for good? The fast Houghton player who was expected to play centre this winter for the local seven left for Renfrew this morning at 7:30. He intimated to friends that he would sign with the Creamery Town and participate in tonight's opening game there. Taylor also stated that he firmly believed the Ottawa club did not want him, and that there was no chance of him catching a place under those circumstances. Manager John Dickson of the Ottawa club got wind of the matter this morning and was very perturbed."

The *Journal* had a similar story under the headline: "Is Taylor Gone? Star Centre Disappears."

At work was the fine Irish hand of M. J. O'Brien and his son, Ambrose. The three-team Upper Ottawa Valley league they were financing was now comprised of Pembroke, Arnprior, and Renfrew. It was strictly an O'Brien family house league, with ambitions. The O'Briens were still building for a shot at the Stanley Cup, and they still coveted Taylor as the catalyst for this challenge.

The Renfrew club, called the Creamery Kings, was the powerhouse of the mini-league that was to have included Cobalt, another O'Brien enterprise, and had won five straight championships. It was their pet, and had been assigned the job of an eventual Stanley Cup challenge.

Within a week of Taylor's arrival in Ottawa, a Renfrew official had arrived in town to sound him out. It took awhile for Taylor to take the overtures seriously, but then all of a sudden he was off and gone, on the early train to Renfrew.

The flight and the chase were right out of a paperback spy

Fred Taylor, age twenty-one, in uniform of Houghton Portage Lakers, 1905.

Fred's mother, Mary Taylor.

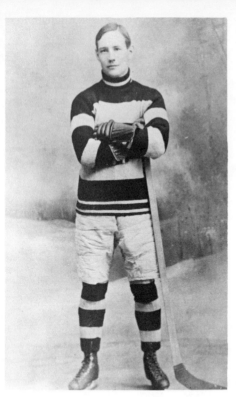

(Left) Houghton teammate Bruce Stua[rt] later played with the Montreal Wandere[rs] and the Ottawa Senators. *(Hockey Hall [of] Fame)*

(Below left) W. M. ("Riley") Hern was t[he] Houghton goalie. He later had a distin[n]guished career with the Montreal Wande[r]ers. *(Hockey Hall of Fame)*

(Below right) Russell ("Barney") Stanle[y] played for Houghton and subsequently wa[s] a teammate of Taylor's in Vancouve[r] *(Hockey Hall of Fame)*

Members of the Ottawa Senators championship team of 1909. (*B. C. Sports Hall of Fame*)

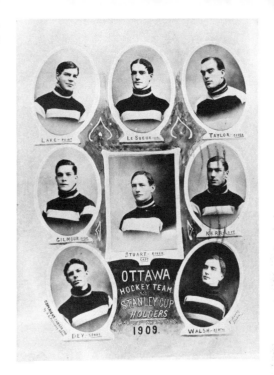

Taylor as he appeared in 1907–8, in Senators uniform.

The Renfrew Millionaires of 1909. Left to right, Bobby Rowe, Herb Jordan, Fred Whitcroft, Newsy Lalonde, Fred Taylor, Frank Patrick, Larry Gilmour, Lester Patrick. *(B. C. Sports Hall of Fame)*

Newsy Lalonde as he appeared in 1906, in a lacrosse uniform.

Headline and picture from Boston *Globe* 1912. *(Bill Cunningham)*

thriller. As the *Free Press* put it when the fugitive was eventually found and returned:

"Upon Taylor's disappearance, the case was immediately turned over to Club Secretary John Dickson, whose subsequent detective work surely caused Sherlock Holmes, Dr. Moriarity and the Old Sleuth to reach up and pull the lid down tight on their coffins."

Nobody could be found who actually saw Taylor board the 7:30 A.M. special to Montreal via Renfrew, but the word was around that he had certainly gone. Dickson had nothing to go on that morning except disjointed evidence from "friends" of Taylor who had been with him the night before, after a team workout. Which, incidentally, had been marked by Taylor's silence.

"Fred," reported Petie Green to Mr. Dickson, "seemed to have something on his mind."

Having deduced that what Taylor had on his mind was a trip to Renfrew for contract talks with the officials of the hockey club, Dickson himself grabbed his hat and caught the 1:45 train out of Ottawa.

Upon arrival in the Creamery Town—so named because of its surrounding green pasture-lands and its Renfrew Creamery—Dickson headed straight for the Dominion Hotel, the hub of local and transient society.

He strode into the lobby, hailed the clerk, and asked if a Mr. Fred Taylor was registered. After consulting the registry, the clerk said that no, nobody of that name had checked in, although there had been a Taylor earlier in the week, from Pembroke, he thought. A traveling salesman, by the look of his large leather satchel.

However, upon hearing an urgent and detailed description from Dickson, the clerk allowed that yes there was somebody like that came in around noon, but had left awhile ago. Without his bag. Dickson fled the hotel to take up the chase and headed up Main Street. Within minutes, he had spied his prey walking slowly up ahead with a large man wearing a coonskin coat and derby. He tailed them to the edge of town, where they wheeled around and headed back toward the hotel. Dickson, keeping out of sight, followed at a discreet distance.

At the entrance to the hotel, Taylor and his friend stopped to chat for a moment, then shook hands, and the gentleman in the coonskin coat departed, obviously in high good humor. At that point Dickson raced forward, blew his cover, and accosted Taylor.

"Fred," he said, "I'd like to talk to you for a minute."

Cool as a cucumber, acting for all the world as if he had fully expected to see the Ottawa secretary there in Renfrew this late Tuesday afternoon, Taylor said, "Certainly. That's fine with me."

Dickson then called for the proprietor and asked the use of a private suite, as he had some important business matter to discuss with his client. There was no such suite available, but Mr. Dickson was informed that they were welcome to use the writing room, which was unoccupied at the moment.

Inside, with the door shut, Dickson motioned Taylor to a chair and said plaintively, "Fred, why did you do this to me?"

Taylor was all innocence. "Do what to you, Mr. Dickson?"

"Look, have you signed with Renfrew yet?"

"No."

"Do you intend to?"

"Well, we've been talking about it, and we're going to talk again in about a half an hour."

"Why, Fred? Why? Why do you want to leave Ottawa?"

"Because I had heard that the Ottawa club didn't want me. That they had been contacted by the Renfrew people and had agreed to release me."

"Who told you that? Did any of our club officials tell you that you weren't wanted?"

"Well, no."

"Then, Fred, all I can say is that you've been listening to the wrong people, and that you've been miserably misled. You've been sold a pretty bad bill of goods. I know things have been said and that there was some resentment among some of the players when you first reported, and maybe even some there yet, but it's up to you to change that by performance. There is already a great respect for you, Fred, and I can tell you that as far as the club executive is concerned we're one hundred per cent with you, and we want you with us. Petie Green told me to tell you exactly the same for himself."

"In that case," said Taylor, "I guess I've been had. If the Ottawa club really does want me, I want no part of playing for Renfrew."

At that point, the door flew open and in charged three representatives of the Renfrew club, one of them the man in the coonskin coat.

They shut the door and closed in on Mr. Dickson.

"What," said the coonskin coat, "are you up to with Taylor?"

"I'm about to take him back to Ottawa, where he belongs, that's what I'm up to. Taylor is under contract to us."

"You have no contract with him, and he has agreed to sign with us."

"The contract," said Dickson, "is in our club minutes. However, I'll leave the matter to Taylor himself. If he wishes to leave the Ottawa team and play here, it's up to him to say so."

After a brief pause, Taylor rose to his feet and in a fine burst of eloquence said, "Gentlemen, now that I fully understand the situation, I wouldn't play here for the whole darn town, with this hotel thrown in." He nodded politely to the open-mouthed Renfrew delegation, smiled agreeably at Mr. Dickson, and the two of them left the room together. They had dinner, a pleasant walk around town, and then caught the train back to Ottawa.

"That Taylor," observed Dickson sometime after, with no lack of admiration, "is a pretty cool customer."

The offer that this cool customer turned down was $2,000 which was $200 more than any existing salary in hockey.

It became apparent why the old guard of the Ottawa team wanted to keep the veteran roster intact as long as possible, and also had some influence in the matter. Four of the veterans, Alf Smith, Harry Westwick, Percy LeSueur, and Harvey Pulford, owned stock, while the others were working for straight salary. However, Taylor was welcomed back into the fold and the Senators got down to business preparing for the league opener in Quebec.

In addition to Ottawa and Quebec, the seven-team league also included the Wanderers, Shamrocks, Victorias, and Montreal, all playing out of the Victoria Street Arena in Montreal. With Taylor yet to make his mark, Ottawa's Tom Phillips was generally considered to be the classiest player in the league, and with that other talented newcomer, Marty Walsh, also in the lineup, the Senators were expected to take a good run at the powerhouse Wanderers.

The Senators managed to look like something less than strong challengers in their league opener on the road, against Quebec. In a frustrating game played on soft, rutted ice, the Ottawas succumbed by a score of 5–2. The new center, Taylor, played well enough in the slush as he scored one goal and assisted in another, but the Ottawas were outplayed and unhappy. The team just didn't jell, and it received a severe roasting in the press. The Senators were rapped as "high priced lemons" as they returned to town for the home opener against the Wanderers in this new arena.

The Wanderers, gunning for their third straight Stanley Cup championship were without their previous year's leader, Lester Patrick, who had stayed out West in Nelson, B.C., to help in the family's booming lumber business. Also missing from the fold was Hod Stuart, the star of some rousing duels with Taylor as a member of the Pittsburgh team in the International League seasons of 1905–6 before he had left to join the Wanderers.

In the summer of 1907, this player who was universally admired throughout hockey for his honesty and stout heart met a tragic end. The event is touchingly recorded in an unpublished chronicle of those years written by Lester Patrick:

"In the month of June 1907, my heart was saddened by news of the accidental death of Hod Stuart, my pal and idol. Impulsively, Hod had dived into shallow water, broke his neck, and died instantly. This was in Belleville, Ontario, where Hod was working on a building contract with his father and his brother, Bruce. I grieved for a wonderful friend."

Lester Patrick's replacement on the Wanderers was a cocky youth from Brandon named Art Ross. At twenty-one, big, strong and immensely talented, Ross was already being touted as a sure-fire star. He played at cover-point, a position that puts a high premium on speed and mobility. Ross had both. So had Fred Taylor, and more so.

The comparison between Ross and Taylor didn't escape the attention of the Ottawa coach, Petie Green. He had been coming to the conclusion that Taylor, with his raw speed just too much for cohesive line play, was miscast as a center. Immediately after the loss in Quebec, Taylor was shifted to cover-point.

Right from the first workout, with Taylor now roaming pretty well at will and able to use his great speed to best advantage, the move looked like a good one. Then, at the grand opening of the new rink, events proved it to be a stroke of genius. It was a milestone evening for hockey in Ottawa, both in respect to the Taylor exhibition and the baptism of the beautiful new arena.

The place was packed to overflowing with a crowd of 7,100 people. The three thousand reserved seats were $1.25 each, and two hundred tickets were sold for a whopping five dollars. Five hundred fans from Montreal had to fight over the hundred seats set aside for their use.

"It was a typically excited first-night crowd, with feelings pent up in anticipation of a great battle. The Wanderers appeared first, and just to release a little of the pressure, the Ottawa people joined in the cheer that went up from the supporters of the red band. But this was just a whisper compared to the shriek that greeted Harvey Pulford as he led the Ottawa team out. Alf Smith followed Pulford, and no sooner had he touched the ice than he flopped on his back. Westwick followed, and went through the same performance. They had neglected to remove the leather runners worn on the skate blades to protect the edge. The incident brought a roar of laughter from the crowd."

Tom Phillips and Marty Walsh also made their debuts with Ottawa that night and were outstanding, but it was Taylor who stole the opening show.

"The contest brought to light a brilliant new star in the Eastern Canadian League. For some time, Fred Taylor, a new member of the Ottawa team, has been in the limelight, not so much through his play, as through certain circumstances which evoked much publicity. Up until Saturday night, he was looked on here as an uncertain quantity—by some. . . .

"Taylor proved the sensation of the night. Such defensive play and individual work up the forward line has never been seen before in Ottawa. Taylor arrived here with the appellation 'Whirlwind of the International League' tagged on him. On his performance Saturday night, he can well be called the 'Tornado of the E.C.H.L.' . . . Toward the end of the half, he brought off the play of the night. He stole possession of the puck near his own goal, made two beautiful shifts to elude two forwards, and then played off the boards as he beat Pud Glass and started a straight run down the side. Both Hooper and Art Ross went out to meet him near the defence, but he swiftly outmanoeuvered both and swept in on the goalie, Riley Hern. Hern had no chance as Taylor deftly slipped the puck into the net."

For the night Taylor had a total of four goals, and the *Free Press* reporter concluded: "With his general play and support of the others, he was worth many more." The Senators won the contest by a decisive 12–2.

The Prime Minister, Sir Wilfrid Laurier, was not on hand at the opening of the new Ottawa Arena to put his government seal of approval on the city's latest twin assets—the rink and Taylor —but the Governor-General, Earl Grey, was suitably impressed with both. He was an avid hockey fan who rarely missed an Ottawa home game. His daughter, Lady Sybil, a member of the exclusive Ottawa Minto Club, was with him at the big game. She was quite a good skater herself, and she knew another good one when she saw him.

Both she and her father were in raptures over the speed and skating skills of Taylor, and showed it. They were followed on their way out afterward by that alert reporter, Malcolm Brice. He was in earshot when the Governor-General was heard to say:

"That new No. 4, Taylor, he's a cyclone if ever I saw one."

Relating the comment next day in the *Free Press*, Brice wrote: "In Portage La Prairie they called him a tornado, in Houghton, Michigan, he was known as a whirlwind. From now on he'll be known as Cyclone Taylor."

This is one of those stories that has been so often repeated that it has become suspect as just another of those little fables that grow around a legendary figure, but this one was exactly true to the facts. And there is some whimsy in the fact that—in the style of the previous Governor-General Lord Minto, whose name eventually graced the Minto Cup of lacrosse—Earl Grey, the rabid hockey fan, would attach his name to the Cup that is now the Holy Grail of Canadian professional football.

The next day, the Governor-General's daughter asked if she

could have one of Cyclone Taylor's sticks, and the request, conveyed to the Ottawa club by the Minto club president, was granted. Taylor only had the one stick, and it cost him $1.50 for another, but he figured it was worth it. This incident has lingered on as another of those treasured memories that Taylor has fondly tucked away.

"I was just a country boy up there in the Capital City, and I was quite awed by it all. I hadn't gotten to meet many Governor-General's daughters up to that point, and this young lady was exceedingly nice. I met her again a few times later on around Ottawa, and when her father finished his term as Governor-General, she took the stick with her back to England. When I met her again in London many years later—I suppose she was in her sixties then—she told me that she still had it."

There was another young lady on hand that night for that spectacular arena christening who was destined to have a greater impact on Taylor's life. She was a Miss Thirza Cook, a pretty, vivacious, golden-haired girl in her early twenties. She had gone to the game with her sister, and was as impressed as the rest of the throng by what Taylor himself thinks may have been the finest game he has ever played.

An avid hockey fan, she was there again two Saturdays later when Taylor was again hailed as the outstanding star on very bad ice. Taylor had just coolly taken over and controlled the game. He himself scored just one goal, but he set up a half dozen others and was all over the ice for the full sixty minutes. The Victorias' Frank Patrick, who played with a sore shoulder, said afterward that it was one of the finest displays of two-way hockey he had ever seen, and called it "remarkable under those conditions."

At work on Monday morning, the spectacular play of Ottawa's No. 4 was the main topic of conversation, as it was throughout the city. By what turned out to be a happy coincidence, Miss Cook was employed as a secretary in the Immigration Department that boasted Fred—now known equally well as "Cyclone" —as one of its junior clerks. The fellow employees, who toiled in separate offices, met for the first time that February morning when Thirza arrived with a group of her friends, all still raving about the cover-point's performance on Saturday night.

That first meeting was just a fleeting one in the main office, with time for little more than a hello and a touch of hands. That was enough for Taylor, who in his own jargon was "a gone goose" over the slender girl with the sparkling personality and the soft, dancing eyes.

The Rideau Canal was frozen over, and an office skating party had been arranged for that night. Taylor, showing moves as fast off the ice as they were on, had asked the Cook girl to go along, and she had accepted.

There, in the crisp cold air of a bright moonlit night on the Rideau Canal, began a partnership that was to last well over fifty years. There was a common bond between them as Thirza Cook was a member of the elite Minto Club, and played on the girl's hockey team there. It was a small thing but a starting point in a marvelous evening that Taylor, with great affection, regards as a milestone in his personal life.

"After the party, I walked her to her home, a fine house in the best part of town. She took me in for a few minutes, and I met her mother. Her mother wasn't pleased.

"Right from the beginning—and it wasn't a very good one— her mother, Amelia, who was a widow, made it quite clear to me that she didn't want her daughter to have anything to do with any hockey player. I had a long walk home."

As the abashed suitor had so quickly discovered, it was going to be a difficult courtship.

There was a social gap between the clerk/hockey player and the Cooks, although the family was not exactly wealthy. Frank, the oldest of the three sons, worked in the C.P.R. freight yards, where he later lost his life in a shunting accident. Thirza herself worked as a government clerk. Still, the Cooks, with four girls and three boys in the family all told, were definitely Ottawa upper-crust and well up in the city's social scale. This was mostly because Thirza's mother was an in-law, by a sister's marriage, to J. K. Booth, the multimillionaire lumber tycoon.

For his part, Taylor's only link with affluence was his $500 hockey salary plus his $35 a month salary in the Civil Service. That and a letter from his mother in Listowel proudly announcing that Archie Taylor had just been promoted to a larger sales territory, a move that—if the market in farm implements stayed good—might push his monthly pay to as much as $80.

For almost all of its six difficult years, Taylor's courtship of Thirza Cook was discouraged by her family, and accepted only with great reluctance. Fortunately, Thirza's brothers and sisters took a liking to Taylor and gave him encouragement. Best of all, Thirza stuck with him without question despite the pressure from her mother.

"After the first few months, we confided in each other completely, and since then I never made an important decision without discussing it with her first. From the beginning, ours was a full partnership. A wonderful partnership."

While the romance moved along, so did that year's league race, and by the last week in February, Ottawa and the Wanderers were tied for first place with identical win-loss records of six and two.

More than anyone else, it was Taylor who had kept the Senators stride for stride with the powerful Wanderers. It was he and the other two new players, Tom Phillips and Marty Walsh, who had kept the fire burning under the steady old guard of Westwick, Moore, Pulford, and Smith. Taylor was the spark of the club's new breed, and despite the early truce there was still a lingering resentment among the old bulls over the fact that Fred was getting by far the bulk of the headlines.

As far as this alleged excess of attention from the press was concerned, the object himself was just an innocent party. He always was and always would be the headline grabber, but he never much minded. If he sometimes played to the crowd, which he did, it was only because his talent was such that it just naturally thrust him centerstage. He just did what he could, with a style and a flair that happened to be unmatched by any other player, and let the raves fall where they may. What the reporters wrote was no more than what the fans had already moved and seconded from their places of judgment in the stands.

Throughout Taylor's career there would be claims for another player or players said to be his equal or better, but there was none more exciting, and nobody disputed that.

A nagging sense of rift that simmered within the Ottawa organization at both the player and management level surfaced in a strange form just before the year's final and critical meeting with the Wanderers in Montreal. Two days before the team was due to leave, there was a dispute among the club executives over which railway line they should take, C.N.R. or C.P.R. It was a seemingly paltry squabble that resulted in the abrupt and angry resignation of the team secretary and manager, J. P. Dickson, who happened to be very friendly with the C.N.R. agent. Dickson was not aboard when the C.P.R. train huffed out of the Ottawa station with the Senators aboard.

As Taylor clearly recalls the weird affair, it came about because of what can best be described as an early version of drag racing, with the steam trains of the day cast in the role of hot rods. "It was a common thing for one train to pull out of the station on schedule a couple of minutes before the other, and then the later train running on a parallel track, would take off and attempt to overhaul and pass it. They'd be going I guess a good seventy miles per hour or so, full steam, with their whistles blowing and the passengers watching from their carriages, waving and shouting when the second train came abreast and the two of them poured it on, racing side-by-side. I tell you, it was a great thrill."

The idea of The Great Train Race didn't appeal to Dickson, who plumped for the lesser excitement on Train No. 2, on the assumption that it would not overtake the first one. He lost. So, eventually, did the spirit of this remarkable Grand Prix on rails. There was an investigation by both rail companies shortly after that ride to Montreal (there is no record of the winner), and the racing was banned.

The Senators arrived at the Sherbrooke station unharmed and were in good spirits as they headed for the rink and their showdown with the Wanderers.

The big game turned into a rugged and at times brutal contest that produced a rousing and historic one-on-one battle between Taylor and his opposing cover-point, Art Ross. The talented pair's first meeting—the opening night 12–2 rout in Ottawa—was no contest, with Taylor the easy winner, but Ross was all primed for the rematch.

Two years younger than Taylor, he too was having a sensational first year in the league. He didn't have Taylor's exceptional speed, but he was tough and smart and cocky and endowed with all the skills. Ross was off on an impressive start on what would be one of the most dominant careers in the game. First a great player and then the shrewd general manager of the Boston Bruins franchise, he would ultimately rank with Jack Adams and Lester Patrick as one of three most outstanding player-executive figures in the history of hockey.

In that game in Montreal there was a special unspoken rivalry between these two superlative players, and from the opening whistle they swirled about the rink like twin shadows, checking like demons and jockeying for a breakaway. Each got one, and each made a furious rink-long rush that was foiled at the goal mouth, first by the Wanderer's Riley Hern and then by Ottawa's Percy LeSueur.

Twice, Ross, the heavier by twenty-five pounds, caught Taylor with a vicious bodycheck and then was rapped himself with a head-on thud that brought blood streaming from his nose, leaving a red wake across the ice as he went back after Taylor. Before half time (the game was still played in two 30-minute periods) Tom Phillips had slipped in alone to beat Hern and give Ottawa a 1–0 lead.

In the second half, the rival cover-points had the packed house of 6,500 in an uproar as their duel heated up, particularly after Taylor broke loose from Ross on a dazzling move to make it 2–0 with a backhand flip over the prostrate form of his old buddy, Riley Hern. It was shortly after that juncture when Ross caught Taylor flying down the boards on what looked like another break, and hit him with a thudding side-long check that laid Taylor out cold. The game was halted while Phillips and two other Ottawa players carried him off the ice.

Then, with one cover-point stretched out on a bench in the Ottawa dressing room, the other one ripped off two end-to-end rushes to tie the game. Teammates Walter Smaill and Bruce Stuart went on to make it 4–2, and it was game over and season over for the Senators.

With one more game to play, the Wanderers had clinched the E.C.H.L. championship. They then went on to defeat the Toronto Maple Leafs of the new Ontario Professional League in the Stanley Cup challenge series. When it was all over, Taylor, not Ross, was named as cover-point on the E.C.H.L. All Star

Chapter Four
THE CLIMACTIC YEAR

With their feud settled for the time being, the Senators and the Wanderers were off for their first stroll on the sidewalks of New York. The Manhattan tournament was promoted by the proprietors of the St. Nicholas Skating Rink, a spacious building in the Sixties that housed an item that was still a curiosity of the times, an artificial ice surface. The only other like it was that in Taylor's old International League haunt, Pittsburgh's Duquesne Garden.

This unique road show was an invitational affair, with $1,000 going to the winner of a three-game series.

Hockey was no stranger to St. Nicks, as the 6,200-seat arena was headquarters for a thriving New York State amateur league. By the standards set a few hundred miles north, the caliber of this league was not very good, but it was good enough to whet the public appetite for something better. This invitational tournament was it, and it would be the big town's first look at hockey, big-league Canadian style.

Although St. Nicks was the only ice arena in Manhattan, it was by no means the largest indoor emporium. The largest was the huge, brick stone-and-stucco monster at 26th Street and Madison Avenue, with its ornate 320-foot central tower that was one of the architectural wonders of the day, built as a tribute to a now-faded Victorian age. This building was the second in the famous line of such edifices known as Madison Square Garden, the latest of which now rises in sterile glass-and-steel splendor over Pennsylvania Station, on 34th Street.

This second of the breed, like the first, was built primarily to house the city's traditional spring circus. In fact, the first, which was erected on the same Madison Avenue site in 1879 and replaced eleven years later, was called Barnum's Hippodrome, after the great showman of the same name, Phineas T. It was built for elephants and trapeze artists and brass bands, and it wasn't until the mid-twenties, when the third Madison Square

Garden opened at 50th Street and Eighth Avenue, that a hockey rink became part of the furnishings.

Here in this sunny week in March 1908, the circus was back at the old stand, with the name Barnum & Bailey up on the Garden marquee. At the St. Nicholas Arena, less than a couple of miles west along Fifth Avenue, a huge streamer was draped across the entrance heralding the arrival of "The World's Greatest Hockey Teams."

The train bearing the players pulled into Pennsylvania Station at midday, Thursday. The first game was billed for Saturday evening. The Canadians were met by a delegation of St. Nicholas Arena officials who had horse-drawn cabs waiting to take them to their lodgings in the Mayflower Hotel on Fifth Avenue. Automobiles were now a fairly common sight on the city streets, but the quaint automated breed of New York cabbie was not yet on the scene.

With their shiny black hansoms clopping smartly up 34th Street to the clang-clang of the passing trolley cars, the visitors were suitably awed by their first look at the bustling metropolis of four-and-a-half million souls, its flamboyance epitomized by Diamond Jim Brady, the one-time bellhop who had made millions as a financier and now cut a dazzling swath on Broadway.

Art Ross, thorough in everything he did, had done some research before leaving Montreal, and had been especially fascinated with the tales of Diamond Jim, who adorned himself with diamond rings and stickpins and beautiful women. Currently, Brady was squiring Lillian Russell, the glamorous star of the new Broadway hit *Wildfire,* co-starring Ernest Truex. This further intrigued Ross, who had listed Diamond Jim Brady as one of the sights he most wanted to see while in New York. Art, who would himself one day become a landmark of sorts up in Boston, simply admired the fellow's style.

Upon arrival at the hotel, the players checked in, unpacked, and then went right out on the town. The majority made a beeline for Times Square, a fifty-cent cab ride away. The boys splurged with the fare, as money was no object. Each player received five dollars a day expense money while in New York, and although it wasn't in the Daimond Jim class, it was quite a lavish sum in those days.

A five-dollar bill went a long way in Manhattan, and some excellent bargains were quickly discovered. Beer was a nickel a glass; six huge foaming mugs for twenty-five cents, with a free lunch on the side. If a fellow wanted to go first-class, he could really lay it on over at the swank Waldorf-Astoria, where cocktails in the Palm Garden were two for a quarter—although as Petie Green noted on being appraised of this rare bargain, "None of our guys would be caught dead with a cocktail."

At the rink, the series was a highly successful promotion, both artistically and financially. It played to packed houses and produced the first faint, prenatal stirrings of the New York Rangers dynasty that would emerge eighteen years later.

Moose Johnson, Art Ross, Ernie Russell, Marty Walsh, and Tom Phillips received raves for their fine play, but the runaway star of the St. Nicks show was Taylor.

When that man in Tin Pan Alley got around to writing "Me and My Shadow," he might well have been thinking of Cyclone Taylor and the headlines that followed him wherever he went. He drew them like a magnet. In this his first of five exhibition series in New York, he was an instant hit with the fans, and he caught the special attention of the reporters who covered the games.

These New York journalists didn't know a great deal about hockey, but they had been around Broadway long enough to know a special star quality when they saw it. They saw it in Taylor. His Manhattan debut was hailed in the New York *Times* with a forthright top-of-the-page headline: TAYLOR WAS MAGNIFICENT.

Said the rival New York *Sun:* "Taylor is by far the fastest man ever seen on New York ice, and his stickhandling is equally marvelous."

On the second night, the arena was hung with great streamers hailing "Little Jeff," and at the third game hucksters were in aisles doing a roaring business selling "Oh you Jeff!" lapel buttons. The nickname derived from Cyclone's resemblance to Jim Jeffries, the former heavyweight champion whose title had been taken over by Taylor's old acquaintance, Tommy Burns. You can bet that nobody loved the name more than Little Jeff himself.

All of the visitors were having a great fun series both on and off the ice. It is not known if Art Ross ever did get to see Diamond Jim Brady, with or without his bosomy chum, Lillian Russell, but there was no dearth of other sights to see. The Times Square bistros and arcades were among the tourists' more popular curios, as was Minsky's Burlesque, the distinguished Manhattan headquarters for culture lovers researching the visual delights of the human torso.

Taylor has insisted that the dishes there were really not his dish. "The boys liked to go where the naked ladies were, but when they asked me to go along I said I wasn't much interested. Now, that might not have been altogether true, but from what I heard they always wanted to sit right down there in the front row."

But as Tom Phillips saw it, "It sure beats hell out of anything back home in Kenora."

Another marvel of old New York of 1908 was the magnificent new subway system that had been opened just two years before with a tube built under the East River to ease the heavy traffic on the Brooklyn Bridge. Taylor took that ride to Brooklyn and back, and was greatly impressed by the speed and luxury of the trains, which had one car set aside exclusively for women.

This too was the year that saw the completion of New York's first giant skyscraper, the 41-story Singer Building. That was certainly an object of wonder to the Canadians, as was the unique 20-story Flatiron Building, set on a wedge of land on 23rd Street, between Broadway and Fifth Avenue. This building was just nearing completion and Taylor and friends were entranced by the huge electric sign that flickered across the face of the site with the more or less breathless message: "Manhattan Beaches Swept by Ocean Breezes."

The sidewalk gawkers had no way of knowing it at the time, but they were witness to a quaint bit of history. That sign attracted so much public attention that it created a whole gaudy new concept of advertising. It became the catalyst for the vast jungle of neon signs that would eventually light up Times Square with a blaze of flashing inducements to buy, buy, buy. As in New York, the urban plazas of London, Paris, Barcelona, Tokyo, et al., would never again be the same.

On Broadway, the new spring season offered the usual glittering array of shows, starring such as Ethel Barrymore, Anna Held, Douglas Fairbanks, Billie Burke, George M. Cohan, Constance Collier, Maude Adams, and of course, the gorgeous Miss Russell. A star of somewhat less eye-appeal, Sir Harry Lauder, had just finished his Broadway stand and was off back to Scotland with his crooked stick and bony knees. To balance this loss, there were the spectacular ladies of the *Ziegfeld Follies of 1908*, starring Mae Murray.

With just six nights in town and three of these on the job at St. Nicks, there was little time left to spend in the theater district except to gawk at the marquees. A few of the boys did take in the *Follies* and recommended the show highly, but Taylor and the others settled for two other live shows: the Circus in Madison Square Garden and *Sporting Days*, a lavish revue playing at the Hippodrome.

Taylor, Marty Walsh, and Bruce Stuart sat in the preferred $.75 seats in the lower balcony to watch the Hippodrome show, and nearly seventy years later Taylor still remembers his entrancement.

"I was awed by a stage that was nearly the size of a football field, or it seemed that way. At one point, there was a race between six horses, running full speed on a treadmill. I got so excited, I almost came right out of my seat."

There were two other memorable acts, the like of which the visitors had never seen and, swears Taylor, wouldn't see again. One portrayed a baseball game depicting John McGraw's Giants in action. The scene was complete with baseball diamond and a grandstand packed with hundreds of fans—well, at least two hundred—and a painted backdrop posing as the pastoral wilds of Manhattan. The only flaw in this remarkable set was that the diamond was a little cramped and the right field foul line led straight into the orchestra pit, which was directly behind first base.

The meticulous Mr. Ross, always thinking, shrewdly calculated that a hard drive right down the line would wipe out the entire trombone section. This never happened, but there was yet another act to astound and astonish the Canadians in the audience. This one showed two flying machines soaring high across the stage, suspended and propelled by invisible wires.

It was just five years since the Wright Brothers had startled
the world by propelling their marvelous contraption over the
sands of Kitty Hawk, North Carolina, in history's first powered
flight. This, in the unlikely setting of the Hippodrome just off
Times Square, was the Canadians' first look, albeit just a simula-
tion, at the scientific wonder of the Twentieth century.

There was a different memory of the visit to the circus in
Madison Square Garden.

The splendor and excitement of the Barnum & Bailey spectacular turned to horror in the final minutes when a trapeze artist
missed a ring in a crossover high up near the roof of the giant
arena. There was no safety net, and the crowd watched in
numbed silence as he tumbled down and thudded into the
sawdust floor more than a hundred feet below. But it was the immediate aftermath that stunned and sickened Taylor.

"We sat there in shock for nearly a full minute with the poor
fellow lying there smashed on the ground, and then a swarm of
circus employees came racing up and literally shoveled the body
into a basket and hauled it off. It was as though they didn't want
anybody to know what had happened. They went on to finish
the show as if nothing had happened." That on the eve of the
final game, was the players last night out on the town.

The teams had played wide-open hockey and split the first two
games, but Ottawa won the decider to take the series.

By that time, the others were reconciled to playing second ba-
nana to Little Jeff, who received a thunderous ovation every time
he took off with the puck. Taylor obliged with a sensational closing display that earned him two goals and a cut of the winners'
$1,000 prize money.

All of the players made it on time and without incident for the
departure the next morning. The train left Penn Station promptly
at 9:20 A.M. leaving behind the seeds of a new era of professional hockey.

When the Senators arrived in Ottawa after an overnight stay
in Montreal, they were met by a large crowd of fans and reporters. The New York victory was really no big deal, but there
was a great public curiosity about the venture, which had been
liberally reported in wire stories from New York.

The Ottawa *Citizen* hailed the trip as "a huge success," and re-

ported that "the victorious hockeyists returned home in a dazzling array of spring styles, sporting the most modern creations
in sky-pieces and top coats. Marty Walsh declared in fact that
they had bought out most of the New York stores."

The "sky-pieces" that helped cause this sartorial stir were, as
Taylor has explained, a style of felt hat that was the new rage in
New York. "They were Christie hats, felt fedoras with little roll
brims, in a sort of bluish-black color. We all had them, and I
must say they were pretty snappy."

Among those in the crowd waiting at the station was Thirza
Cook, and the romance was resumed. It now had lots of time to
prosper, for with both his girl and his job there, Taylor's summertimes would now and for the next few years be spent in Ottawa. Both of the foregoing distractions, of distinctly contrasting
appeal, left ample time for his old summer love, lacrosse.

He signed on with the Ottawa Capitals of the National
Lacrosse Union. He played the inside-home position, and well
enough to be described in the Montreal *Gazette*, during an away
game in that town: ". . . just now the biggest attraction in the
national game . . ."

It is likely that Taylor's reputation as an outstanding hockey
star influenced judgment of him as a lacrosse player. He was a
good, effective player and had his brilliant moments, but he
thrived mostly on his natural athletic ability and his tremendous
competitive spirit. He at one time told a reporter that he "never
really liked lacrosse." Still, he was in demand in the game, and
he always produced results and generated excitement.

At one point, "the biggest attraction in the national game" got
himself into a pot of trouble over that fiery spirit of his. He did it
by a means that belied his public and self-avowed reputation as
a nice guy who wouldn't harm a fly. Unless, that is, said fly happened to be crawling his way in a potentially menacing manner.

The Capitals were hosting Toronto at Lansdowne Park, and
Taylor, moved that day to defense, was getting a lot of extra loving care and attention from the visiting players. After he had
scored his third goal in the opening period, he was lustily decked
by the Toronto cover-point, Tom Harshaw. Taylor got up, and
Harshaw decked him again, with an exceptionally good right

cross. The newspaper account of the ensuing events pretty well match the Taylor version—to a point.

This is how Taylor saw it: "Harshaw had been giving me a lot of punishment right from the opening whistle, and that last lick, from the blind side, did it. I went after him, caught up with him, threw away my stick and knocked him down with a punch to the jaw. I put my foot on him to hold him down, and the referee, Tom Carlind, came racing up to intervene."

Here the Taylor story and the press account differ somewhat.

The newspaper report said: "Taylor left Harshaw and turned on the referee, Carlind, who just wanted to stop the fracas. The Ottawa player swung at Carlind and struck him in the face with his fist. It appeared to be an unprovoked assault, calling for Taylor's suspension."

Taylor's version: "While I was involved with Harshaw, I heard footsteps coming up from behind, and I thought it was another Toronto player coming to Harshaw's assistance. I just wheeled around and let one go. Next thing I knew, two big policemen came running out onto the field, grabbed me and hauled me off. They put me in a paddy-wagon, hauled me off to the police station, and tossed me in jail."

The headline in the next day's Montreal *Gazette* was straightforward enough. It said simply: "Taylor Jailed." For a God-fearing, church-going Ottawa scoutmaster beloved by his troop, this was somewhat of an embarrassing situation. However, the incarceration in the pokey lasted for just six hours.

The Ottawa team manager went to the station house to talk to the police, but the clincher came when the referee, Carlind, also showed up to plead for the new lodger. As Taylor commented later, Mr. Carlind was very sporting about the whole thing, even if he did have a very sore nose. "I told Tom what had really happened—that I didn't know it was he running up behind me, and that when I turned around, thinking it was a Toronto player out to get me, I couldn't see who it was because the sun was in my eyes."

Taylor has sworn that Carlind looked only mildly skeptical. In any event, that may have been the first and last time a player in any sport has used "but the sun got in my eyes" as a defense plea in an assault case.

Carlind was quite willing to let bygones be bygones, but not the league governors. They took a very stern view of the incident. There was the devil to pay at a special meeting called at league headquarters in Montreal, with representatives of some teams angrily demanding Taylor's outright expulsion.

"That man," roared Shamrocks' manager Harry McLaughlin, "should be barred for life. He is being protected only by politics and because he is a big gate attraction!"

Three teams supported the demand for expulsion, but in the end, obeisance to the economics of a gate attraction being no less than it is now, it was agreed that the league president merely write Taylor a letter of censure.

In Ottawa, there were several indignant and sorrowful letters to the editor lamenting the incident. One said: "Yes, I am sure that Fred Taylor is as much ashamed of himself as we are. Off the field and on, he appears to be two different persons. Sort of a Jekyll and Hyde. Perhaps he shouldn't play lacrosse, as it seems to warm his temper too much, and he is too much of a gentleman to be involved in such a sordid business as he was guilty of on Saturday."

Taylor, properly censored but not necessarily chastened, turned up at Lansdowne Park the next Saturday for a repeat game against Toronto. There is no ready record of the game's outcome, but apparently nobody was mortally hurt, not even the referee.

At about this time, a different sort of Taylor headline appeared in both Ottawa papers, as this one in the *Citizen:*

NEW TROOP FORMED
Famed Hockey Star Fred Taylor
To Lead Dominion Church Scouts

The Boy Scout movement recently founded in England by Lord Baden-Powell was spreading fast throughout the civilized world, and Scoutmaster Taylor's troop was the eighth in Canada. Here was the reaffirmation of a boyhood fascination with the affairs of the British Boer War hero that had surfaced during the days in Listowel, back at the turn of the century.

As Cyclone Taylor moved toward the first peak of his career,

1908 became a year of high drama for three of his boyhood friends. They were Tommy Burns, who now reigned as king of the world's heavyweight boxers; Tom Longboat, the Indian youth who was now acclaimed as one of the world's greatest marathon runners; and Cal Bricker, the Listowel school chum who was Olympic-bound as a superlative track and field athlete.

With Taylor, this group formed a foursome remarkable in the fact that all four came out of that small piece of western Ontario that stretches from Tara to Brantford and all were born within a six-year span in the 1880s. Their paths had crossed many times during their younger days, and they all shared a common admiration for each other's exceptional athletic skills.

The affairs of his boyhood friends were of much fascination to Taylor as he followed their adventures through the newspapers and word-of-mouth from Listowel or Hanover or Brantford. There was even at times a touch of envy as he read of exploits that took all three abroad, far beyond the boundaries of Taylor's own considerable travels.

Of the three, Bricker had been the closest to Taylor, and his relatively modest career would not meet with wide public acclaim until July of that summer over in London's White City Stadium.

When Taylor had left Listowel in the cold winter of 1904 to play hockey in Portage la Prairie, young Bricker was just a good track and field athlete with little reputation beyond the immediate area. By the time Taylor got to Ottawa three years later to lay claim to his status as a big-time hockey star, Bricker had gone to college in Toronto, won two intercollegiate all-round championships there, and was now a candidate for the Canadian Olympic Team as a broad jumper. At the Olympic Trials in Montreal on the very day Taylor was involved in his the-sun-got-in-my-eyes gambit with the lacrosse referee, Bricker set Canadian records in the broad jump and triple jump and was named to the Canadian team bound for the London Olympics.

In London's giant White City Stadium, pitted against the best in the world, the twenty-four-year-old from Listowel was rated little chance of finishing among the elite top three medal winners.

Taylor had just finished breakfast in his Ottawa boarding house that July morning when a friend from the downtown telegraph office came to the door with the news that Bricker had won an Olympic bronze medal with a leap of twenty-three feet, six inches. Fred was delighted with the news and immediately phoned home to Listowel. The folks there already knew.

True, their boy's feat was upstaged that week by the double-victory of Toronto's Bobby Kerr in the sprint races, but it was an outstanding accomplishment by the hometown boy nonetheless. Bricker's medal was Canada's first ever in an Olympic field event. It would not be his last.

Still, the high drama of that 1908 Olympiad was in the classic marathon, which is traditionally scheduled for the final day of competition. In this race, the Canadian hope was Tom Longboat, and back home there was tremendous public interest in his venture. No Canadian was more intrigued by this lonely challenge than was Fred Taylor, who as a pure athlete admired Longboat over all others.

Tom was thirteen when Taylor first saw him, already strong, lithe, and supple as a willow reed.

"I had never seen anything so smooth and effortless. He just seemed to flow over the ground. I don't remember much about the race except that Tom won, and with the greatest of ease. He fascinated me. I went to him after the race and said hello. I was a couple of years older than he was and I wasn't too conversational myself, but he was much less so. He was very quiet and painfully shy. He just answered in grunts and monosyllables, but he smiled when he got up to go, apparently pleased that I had spoken. I'm sure he was a lonely lad, but he didn't know quite what to do about it. I saw him at meets many times after that, and I got to know him better. We got along fine; understood each other, I think. He was a fine person, and oh my, what an athlete!"

By 1908, with the prestigious Boston Marathon numbered among his spectacular string of victories, Longboat was acclaimed as one of the world's greatest runners. That summer, after an emotional ceremonial send-off by his people of the Onandaga Indian Reserve, he went to London as one of the favorites to win the classic Olympic marathon. With him was his manager, the flamboyant Toronto-Irishman, Tom Flanagan, a promoter who had long been suspected of manipulating Longboat for his gambling profit. This suspicion boiled into a great furor in the English press, and the U. S. Olympic team made an unsuccessful request to have Longboat declared ineligible on the grounds that he had violated his amateur status.

Holding a commanding lead for six miles of the grueling 16-mile route from Windsor Castle to the gates of White City Stadium, Longboat inexplicably faltered and dropped back into the pack. In obvious distress, he finally stumbled to halt and dropped to the ground. For him, the race was over.

The winner of what was to be remembered as perhaps the most dramatic footrace of all time was America's Johnny Hayes, whom Longboat had beaten in the Boston Marathon. Italy's Pietri Dorando, the heroic little pastry-cook from the Isle of Capri, collapsed in the final stages and was dragged to the finish line by Italian team officials. He beat Hayes to the finish but was disqualified.

Utterly downcast, Longboat was later that day questioned by English and American reporters about the pullout.

Flanagan was himself unusually subdued.

"Tom," he said, "suddenly became very ill. Very ill. That's all I know."

"We know that, Flanagan," said a reporter, "but what about the stories going around that your boy was doped?"

"I don't know anything about that."

"But you know that there was a lot of last-minute money bet on the race, most of it, we hear, against Longboat?"

"Look, I've heard the same story. And I don't know. All I know is that Tom was very sick. Ask him. Well, Tom?"

Longboat, with his head on his chest, was barely audible.

"I don't know about any dope. I just got sick and I couldn't run any more. That's all."

And that's how the story rests today.

Upon his return to Canada, none of his friends, including Taylor, could get any more out of him than could the London reporters. The only thing sure was that the lonely, confused youth had passed his zenith, and his star was on the decline. The descent would be slow but, in the end, tragic.

As Longboat tried to pick up the pieces, Taylor was finishing the lacrosse season and getting ready for another hockey cam-

Ernest ("Moose") Johnson turned professional with the Montreal Wanderers and played with them on four Stanley Cup-winning teams. He was renowned for the length of his reach—and the length of his stick. *(Hockey Hall of Fame)*

Arthur H. Ross, a frequent opponent of Taylor's, was a top goal scorer for the Montreal Wanderers. He later coached the Boston Bruins to three Stanley Cups. *(Hockey Hall of Fame)*

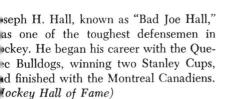

seph H. Hall, known as "Bad Joe Hall," as one of the toughest defensemen in ckey. He began his career with the Que- c Bulldogs, winning two Stanley Cups, d finished with the Montreal Canadiens. *ockey Hall of Fame)*

The Vancouver Millionaires, Stanley Cup champions of 1915. Back row, left to right, Fred ("Smoky") Harris, Fred Taylor, trainer Pete Muldoon, Mickey McKay, Frank Nighbor. Front row, left to right, manager Frank Patrick, Si Griffis, Lloyd Cook, Hugh Lehman. *(B. C. Sports Hall of Fame)*

Taylor (left) at lacrosse face-off in 1913, when playing for the Vancouver Terminals. Mayor Baxter is the referee.

Frank Patrick, player-pre-ident of the Vancouver M—roons, Stanley Cup cha—pions, 1915. *(B. C. Sports H— of Fame)*

Lester Patrick with his sons Lynn and Muzz.

Cyclone Taylor, hair thinning but still in top form, in Vancouver Millionaires uniform. *(Hockey Hall of Fame)*

Harry ("Hap") Holmes was beaten for three goals by Taylor in his last game, March 11, 1921, in Victoria.

Tom Longboat, the great marathon runner, in his prime. *(Wide World Photos)*

Tommy Burns in the fighting trim tha
made him heavyweight boxing champio
of the world, 1906–8. *(Canada Sports Ha.
of Fame)*

paign. In the early autumn some player switches were confirmed, including Bruce Stuart's departure from the Wanderers to join his one-time Houghton teammate, Taylor, with the Senators.

Before the new season got under way, there was a stormy interlude in Pittsburgh, in the old Duquesne Garden haunt of the Houghton days. Taylor was invited to join some other select E.C.H.L. players in an October tournament featuring the teams of a Pittsburgh amateur league, bolstered by the imports. He took leave from his government job for the two weeks of play, for which he was to receive expenses plus $100. At least, there was to have been two weeks of play, but it didn't turn out that way.

Taylor was cover-point on the favored arena team that became involved in a wild melee in the third game of the series. The fracas turned into a full-scale battle with great amounts of blood spilled and at least a couple of cracked heads. The police were called in to halt the hostilities which had been enjoined by the fans and threatened to spread into the neighboring state of West Virginia.

Although Taylor claims to have been an innocent party to the long-forgotten incident that sparked the free-for-all, he did take an active part in the subsequent proceedings, and had a gash in his scalp to prove it. With the whole arena in an uproar and the gendarmes hard-pressed to contain the exuberance, the game was called and the players of both teams were expelled from the series. Taylor packed up and went home to Ottawa with three souvenirs: the crack on his skull plus Fred Lake and Dubby Kerr, two talented wingers who were to join him on the Ottawa club.

The fiery Art Ross, who was bidding to be as controversial as Taylor, was involved in a player deal that led to the departure of two Eastern Canada Amateur Hockey League franchises, reducing the roster to four. Always, like Taylor, on the hunt for a better dollar, Ross had quit the Wanderers to sign with Montreal, taking goalie Riley Hern with him. To stop such trafficking, the Wanderers and the Shamrocks immediately got together and prevailed upon the league executive to ban jumping by players of the previous season's squads. Montreal fought the move, lost, and quit the league in a huff. The Shamrocks followed.

Ross went back to the Wanderers, demanded and got a record $1,600 contract. With that kind of money out in the open, the league brass were somehow inspired to drop the long-outmoded word "amateur" from the name, and it was now simply the Eastern Canada Hockey League. That seemed sensible enough to Taylor, who was again getting feelers from the O'Briens and had his eye on a lot more than Art Ross's $1,600 talent fee.

Going into December, some Ottawa changes were confirmed. Bruce Stuart was now in the fold, Pulford had retired, and Tom Phillips was off to join Edmonton in the Western League. Fred Lake and Dubby Kerr, Taylor's friends from the recent Pittsburgh combat zone, were two of the replacements.

With their league opener against the Wanderers scheduled for January 6, the Ottawa players broke training for a couple of days off over Christmas to spend the time with their friends and families. Back in Listowel, Mary Taylor was planning the usual family Christmas dinner of roast goose, and Fred would of course be there.

These Christmas feasts in the Taylor household were always warm and affectionate reunions, in the past marred only occasionally by the excessive conviviality of the head of the family. Taking the holiday spirit too literally, Archie Taylor sometimes overindulged after dinner and became, as Fred delicately puts it, "a trial."

He was due out on the 4:00 P.M. train to Listowel Christmas Eve, but first there was a date with Thirza Cook on the previous night. He picked her up at her house and they went for a skate on the Rideau Canal, the scene of their first date nearly a year before.

It was another crisp, clear night with the city clean and still under a fresh fall of snow. A stretch along the Canal had been cleared by the skaters, and there was a swarm of them out, mostly couples, moving indolently, gracefully along with the rhythmic scrape of their blades. They were all well bundled against the cold, and Taylor himself wore a bright red woolen toque that would become a familiar sight that winter in the hockey arenas as his thinning hair receded. Although Fred was just twenty-four, this was already getting to be an area of sensitivity.

Fred had been invited back to the Cooks' house for late supper after the skate. This didn't exactly mean that there was a thaw in the cold war between the pro hockey player and Mrs. Cook, who just happened to be out for the evening. There were still three years to go before a full truce, and for the present the couple knew they'd just have to wait it out.

The carolers were out along the Canal banks when Fred and his girl left and headed along the homeward route up past The Hill, where the Parliament Buildings were bathed in the soft glow of Christmas lights. As they turned into Wellington Street, they heard the then familiar city cry of: "Extra . . . Extra!" and an urchin hove to with a thick bundle of newspapers under his arm, hawking his wares.

Taylor hailed the boy, bought a paper, and walked swiftly to a street lamp to scan the headline. He had an idea of what it might be about, and the premonition was correct. A streamer across the top of the page read: BURNS BADLY BEATEN, JOHNSON CHAMPION.

The story was datelined Sydney, Australia, and Taylor just took a cursory glance at the lead before he folded the paper, took Thirza's arm, and continued the walk. The first few lines of the story simply confirmed the headline: Tommy Burns, the first Canadian to reign as World Heavyweight Boxing Champion, had surrendered his crown after a savage beating by the Galveston Giant, Jack Johnson.

In the silent walk through the streets of Ottawa, Taylor felt a great sadness for the young man he had known as Noah Brusso. As Tommy Burns, he had worn the champions' mantle with grace, but was never accorded the deference his title merited. First scorned by the American press as a "freak" champion unworthy to follow such heroes as John L. Sullivan and Gentleman Jim Corbett and James J. Jeffries, and then hounded by the malevolent black, Johnson, Burns had now succumbed to the full bitterness of defeat down in far-off Australia.

Taylor, and the rest of the World, had reckoned this fight with much bigger, stronger Johnson would be a mismatch, and for the past years Burns had been scorned and blasphemed for evading it. But as Taylor knew, "evade" wasn't Tommy's word for it. He had defended himself this past summer in a fascinating and courageous confrontation with his taunters in the famous London boxing arena known as the Sporting Club.

On his European tour through London, Dublin, and Paris, Burns had met and knocked out four top foreign challengers in defense of his title. He could have done no more, but as he rested in London before returning to America, he was derided by a harsh British press that had picked up the U.S. charge of a runaway flight from the real challenger, Johnson.

That night in the Sporting Club, where he had appeared at ringside as a spectator, Burns was greeted by a derisive cry from the gallery: "Hello, is that Tommy Race-Horse Burns down there?"

The ring announcer wanted to introduce Burns, but was hesitant about it, concerned over the possible nasty reception.

"Go ahead," said Burns quietly, "introduce me."

He climbed into the ring and the announcer called out:

"Ladies and gentlemen . . . I would like to greet the World Heavyweight Boxing Champion, Tommy Burns . . ."

The fans obliged, with a raucous chorus of catcalls. Burns waited awhile, raised his hand for silence, finally got it, and then spoke.

"Gentlemen, you abuse me because I have not yet signed to meet Jack Johnson. The fact is that I have refused to accept a purse of £3,000 that has been offered for such a match. I am my own manager. Now, I put it to you that if you could get double that sum—£6,000—would you sign for the lower figure? Well, I know I can get £6,000 to fight Johnson, and when I am offered that figure, I will fight him. That is a promise."

There was scattered applause for the man's courage in facing the hostile audience. Here in London, as it would be in Sydney, Australia, it was Noah Brusso, the man from Hanover, against the world.

At the Cooks' house, Taylor sat and read the full account of the fight in Sydney, but it would be many years later, at a reunion with Burns, before he could patch together the full story.

Burns had gotten his £6,000 guarantee from a Sydney promoter, and he had signed to meet Johnson, as he had promised. In addition to the £6,000, Burns also received £1,000 expenses. Johnson, who had been waiting in Australia, got £1,000 flat.

"What Johnson gets," said Burns, "is his business. I'm the champion."

Tommy went off to the mountains to train, and when the fight was postponed several times because of promotional problems, he was stricken with influenza and went to bed for a week. On the day of the fight, he checked in at 163 pounds, eleven pounds under his normal weight and more than thirty pounds lighter than Johnson's tiger-lean 195. There was talk of another post-ponement, but Burns acceded to the pleas of promoter Hugh McIntosh and agreed that there should be no further delay.

Sullen and bitter after three years chasing the title that he thought should have been his long before, Johnson was in a mur-derous mood. The early round-by-round dispatches from ring-side showed that Burns was doomed to defeat from the minute he touched gloves with his tormentor. The Canadian had not the height, weight, or reach of Johnson, nor had he Johnson's pent-up store of hate and his burning lust for revenge.

They say that Johnson could have picked his round to put away Burns that night, but that he deliberately delayed the end so that he could administer a slow, savage beating. There were times when Johnson just seemed to be propping up the battered, bloodied champion, and others when Tommy just stubbornly re-fused to go down, and went hammering away at Johnson's ribs.

As Burns staggered from his corner to start the fourteenth round with the mob up and screaming for the referee to stop the slaughter, police swarmed into the ring and halted the contest. The fight was recorded in the books as simply a win for Johnson in the fourteenth round.

The round-by-round account that Taylor read in the Cook par-lor was full and concise, and there was a special sadness to it that only a friend and a fellow-professional athlete could appre-ciate. At that moment, with two ex-adversaries of the younger days more than half-a-world apart, his heart went out to Noah Brusso.

Still, as Burns took off for a ranch in the Australian bush to rest and ponder his future, there was work to be done in Ottawa, and Taylor was off on his second season with the Senators. And as the quirk of coincidence had already taken the careers of three old friends to their various peaks in the past few months, so it would be with Taylor.

It was evident from the opening week that Ottawa and the Wanderers were the class of the Eastern Canada Hockey League, and with the Wanderers in possession of the Cup, it became increasingly obvious that their challenge would come from the Senators. In the absence of any substantial challenge from elsewhere, it was decided that the team that won the E.C.H.L. title would also be the Stanley Cup champions. This formula made sense as the league race would culminate with a showdown between Ottawa and the Wanderers on their last meeting of the season.

Before that, Ottawa's new center, Marty Walsh, was off and running wild, enroute to a bag of thirty-eight goals in the twelve-game schedule. Yet it was still the Ottawa cover-point, Taylor, who was getting the headlines. His own season goal total would be a relatively modest twelve, but as the playmaker and the spark of much of the scoring action he was worth far more than that. Although his position gave him license to act as sort of a fourth forward, a cover-point is essentially a defenseman, and while centers and wingers of that free-scoring era were collecting up to six and even seven goals a game, he had to settle for much less. But had assists been tabulated in these days, the Lord only knows what point totals Taylor might have recorded. Also, in those days the fans did not necessarily regard the high-scoring player as the super-player, nor was the press obsessed with goal scoring as the sure criterion of greatness.

As far as the press of 1909 was concerned, it was business as usual, with no shortage of colorful material with Taylor around. He was again the center of attention on the ice and in the newspapers as the Senators took off in pursuit of the Stanley Cup.

The start did splutter a little when Art Ross and the Wanderers breezed into town and won the league opener 7–6 in overtime, but there were signs that this would be the year. Taylor and his new teammate Fred Lake were described as "magnificent" on defense, and Taylor himself managed to slip away for a pair of goals in the losing cause.

Then Ottawa whipped the Shamrocks 11–3 as that other survivor of the guerilla warfare in Pittsburgh, Dubby Kerr, scored a hat trick. Then there were home-and-away wins over Quebec, and by brutal margins—13–5 and 18–4. In the second victory, Ottawa's bustling new acquisition, Bruce Stuart, gave a boost to his local shoe-store business by firing in six goals. Four came from plays made by Taylor, who, according to the newspaper accounts, had in those two games amassed eleven of what today's statisticians would record as assists.

It of course had to happen, and it did. There was another mad flurry of headlines concerning the disposition of the flying twenty-four-year-old with the woolen toque. Behind it all again was the fine Irish hand of the O'Briens, who were still digging in down in Renfrew for their own cup challenge.

Ambrose had been sighted wheeling around the downtown area in his carriage, engaged in what he blandly termed "sightseeing." It was no secret that one of the sights he had been seeing was Fred Taylor, who claimed a more-or-less pristine innocence as a mere passing object of interest. And, really, what could he do if visitors from Renfrew occasionally stopped to gawk, and maybe say hello, or something.

"Is Taylor Going?" . . . "Will Taylor Jump?" . . . "Taylor Not at Practice. Renfrew Again?" . . . "$3,000 Creamery Kings Offer for Taylor" . . . and so on into the night screamed the headlines.

Taylor then and later denied that he was having contract talks with Renfrew, although he could not deny that Ambrose O'Brien was interested in more than just his nice manners. Taylor, in fact, was engaged in what was for him a rare game of patience. He had no intention of leaving Ottawa—yet. And he knew that O'Brien would be back.

Headlines or no headlines, he was giving his money's worth and more to the Ottawa fans as his all-round play led the Senators to a fine season that gave them a record of eight wins and two losses with just two games to go. The Wanderers, with Joe Hall and Moose Johnson playing superlatively, had an identical win-loss record.

In Ottawa's eleventh game, a Saturday night contest with the Montreal Shamrocks just prior to the pending Wednesday night confrontation with the Wanderers, Taylor suffered a severe foot injury.

There was grave concern in the Ottawa *Free Press:*

"The accident took place shortly after Taylor had electrified the crowd by a run the length of the ice, winding up with a deft shot that found the back of the cage. He tore in on another of his celebrated dashes a minute later, but lost the puck to Jack Laviolette, the Shamrocks defenceman, who knocked it behind the net. When the two went to retrieve it, Taylor fell down and his right foot was caught by Laviolette's skate between the ankle and the heel. A jagged gash cut three inches deep, right to the bone. . . .

"Blood gushed from a triangular rip in the thick leather of the boot. The skate was removed and although Taylor was asked not to butt in, when the stocking was removed he inspected the ugly, sickening gash and said, 'Well, I hope it won't keep me from playing on Wednesday.'"

"Dr. Sarse Nagle, the club physician, dressed the wound and put in some temporary stitches. There was quite a lot of excess flesh hanging from the stitches, and with a grimace from Taylor, Dr. Nagle just trimmed it off. He was then taken to the Water Street Hospital."

The Senators won that game 11–2, but all the talk afterward was as to whether or not Taylor would be ready to play the next game.

An Ottawa *Citizen* reporter wrote of the scene in and around the Arena on the night of the game.

"Ice like polished marble has been prepared for Ottawa and the Wanderers tonight. The perfect setting is made to order for the most talked-about hockey match ever played in Canada. At stake together is both the E.C.H.A. Championship and the Stanley Cup. No wonder fans have come from Halifax, from Winnipeg and even from the U.S.A., for there is a large-sized party from Philadelphia.

"The Wanderers team and their executive officers and over 300 supporters arrived at Central Station shortly after seven on the Grand Trunk Special. They were met at the station by ticket scalpers offering their wares at $5.00 and more a ticket. The big noise was in the Russell House Rotunda. There a seething mass swayed back and forth, some wearing the red-and-white ribbon and chicken feathers of the champion Wanderers, and others with the red, white, and black of Ottawa. It was not long before the money commenced to show itself. Ottawans offered $100 to $80, and there were ready takers. The big money men from the Silver Nugget country were flashing rolls so big that they rather intimidated a modest $100 bet, and the Ottawa people soon pulled in their horns.

"The first question asked by the Wanderers players wasn't surprising: 'Is Fred Taylor going to play?' Of all the men the Wanderers don't want to see on the ice, it is Taylor. His presence means 50 per cent extra work for them and depreciates their chances by as much."

The score that Wednesday night was Ottawa 8, Wanderers 5.

Ottawa had the Stanley Cup again after what was described as "a furiously fought game that was perhaps the finest and most exciting ever seen in this part of the world."

The winners got five goals from Dubby Kerr, two from Marty Walsh, and one from Fred Taylor. This last statistic drew special note: "Fred Taylor played. With his injured right foot bound in cotton batting and lint, encased in a boot protected by a broad welt of stiff leather extending from sole to top, he skated onto the ice and immediately received a roar from the record crowd of 7,500 that packed the arena.

"His first attempts at circling about and rushing up and down the ice in the warm-up did not reassure the anxious fans, for he showed a very perceptible tendency to drag the right foot. The crowd seemed to ask in one breath: Can he hold out?

"But Taylor knew what he was doing. He took matters easy until his foot got used to the strain. There was a long wait until the game started, and so he had plenty of time to shake out the stiffness. He soon showed some speed and with Lake took off on a run down the ice. That tickled the crowd, for it was evident if he could whip around on the run and break fast, he would be okay.

"When the game began, he seemed to be back at his old full speed, and one of the Wanderers' officials was heard to remark, 'Why, that Taylor is no more hurt than I am,' but of course he was.

"Taylor got his goal, Ottawa's third, to make it 3–1, in the first half, and it was a vintage effort.

". . . at this juncture, Cyclone Taylor effected the most sensational piece of work of the night, taking the puck behind his own goal, outskating everyone who tried to stop him and scoring on a marvelous side shot from a very acute angle. It was a typically magnificent piece of work, and Taylor received an ovation from the crowd.

"At the finish, with the ringing of the gong, thousands of fans swarmed onto the ice. The Ottawa cheer thundered out as if to lift the roof, hailing the return of the Cup after being away for three years."

The champions were not allowed to escape to their dressing room.

"Lake, whose face was badly cut and swollen, fought to get away but was lifted off his feet. Taylor, who was trying to help Lake, also offered some feeble resistance, but he too was seized and raised shoulder high, as were the rest of the victorious team. Taylor was robbed of his stick and his gloves in the struggle, and somebody even tried to remove that famous right boot, but this time Taylor, his face pained, resisted too strongly. The exultant crowd then poured out of the rink and into the streets, still cheering, headed for a night-long celebration.

"In the Wanderers dressing room, Art Ross, the outstanding player on the ice that night for the defeated champions, echoed the general sentiment when he said, 'The best team won. And the best man was Taylor.' Indeed, Taylor was the hero of the night and his popularity here was never more demonstrated than when he scored that third Ottawa goal. It brought every fan to his feet, and Taylor's name was cheered and shouted to the rafters.

"The work this Ottawa man did in last night's struggle and the knowledge of the heavy handicap he was bearing will always live in the minds of those who witnessed the game. Sent slamming into the boards many times as he battled his way down the ice, he took punishment that would have put the ordinary man in hospital."

For Taylor, the extraordinary man, this was his Ottawa swan song. He would not play again with the Senators. He would return again to the big rink on Laurier Avenue, but next time there would be no cheers from the gallery.

Chapter Five
TO NEW YORK AND BACK

New York, New York, it's a wonderful town! And here they were again, resplendent in last year's Christy fedoras, back for another look at the bright lights and the nickel beers. Following the great success of 1908, there was no doubt that the invitational hockey series would be repeated in 1909, or that the Senators would be there.

The Ottawas were picked again not only because they were the new Stanley Cup champions but also and especially because they had Fred Taylor aboard. Now and for the next few years, the team that could deliver Cyclone Taylor, alias Little Jeff, was assured of an invitation.

The promotion of this second series was built around the return of Taylor, who was firmly established as the big town's first hockey hero, and when the teams arrived in New York, banners hailing the return of "Little Jeff" were already being hung in the arena. Once again, the colorful Wanderers joined Ottawa on the trip south, and this time the winner's prize was increased from $1,000 to $1,500.

Because of a clash of arena bookings, the series was cut to a two-game total-goals competition, but the end result was no different from the year before. It was Taylor, slipping around the prostrate figure of Moose Johnson, who scored the goal that won it all for the Senators, six goals to five. The fans greeted this final flourish with unrestrained delight, and at game's end they swarmed onto the ice to pummel their hero. And as far as the New York press was concerned, this was just a replay of the previous March, with Taylor again getting far more than one man's share of the raves.

Grumped Johnson on the ride back home: "They'd give that crafty little sonofabitch a headline if he just walked out there and blew his nose."

Taylor nodded agreeably at this as he counted his share of the $1,500 winners' purse, and mentally popped it right into his piggy bank.

It wasn't much, but it was all clear. He was now embarked on a strict savings program, with a target figure of $10,000 in mind, a sum that would have staggered his teammates had they known about it. However, this was a private matter, involving himself and Thirza Cook.

With the Senators back in Ottawa again after this second sojourn in Manhattan, the romance was going just fine despite the continuing freeze by the lady's mother. Still, there was no talk of a marriage pact, nor would there be until Taylor had $10,000 in the bank. This was his idea.

Hurt and frustrated at being rebuffed as socially unacceptable to the widow Cook, he decided to try a practical route to better popularity. If it was financial security they were worried about, he was going to show them he could provide it. A $10,000 bank account should do it, for in those days that was a lot of money.

So was Taylor's annual income, which with his hockey salary and his Civil Service pay now totalled more than $2,800. That was more than double the earnings of his father after thirty years toil as salesman for the Cockshutt Company.

In those days a man could get a good tailor-made suit in Ottawa for $15, a pair of quality shoes for $3.00, and as Taylor himself fondly recalls, "you could get the best meal in Ottawa at a lunch-counter for fifteen or twenty cents . . ." For a God-fearing young Methodist who walked swiftly past taverns, shunned the demon tobacco, and considered thrift one of the nobler virtues, there was no great problem saving a dollar or two. Yet it would take longer than he'd like to build the $10,000 marriage stake without help from some substantial source, like, say, the old established firm of M. J. O'Brien & Son.

It was well known that the O'Briens, proprietors of a million or two in silver mine stocks, a construction company, and also the three-team Upper Ottawa Valley League, were still slavering after a Stanley Cup championship. It was just as well known, especially to the principal himself, that Cyclone Taylor remained a prime target. Fred knew that he had the O'Briens on the hook, and when the time came he would look kindly on reversing the situation.

Before then, there was another summertime ahead, and this one, for the first time since he was old enough to lace up his own boots, would be without lacrosse. He had just decided to pass it up for a year.

His scout troop continued to keep him occupied. And an added diversion that summer was an occasional trip down to Detroit to watch a famous baseball contemporary at work in Navin Field, home of the American League Tigers. In that Detroit ball park, as in all others throughout baseball, Ty Cobb was hailed as the game's new wonder-player, and he was no less admired north of the border.

Cobb was in his fifth year with the Tigers, and the matchless career that was to cover twenty-four seasons was already approaching full bloom. The Georgia Peach was also in the third year of an unparalleled streak of nine consecutive American League batting championships, on his way to a brilliant .385 average as a prelude to his epic .420 in 1911. Cobb had already been the key player in three Detroit pennants, and was the most talked about athlete in America. The fellow was well worth the five-hour train trip from Ottawa, followed by the nickel ferry ride across the Detroit River.

Taylor had picked this particular Saturday in September for the outing because the Washington Senators were in Detroit for a four-game series, and the fast-rising young pitcher, Walter Johnson, was scheduled for the series opener. Johnson's blazing fastball was almost as much talked about as Cobb's sensational hitting and baserunning, and the youth who would become known as the "Big Train" was edging toward his own remarkable streak of ten consecutive seasons with twenty or more victories, two with over thirty.

With Taylor as he boarded the Windsor-bound train in Ottawa were two close friends, Hollie Hemphill and Harry Krotiz, a pair of pretty good soccer players who were also avid baseball fans and admirers of Ty Cobb. After an early A.M. departure, the train huffed into Windsor station just before noon, and by 1:00 P.M. the three fans had disembarked from the Detroit River ferry at the foot of Woodward Avenue and were hiking briskly up

Michigan Avenue toward Navin Field. It was nearly an hour's walk, but as Taylor, the leader of the safari, pointed out, it beat taking the trolley, which cost another nickel.

It was an unusually quiet Saturday afternoon for that part of downtown Detroit as most of the action this day was out Woodward Avenue between the Six and Seven Mile Roads. There, thousands had gathered to watch daring young autoists in their gas buggies hurtling along at up to 40 m.p.h. over the World's first one-mile strip of paved road. Henry Ford's town had gone ga-ga over the new auto age, and this urban raceway on the city's main street was the world's first drag strip. One driver snorting along in a jazzy new Overlander sported a revolutionary new piece of equipment: a glass windshield.

The Ottawa delegation got to the ball park a bit late for batting practice but were in their thirty-five-cent seats in the leftfield pavilion in good time for the start of the game. Taylor, a devotee of the sport ever since his own baseball days of early Listowel, was in his glory. Given a sunny day such as this one was, there was nothing he loved more than watching a ball game, at least as a second choice to playing in one. There was a contemplative charm about baseball that he deeply appreciated, what with the players set out on the field like a lot of pawns in an animated chess game. He was fascinated by the endless strategic opportunities for moves and countermoves, and in the deceptively leisurely pace that was so different to that of the pell-mell world of hockey.

Yet, lulls could be suddenly broken by quick bursts of action, and Taylor liked that. In a way, although his lulls on the ice were never much less than a swift half-speed, this was how he played hockey. A deceptively tentative move down the ice, a feint, a thrust, and he was off, racing down the rink at a dazzling speed with the puck cradled on the blade of his stick, then angling in for the shot or the pass to set up the goal. Although on the ice Taylor looked all speed and reflexes and automatic turned-on response, he was in essence a thoughtful hockey player. And baseball, with its different style of pace, was a thoughtful game. As in hockey, it required a high level of patience and native intelligence to play it at its best, and Cobb, like Taylor, certainly had that.

But this, if you were looking for the vintage Cobb at bat, wasn't Ty's day. Johnson, on his way to a 4–0 shutout, had Ty and the rest of the Tigers almost completely muffled with his dancing fastball. Then, in the eighth inning, after taking two strikes, Ty coolly squared around and laid down a perfect bunt.

He beat the throw to first, and then stole second on the next pitch.

As if putting on a show especially for the visitors from Ottawa who were perched just up over the left-field line, Cobb then took off for third. He came roaring in with his spikes high and ripped right into the third-baseman, sending him flying across the coach's box and all but into the Tiger dugout.

Cobb just grinned as he got up and dusted the dirt from his pants and stood, arms akimbo, huge chaw of 'baccy bulging from his right cheek, glaring defiantly at Johnson.

Each time now as Johnson went into his stretch, Cobb danced off third, all insolence as he taunted and jibed, daring a throw as he threatened to take off for the plate. Twice he drew throws and twice he beat the tag at third with a dive into a thick swirl of dust and imprecations. The crowd loved it. Just standing there on the base line, casually dropping into his crouch, Cobb was pure excitement. Taylor, the hockey player who had his own brand of pure excitement, was entranced.

If young Walter Johnson was as impressed, he didn't show it. The unflappable fastballer kept his cool and struck out the batter for the third out to end the inning and leave Cobb chafing angrily at third. However, Taylor had had his treat and his reaffirmation. No doubt about it, this Cobb was something to see. As an alter-ego, he'd do.

In a race for the ferry after the game, the trio got into Windsor in time to catch the evening train, and they were back in Ottawa by midnight. There, even though the start of the hockey season was still several weeks away, the headlines were heating up as Ambrose O'Brien, backed by the family's bankers, began taking dead aim at Taylor for the superteam he was assembling in Renfrew. By December, he would in fact go after the entire roster of Ottawa's Stanley Cup championship team, but it was the hunt for Taylor that really stirred up the sports pages.

It was that time of year again, and the headline writers were off on another Taylor binge. By the time training began, they were in full cry. "Taylor Going to Renfrew" . . . "Taylor Will Play Here" . . . "Taylor Won't Play Here" . . . "Taylor Already in Renfrew?" . . . "Mystery: Where is Taylor?" It was a riot of bannered speculation.

Taylor had missed the previous night's practice, and rumors were flying. At least two people claimed they had seen him board the train for Renfrew.

The fact was that Taylor had gone nowhere. During the hunt, he had been holed up in his boarding house on O'Connor Street, where he had been found by the Renfrew agent, George Martel. The O'Briens had assigned Martel the job of getting Taylor's name on a contract, and he had been in town for the past week, trying to do just that.

"That fellow," recalls Taylor, "got to be an awful pest. He followed me everywhere. That wasn't the first week he'd been in Ottawa."

There had been times though when Taylor had followed Martel, accompanying him on secret trips to Renfrew. The hunted had joined the hunter "four or five times" in November and December as he traveled with Martel to the O'Briens' lair, but nothing had yet come of it all.

Ottawa official John Dickson always seemed to get wind of these illicit journeys and went right down to Renfrew after Taylor, trailed him to the hotel or a cafe, and talked him into returning on the next train. But the O'Briens' raid was now out in the open, and the brazen pursuit of Taylor and other top stars of the Eastern Canada League set up what eventually amounted to the troubled loop's suicide pact.

At the league's November meeting, the rattled executive, concerned over the loss of their top players and the subsequent threat to their attendances, ousted the Wanderers over a petty dispute concerning the size of the gate splits. The Wanderers' new owners had announced that in order to cut expenses they planned to move their home games from the spacious arena on Wood Avenue to Montreal's smaller Jubilee Rink. The other league members didn't like the prospect of lesser revenue from the visiting team's traditional 50–50 gate split, and opposed the move. The Wanderers stuck to their guns, there was a great squabble at an executive meeting, and the club was expelled from the league.

Then, striving for a big-league image to counter the Ambrose threat, the executive dissolved the now shrunken E.C.H.A., reformed, and called their league the Canadian Hockey Association. Franchises for this new so-called national league were granted to Ottawa, Montreal Shamrocks, Quebec, the Montreal Nationals, and All-Montreal.

This was a questionable maneuver, but the real blunder followed when both Renfrew and the exiled Wanderers applied for membership. Both bids were summarily rejected, and the obvious happened.

Furious at this rebuff, Ambrose O'Brien and the Wanderers got together and formed their own league. They labeled it the National Hockey Association of Canada. It was a four-team organization that included Renfrew, the Wanderers, and the other two O'Brien-backed teams in Cobalt and Haileybury. The battle lines were drawn, the war was on, and the O'Briens rolled out their big guns.

"Fred Taylor," said Ambrose O'Brien, "is our first priority. If we land him, the others will follow. And, we intend to land him. Money is no object." Ambrose was as good as his word, and his money.

By Christmas week, ten days before Ottawa's first game in their new league, Renfrew had Taylor's name on the dotted line. With him on the way into the fold, Renfrew had also lured both Lester and Frank Patrick from Edmonton, and the O'Briens were almost halfway there with their Dream Team.

Lester signed for $3,000. Frank for $2,000. Both, pending the announcement of the Taylor contract figures, were record sums. Said Lester afterward of his $3,000 pact: "That's what I asked for. I was amazed when I got it."

But, as was always the case, it was the Taylor story that caused the greatest stir and generated the greatest publicity. An Ottawa *Free Press* headline trumpeted the news that Renfrew had signed Taylor for $3,000 plus "A Steady Job."

Reports were that Taylor would receive more than $3,000 for the year "plus a soft job at $1,200 a year." Renfrew officials would only say that he was "getting more money than any other hockey player has ever received."

Taylor did get more than $3,000. His payment for the one season's play with Renfrew was $5,250, with the entire sum deposited in Taylor's Ottawa bank before the start of play. It was far more than had ever been paid any other hockey player, and in this one move at least, Taylor had upstaged his personal sporting idol, Ty Cobb.

Cobb, the brightest star in baseball, had just signed a new contract with the Tigers that called for a salary of $6,500. That was for seven months of play over a season of 154 games. Taylor's $5,250 was for a two-months' season of twelve games. On a per game or per month basis, he was now far and away the highest paid team athlete in history—in any sport.

Yet, nearly seven decades later, the star of that coup still had second thoughts concerning the full merits of the historic contract.

"You know," he said, "if I had held out, I could have got a lot more money. They would have paid almost anything to get me, and they said so. Why, if I had had this fellow—what's his name . . . Eagleson . . . then, I could have got $10,000 for sure." But, of course, Alan Eagleson, superagent, was not around then.

Fortunately for Taylor, a gentleman by the name of Jack McGinnis was. McGinnis was a bright young schoolteacher from Vancouver. He lived in Taylor's O'Connor Street boardinghouse, and they had become good friends. Taylor respected McGinnis as "a very smart young fellow with a sharp eye for business," and when the two of them got talking about the Renfrew proposition, McGinnis volunteered his advice. Taylor said he would be very happy to have it.

"When we met with George Martel in Martel's Ottawa hotel room to really talk turkey, Jack was with me, and I just let him do all the talking. It was McGinnis who mentioned the sum of $5,250, although I don't recall how he arrived at that particular figure. Martel sat there for a minute thinking it over and then just nodded his head and said that it was okay. I almost jumped out of my chair. I thought I had myself a fortune." At 1909 prices, he wasn't far wrong.

Maybe because of Taylor's reputation as a man of many

minds, all sworn to be of good intent but inclined to be confusing, the unique cash-in-advance clause arranged by McGinnis had a condition attached: The entire sum was to be deposited in Taylor's bank, but was to be held for withdrawal at the end of the season. It was Renfrew's way of being sure that Taylor would show.

It would seem that the conclusion of a historic deal like this would call for some kind of celebration by the schoolteacher and the superstar, and there was one. "Oh yes. After leaving Martel's hotel, we stopped off at a place downtown and, as I recall, had a couple of very nice ice-cream sodas." Eagleson and any one of his clients would probably blanch at the thought.

But now the Renfrew Creamery Kings, to be later and inevitably known as the Millionaires, had their nucleus for a Stanley Cup challenge plus the biggest gate draw in hockey. Yet even as Taylor headed for Renfrew, Ottawa fans still refused to give up hope of keeping him in town.

There was a report that Renfrew had made Taylor post a $1,000 appearance bond, and a public subscription immediately raised the full amount as compensation for Taylor if he would change his mind and refuse to report. The offer was made through the Ottawa club, but Taylor denied that he had been asked by Renfrew to post any such bond.

The deal was final, Taylor was in camp, and the first test of the O'Briens' powerhouse team was assured when at a meeting in Montreal's Windsor Hotel the league roster was finalized, with a fifth team added to Ambrose & Company's National Hockey Association.

The new team was to be called Les Canadiens, and it was agreed that to give the franchise special appeal in Montreal the club would get first pick of French-Canadian players, and sign them exclusively. The other teams in the league would respect this priority. And so it was that this rebel amalgamation of Renfrew and the Wanderers, an act born of pique, led to the founding of what has become one of sport's most colorful and successful dynasties, that of the Montreal Canadiens.

When Didier Pitre and Newsy Lalonde joined Les Canadiens in the early days of 1910, they became the first of that distinguished Montreal Forum bloodline that was to produce such

French-Canadian stars as Georges Vezina, Aurel Joliat, Maurice and Henri Richard, Jacques Plante, Bernie Geoffrion, Jean Beliveau, Jacques Laperrière and Guy Lafleur.

After the first weeks of play it was clear that the maverick league was superior to its rival organization. It had the better players, the more exciting play, and was drawing the bigger gates. The O'Brien house league—after all, the O'Briens controlled three of the five franchises—was No. 1.

Suffering badly at the turnstiles, the Canadian Hockey Association was paying the price for its arrogant blunder in ousting the Wanderers. The price of this was dissolution, which came about before the end of January, when the league folded. Hats in hand, the Ottawas and the Shamrocks went to the rebel league and meekly asked permission to join and compete there for the rest of the season. The request was granted, but it was one-up for the O'Briens.

It was the O'Brien purchasing power and the star-laden team it had brought to Renfrew, with the help of another well-heeled citizen named Alexander Barnett, that began the new order of things. And it was Taylor more than any other player who gave the upstart league instant status. There is no doubt that he had lots of help from that first lineup of the Creamery Kings that had Bert Lindsay in goal, Frank Patrick at point (defense), Taylor at cover-point, Lester Patrick at rover, Herb Jordan at center, and Bobby Rowe and Larry Gilmour on the wings.

Although surrounded by this fine collection of talent, Taylor still stood out as something extra despite the fact that others would score more goals and dominate the individual statistics. In any trade it takes a tradesman to judge the real worth of another, and an outstanding player of the day named Fred Whitcroft offered his assessment of Taylor during the Creamery Kings' first meeting with Les Canadiens in the Renfrew rink.

Whitcroft, a talented center from Edmonton, was in town prior to signing on with the Renfrew club and watched the Les Canadiens contest from the stands. "Taylor," he told a visiting Toronto reporter, "is the greatest player I have ever seen."

The Ottawa *Free Press* also had its man there to record the Creamery Kings' 9–4 victory and to report on the play of the Ottawa refugee. Said this reporter, noting that Rowe (four goals for Renfrew) and Newsy Lalonde (two for Les Canadiens) were impressive: "Still, the outstanding feature of the night's play was the remarkable work of Fred Taylor, the Renfrew cover-point. He gave a wonderful exhibition of skating and shooting and was responsible for several of the Renfrew goals. The Cyclone showed all of his old skill, and his marvellous swoops down the ice with the puck sent the crowd into a frenzy. Taylor is already the favorite in this burg, and his every move is greeted with cheers. Lester Patrick, the tall Renfrew captain, was a close second to Taylor and netted two goals . . ."

Lester Patrick, who would one day be known as the distinguished and dignified Silver Fox of the New York Rangers, had spent an undignified evening with the visiting roughhouse, Lalonde.

"Lester Patrick and Newsy Lalonde were each banished three times as play got very rough, with the rival captains slashing with their fists on several occasions. In the second half, Patrick cut Lalonde's head open with a swing of his stick, and as soon as the Renfrew leader got back onto the ice, Lalonde got him with a wicked cross-check that sent the famous rover into the air as if shot from a cannon."

The attendance at that game was "about 1,400, a little under capacity." These figures, as Taylor has suggested, indicate the "lunacy" of spending all that money to put a team into Renfrew. Why, there were less than 4,000 people in the entire community, and if the rink were three times its size and every person in town showed up, they still couldn't pay the bills. "Those O'Briens had simply bought themselves a golden toy, and it was going to cost them an awful lot of money. The Renfrew situation just couldn't last."

He was right. It couldn't. But gee, as they say in that song, it was swell while it lasted. Especially for Taylor, who had himself the best of two worlds, at top rates.

He had not, as had been reported in the Renfrew papers, quit his job in Ottawa to take another one in Renfrew as part of his salary deal. He had simply taken leave of absence, and although living in a Renfrew boardinghouse, he traveled to Ottawa frequently to see Thirza Cook.

At his Renfrew abode, he shared mealtimes with fellow dodgers Lester and Frank Patrick, Bert Lindsay, Bobby Rowe, and later, when he joined Renfrew from Les Canadiens, Newsy Lalonde. Even then, the two Patricks stood out from the crowd as superior students of the game of hockey, and the seeds of many a future Patrick innovation that would help revolutionize the game were sown at that boardinghouse dinner table. Taylor himself was tremendously impressed with the Patricks' thorough knowledge of hockey; of what made it go, and what might be needed to make it go better.

"Frank in particular had an amazing grasp of the science of hockey, and they were both already dreaming about changes that would improve the game. Lester eventually became the better known of the two as both innovator and executive, but Frank was always very much underrated. He was the solid, down-to-earth practical man, much the quieter of the two. Lester was the likeable good-time-Charlie, the hail-fellow-well-met, always the life of the party. He was a great storyteller, and sometimes in the parlor he would recite poetry in French. Frank just stayed in the background.

"But at dinner, the talk always got around to hockey. Frank was always there with his ideas and views, Lester embellished them, and the rest of us would just sit and listen with the greatest respect. Of course, none of us dreamed then that Frank and Lester between them would eventually change so much of the game, but if anyone had suggested to us that this might happen, we certainly would have believed it."

With Renfrew the small town it was, the hockey players quickly became familiar figures on the streets and were soon very friendly with the natives and special favorites with the young people. One of these was a sturdy youngster named Charlotte Whitton.

Charlotte was a rabid hockey fan and became a particular favorite of the players. She watched all the workouts, knew all the players, and on her thirteenth birthday, she was presented with a stick by Fred Taylor and given a ticket to that night's game. The ticket entitled her to a seat in the box reserved for dignitaries, and Renfrew had the first Queen for a Day. The young lady was entranced, as she considered the local hockey heroes to be the most talented and colorful creatures on earth.

Miss Whitton grew up to be a very talented and colorful

person in her own right in the early sixties as the unsinkable Mayor of Ottawa. And of those early days in Renfrew, she once wrote: "The players were especially kind to the young people. They spent a lot of time with them, coaching them and teaching them all they could about hockey."

She also recalled that the players were a thirsty lot and some-times drank too much. "Every day that was halfway decent, they could be seen on the street outside the Renfrew Mercury Build-ing, sitting there in the sun like graven images."

Considering all the facts, it is somewhat difficult to conjure up the titillating image of a long winter's orgy in the taverns of Renfrew, starring either the hockey players or the townsfolk. In addition to Taylor, both of the Patricks and Newsy Lalonde were teetotalers.

There was also the matter of a referendum that had a definite effect on the issue. The referendum was for the continued legalization of the sale of alcoholic beverages in Renfrew. It had just been put to the citizenry, and they had voted it down.

This action provoked amused comment from the city slickers up in Ottawa. "My goodness," chided the *Free Press*, "hockey players without a saloon? Why, this is about as unheard of as a saloon without hockey players . . . Drink up lads, but where . . . ?"

However, a shortage of saloons could not be cited as a decent excuse for the fact that the Renfrew team, built at much expense to dominate the league and win the Stanley Cup in the first year, failed to do either. It was the Wanderers who won the league championship with a record of eleven wins and one loss. The Creamery Kings, now also known as the Millionaires, were third, behind Ottawa, with eight wins and a tie in twelve games.

As has been pointed out by several observers of the scene since then, this was perhaps the first glaring evidence of the truth in the old saw that says a Stanley Cup can't be bought; that there is more to the exercise than just laying cash on the line.

The season had its share of highlights, among them a 1–1 tie between Renfrew and the Shamrocks in a game that was never actually finished. The players themselves barely survived the mixed perils of a flooded rink and their own tattered tempers.

Calling on a saving sense of humor, the *Mercury* reporter who covered the affair took the light approach in his report. Among other things, he noted that "the unseasonable mild spell had turned the ice to mush that then turned to water, that then turned on the players, and spread its misery throughout the arena.

"Throughout the game, attendants came constantly out and took up the water by the bucketful. They scraped and rescraped the mushy surface to no purpose. The pools gathered again, skates stuck in the soft ice, and the wearers went tumbling into the water. The dripping figures, putting on double strength when they got up and bore a miserable sight as they tore through the slush, yet they continued to play hockey—strong and capital hockey.

"Despite the horrible conditions, the eccentric Fred Taylor was there playing in all his glory, with his old tricks, his speed, and his elusiveness. Always he kept an opponent guessing. He loved to feign a run ahead and then suddenly double back on himself. This was exasperating to the enemy, but the coolness of it all always provoked thunderous cheers. This is not a play that scores as a rule, but it is a joy to watch, and every creature in life has the grandstand in mind."

By the second half the deteriorating conditions proved too much, and hockey gave way to pandemonium. It began when Barney Holden of the Shamrocks took a swipe with his stick at Taylor's head. Cyclone returned in kind, bloodying Barney's nose. "Then suddenly they all seemed to be going at it, slashing and swiping, with the water flying and the puck trapped and immoveable in great thick puddles of slush."

But for the delighted fans the game's highlight came in the closing minutes. It was then that the smoldering feud between "Renfrew's gentlemanly Frank Patrick and the Shamrocks' Bad Joe Hall" finally burst into flame. Throughout the contest they had been exchanging pokes and chops. Already bloodied once by Patrick's stick, Hall eventually had had enough. "After taking more of these knocks, Joe went splashing up the ice again after Patrick, who hit him again. Hall stopped in his tracks and struck back with his stick, slicing Patrick's cheek. A lively scrap followed during which Hall received another nasty gash over the eye. . . .

"The referee, Kennedy, tried to hold Hall back but Joe, confused, struck Kennedy, for which he was banished from the game. Before he left the ice, Hall slipped and fell into the water and refused to be helped up, kicking his legs furiously and tearing Kennedy's pants. Don Smith held Frank's brother, Lester, pinned against the boards with his stick as Hall, screaming epithets, was helped to the dressing room.

Chaos still reigned as the game at last ended with the score tied 1–1. No play-off could be arranged since Renfrew refused to take the ice again if Hall were permitted to play, and the referee had so ruled. "Afterward, Joe Hall went out to Mr. Kennedy, shook his hand and apologized for the swelling on his eye, stating that with blood in both his own eyes he did not know who he was hitting. . . ."

And so it was on that tumultuous afternoon in the Jubilee Arena. It is good to be able to record that both teams recovered from their mixed ordeal and seemed none the worse for it. And that a week later the teams were at each other again in Renfrew with the Creamery Kings winning 10–2 as Lester Patrick and Cyclone Taylor split six goals, and Bad Joe Hall was never once slugged by Frank Patrick, or vice versa.

As can be seen from such references, extravagant prose and an uninhibited sense of lyrical expression was the order of the day among the nation's sporting scribes. This may perhaps be explained by the fact that there was no radio or television to subvert the spirit or the imagination, and no "color commentators" to dispense their infinite wisdom. It was probably quite natural then that the reporters felt obliged to bring flaccid scenes to florid life for the reader, and to paint the livelier scenes in the brightest colors their pens could summon.

This view gave them license to romanticize, and they did. Even—or perhaps especially—when reporting a trifle such as, say, a ladies' hockey match. One such match, played in Pembroke, Ontario, had as principals Fred Taylor and Lester Patrick. The report of the game occupied a full quarter page in the local paper under the heading: "Ladies Hockey Match a Brilliant Function."

The teams, named appropriately the "Cyclones" and the "Whirlwinds," played the full sixty minutes, but the reporter who covered the game seemed less concerned with its outcome than with such fine points as the design of the girls' uniforms. Certainly the visual delights of the contest received prime attention. "Under the brilliant lights of the rink, the red and white uniforms flashing backward and forward, hither and thither, now mingling, massing, wheeling and scattering as they produced kaleidoscopic effects, the pictures presented were colorful, brilliant, and vibrant with shimmering animation."

Apparently the visiting celebrities acquitted themselves well. "The Messrs. Taylor and Patrick who acted as referee and judge of play while making no effort to attract the attention of the assemblage, could not fail to win the wondering admiration of all as in the discharge of their duties they threaded their way among the players, skating now forward now backward as occasion demanded, with unvarying skill and celerity, and never by chance colliding or in the slightest degree interfering with any of the players. As one watched these evidently unconscious displays of skill, it did not appear at all astonishing that these men should earn enormous remuneration for their services during the short hockey season."

Throughout this pleasant time of ardent acclaim and close personal identification with the community, it was this twosome, Cyclone and the elder of the two Patricks, Lester, who were the "front" men in the team's social life.

Taylor, twenty-six, known as a "snappy dresser" but not quite a dude, was admired for his easy, courtly manner, and his way with words. Patrick, twenty-seven, had a style and a confidence and a *savoir-faire* that made him a natural leader and an asset to any party. Of these, in the chill of the Renfrew winters, there were many. There were sleighing parties, snowshoe parties, skating parties, and just plain parties, many of them hosted by Ambrose O'Brien in the large and comfortable home he kept in Renfrew.

Perhaps, in the interests of the O'Briens' dream of a Stanley Cup, there were too many parties and too much socializing between work nights at the hockey rink. If this were so—and it sounds quite reasonable—the theory was never broached at the time, and hockey in Renfrew, in Taylor's long-considered reflection, was "just a wonderful fun time."

The Ambrose family and their partners in this gilt-edged

money-losing enterprise may not have been the very last of the carefree owners, but they were certainly part of a dying breed. It may have been that the O'Briens & Friends reaped their dividends just from the fun of tinkering with what Taylor called their "golden toy," and that the blithe spirit displayed by their hired hands rubbed off on them.

Ambrose O'Brien was particularly taken by the bandy-legged, cocky, uninhibited and otherwise delightful Newsy Lalonde, who had—aided by some urging and a $2,000 contract—quit the Canadiens and switched to Renfrew late in the season. Ambrose was there the day—one of those when Taylor had gone to Ottawa to visit Thirza Cook—when Newsy decided to skin Larry Gilmour out of $5.00 in a snowshoe challenge race.

With a heavy late fall of snow on the ground and nothing much else to do after a brief workout at the rink, Newsy drifted over to the O'Brien house with Gilmour, the local boy who had made the Renfrew team on his merits as a superlative hockey player. Gilmour was also known as the team coach, although this was more honorary than actual, as Lester Patrick was really the man in charge on the ice.

There was nothing in life Newsy loved more than competition —of any kind—even if he had to invent it. There was nothing he liked less than parting with money. It was claimed by those who knew and admired him that he still had the first nickel his mother gave him to put in the church collection box as a boy back in Cornwall, Ontario. These endearing qualities led to numerous fascinating Lalonde episodes, such as one in this late winter in Renfrew.

Ambrose O'Brien was home for one of his frequent returns from his wide world of business and was the host at lunch. Afterward, for no apparent reason other than that of the inexplicable Lalonde whim, Newsy challenged Gilmour to a snowshoe race for a $5.00 bet.

Gilmour accepted, and a farmhouse approximately three miles to the south of town was designated as the finish line. The two of them took off, with O'Brien accompanying them in a cutter, as referee. After little more than a mile, Lalonde knew he was beaten, and that he had picked himself a ringer. It happened

CYCLONE TAYLOR

that local-boy Gilmour was an expert on snowshoes and was far too good for his floundering adversary.

He probably would have continued the futile chase to the bitter end and surrendered the five-spot had not Gilmour had the impudence to stop, turn, grin amiably and doff his fur hat at his fading pursuer. And when Mr. O'Brien added insult to injury by sitting back in his cutter and laughing uproariously at the sight, well, that did it.

Putting on a furious burst, Newsy forged ahead with arms and legs flailing wildly away in what appeared to be a formidable late challenge. But he had gone no more than a few frantic strides when his feet tangled, his snowshoes crossed, and down he went into the snow, in a crumpled heap. He lay there inert, issuing little moaning sounds that brought O'Brien out of his cutter and racing to the scene of the accident. Newsy moaned and pointed to his right ankle.

"My God," cried O'Brien, "it's broken!" Newsy nodded helplessly and as Gilmour hurried up, visions of the loss of his newly acquired $2,000 hockey star danced through O'Brien's head. Gilmour's face reflected the boss's concern. Together they lifted the groaning Lalonde into the cutter and bundled him beneath the fur rug. Newsy was all pain and gratitude, as he was being tucked in he smiled wanly, reached under the rug and rummaged around in his pocket as he said plaintively: "You were too good for me, Larry. You beat me fair and square. Here's your five dollars."

He was still struggling gamely in his pocket when O'Brien clutched his arm and said chidingly, "I won't hear of it, Newsy. The way you were going when this happened, there's no telling how it might have turned out. Now, don't you go worrying about that five dollars."

Stripping a crisp banknote from his wallet, O'Brien handed it to Gilmour. "We'll see you at the house, Larry. We've got to get this ankle seen to right away."

Clambering in beside his doleful passenger, O'Brien flicked the reins and the cutter sped off, Newsy's homely face grimacing with pain as he turned with a forlorn wave for the lone snowshoer.

O'Brien had to hurry off to catch a train as soon as he got back to the house, leaving Lalonde to the tender ministrations of the family doctor, who as it happened, had good news for his patient —the injury was not a break.

The next evening Newsy was the life of the party as he scored five goals in a 17–3 rout of Ottawa. All concerned agreed that it was indeed a remarkable recovery.

While all of the Renfrew players admired Ambrose O'Brien's money, Lester Patrick held a particular admiration for Ambrose's daughter, Stella. Taylor remembers her as "a lovely girl, vivacious and full of life." Just the sort who would appeal to Lester. And she did. Whenever there was a party and Stella was around, Lester would be right there with her, all charm and smiles. "They became quite fond of each other, but nothing ever came of it. It was just one of those winter romances that you'd see every hockey season, wherever you might be at the time."

Taylor's own romance entailed commuting the fifty-odd miles to Ottawa, and he took the return train ride at least two and sometimes three times a week. Thirza Cook herself never came to Renfrew to watch a game, being content to stay and wait for the Renfrew to come to the rink on Laurier Avenue.

In Ottawa, despite his defection to a foreign country, Taylor remained a hot topic of discussion. The fans still continued to regard him as theirs and were just refusing to let go. The Ottawa hockey club had the same stubborn hang-up, and the new season in the new league was barely under way before the Senators were again claiming that he was still legally their property and demanding his return from the pirates of Renfrew.

As the club made its demands official, the press took up the hue and cry to a point where one letter-to-the-editor complained angrily that "this man Taylor is getting more newspaper space than the British elections. . . ."

What the Senators did in an effort to bring Taylor "home" was appeal to the new league to recognize a verbal agreement they'd had with him, and thus declare the Renfrew contract null and void. "Taylor," said a club official, "would be welcomed back like the flowers in May, and I happen to know that he would be delighted to return."

"Not a chance," huffed Renfrew. "We signed him, he is under contract, and he is our property."

Taylor agreed. "I'm happy here and I intend to stay. I fulfilled all my Ottawa commitments and that's all behind me."

The Ottawa appeal died in the league committee room, and the matter was again closed. In the Capital City, world news crept back into the headlines, for a while, at least. The "Case of the Restless Cover-point" was far from closed. The furor was merely in limbo, awaiting the next move.

The Renfrew Millionaires' first game in Ottawa came in mid-February, with Taylor firmly established as the star of the team. It was also the occasion of Taylor's first appearance in the Ottawa rink since his dramatic departure, and he was headed for a rough reception.

If Taylor was concerned, he didn't show it. All that this talk of retribution did was bring out the showmanship in him. He may have been the sport's first willful practitioner of the art. With his special eye for the gambit, he even picked his spot for a full and proper reporting of his personal response to the hostile atmosphere: the newsroom of the *Citizen*.

He had dropped in to renew old acquaintance, and the conversation naturally got around to the up-coming big game. Also visiting the newsroom was the Ottawa goalie, Percy LeSueur. When the talk got around to the matter of the Ottawa defense, Taylor coolly observed that he didn't think much of it. That got LeSueur's hackles up, and Fred added, just as coolly: "Tomorrow night I'll score a goal by skating through the Ottawa defense —backward."

The remark was headlined in the next day's edition and became the instant talk of the town. The story observed that the boast might have been made tongue-in-cheek, but the nettled LeSueur wasn't so certain. "This Taylor," he said, "is a pretty cocky customer, but he usually backs up what he says."

The rival *Free Press* got into the act with a story dissecting the Taylor statement, and more or less debunking it.

"If Taylor did say it, he must have been joshing. If he wasn't joshing, then he never said it. However, there is no doubt that Taylor is the man of the hour, and all eyes will be on him tonight. A hockey game without Fred Taylor is like 'Hamlet' with-

out the Prince . . . if anyone can score a goal backward, he
can . . ."

Some of the outraged Ottawa fans were taking the gambit
seriously enough. One of them phoned the *Citizen* office and announced that he wished to wager one hundred dollars that
Taylor would not make good his boast. The hundred dollars had
been deposited at the King Edward Hotel, and it could be
covered by application to a Mr. Peter Danis.

Mr. Danis was on to a good thing. It is not known who covered
the hundred-dollar bet, but it is known that Taylor didn't score
a goal, either backward or forward, as Ottawa won the game by
the score of 8–5. Still, the papers described the contest as "one
of the most tremendous battles in the history of this fascinating
sport, and undoubtedly the hardest-fought match ever seen in
Ottawa . . ."

Fred Taylor would certainly vouch for that.

He found himself in the eye of a storm that swept through the
Laurier Avenue arena, a storm whipped up by a hostile crowd
that seemed literally out for blood—Taylor's. He had expected
something like this, but nothing like the eruption that engulfed
him.

As the *Free Press* reported afterward:

"Taylor knew that a hot reception had been prepared, and it
began early. He was the last of the Renfrew team to appear on
the ice, skating out amid shouts of 'Here he comes . . . ! Here he
comes . . . !' and then an angry chorus of boos and hisses as he
went to his position. When he arrived there, it was the signal for
a wild demonstration as shouts of derision fairly shook the
building. Invective still thundered down after the puck was
dropped, and continued for minutes almost unabated.

"Lemons, oranges and other fruit and a variety of objects were
hurled at the great player as he skated along the boards, and at
one point a whiskey flask smashed at his feet.

"Players of both teams helped sweep up the broken glass, with
Taylor urged by them to go to center ice, out of range. But when
play was resumed it began again. Another shower of rotten fruit,
copper coins and rubbers came raining down onto the ice amid
more boos and shouts of 'Go home to Renfrew, Taylor' . . .
'Back to the bushes . . . !'

There was an accompanying, non-stop stream of epithets that were delicately reported as "of shocking vulgarity . . ."

Amidst it all, Taylor played as if nothing unusual was happening, ignoring the demonstration. He tried hard not to look rattled when another whiskey flask came hurtling down from the gallery just before the end of the first half, narrowly missing his skull.

He knew that he had provoked much of this by his cocky promise to score a goal while skating backward through the Ottawa defense. The remark had been made in jest, but the reaction was somewhat less jocular, and Taylor was paying for his brashness.

Still, there was sympathy for his plight, and admiration for the way he handled it. Said the *Citizen:* "Seldom if ever has an athlete been forced to endure what Taylor was subjected to. To his great credit, it must be said that he bore himself remarkably well. Despite all the abuse and violent attempts to rattle him, he was at all times cool as a cucumber. He merely smiled at the hoots and the hisses, showing remarkable nerve throughout.

"Taylor did not produce his usual spectacular game, undoubtedly because he was so closely marked by the Ottawa team, who had sworn not to let him score. However, he was still brilliant in spots, and his gameness was unquestioned."

One reporter in particular was repelled and upset by the demonstration. This was the *Free Press* sports editor, Malcolm Brice, the man who had journeyed to Listowel in the summer of 1907 to recruit Taylor for the Senators.

By the time the second whiskey bottle was hurled onto the ice, Brice had become concerned about Taylor's safety, a concern that was hardly lessened by the torrent of abuse that followed Taylor up the ramp to the dressing room when the first half ended. The likelihood of an ugly incident in the second half worried Brice, and he decided to go to the Renfrew room and talk to Lester Patrick about it.

He was going to suggest that Taylor be either removed from the game and replaced by a spare, or that Patrick simply come out and announce that he would withdraw the whole team and forfeit the game if the demonstration was continued. Brice, who remained a lifetime admirer of Taylor, probably knew that any such pleas would fail, on both counts.

In the first place, Lester Patrick, the spokesman for the Renfrew team, would never consider such a proposition, and Taylor, tough and stubborn competitor that he was, would certainly reject any suggestion of "surrender" out of hand. As it was, Brice never got to make his proposals, as the dressing room door was shut and locked and his urgent knocking went unheeded.

What happened inside the dressing room?

Apart from some soft and colorful cursing as the players sank onto the benches for their fifteen-minute rest, nothing much was said about that stormy first half. Taylor just unlaced his boots to ease his feet and sat quietly awaiting round two.

With Taylor effectively bottled up and Ottawa eventually in control in a furious game that went into overtime, the abuse, although it continued until the final whistle, was a little more subdued than it had been. To Brice's relief, Taylor survived unharmed, and with his dignity intact.

As Brice wrote: "Few expected Taylor to take such a terrible amount of abuse and punishment without getting rattled or retaliating in some way. He failed to score his so-called 'promised' goal, and at least one Renfrew man is out $100 as a result. But from the beginning to the end of a painful and losing cause, Taylor's work was always cool, clean-cut and effective, and he conducted himself in a decidedly creditable manner. At the finish, he was physically bruised and battered from the beating he took on the ice as a marked man, but he was the first to offer his congratulations to the victorious Ottawa players."

There was a long and emotional editorial in the *Free Press* deploring "this despicable display" by Ottawa fans while praising Taylor for his "admirable and courageous conduct" throughout the ordeal, and that was almost the end of the backwards-goal episode.

The two teams met again three weeks later at the Renfrew rink and this one was a slaughter with the Millionaires winning 17–2. This was the game in which Lalonde had made his miracle recovery from a "broken" ankle by scoring six goals—all in the second half. In that game too, Lester Patrick poured four goals past the helpless Ottawa goalie, Percy LeSueur and Taylor added one. That lone goal received more attention than the

other sixteen put together, even upstaging Lalonde's spectacular bag of six.

Meaningless in the 17–2 rout, it was just a little pizzaz tossed
in by Taylor to tickle the fans and undoubtedly himself. With
time running out in the game, Fred the Showman stole the puck,
sped down the boards through the Ottawa defense, wheeled
around, skated backward for the last few strides, and then
flipped a neat backhander past the startled LeSueur.

There was a sizable delegation of Ottawa fans in the audience,
undoubtedly some of whom had been in the Laurier Avenue rink
just three weeks before when Taylor's boast had backfired. Now,
as LeSueur retrieved the puck from the back of the net and
Taylor skated away with a big grin and his stick held aloft, they
were up on the feet with the rest of the fans, applauding. The
prolonged ovation was music to Taylor's ears. It had been
shrewdly orchestrated. Lalonde, who had reasonably theorized
that a six-goal performance was good enough to make the author
the star of the show, once again left the ice muttering to himself.

Newsy's day was to come a couple of weeks later, against a
team from Cobalt that had the misfortune to come up against a
Renfrew team that was running hot.

It was the final game of the home season, and Lalonde, who
had been sensational since joining Renfrew, had a total of
twenty-five goals in his ten games split between the Canadiens
and the Millionaires. He was still seven goals behind the league
leader, Ernie Russell of the Wanderers. Going into the Cobalt
game, the Millionaires had made it known that they wanted their
boy to win the scoring title, and they really turned it on for
Newsy. The final score was 15–4 for Renfrew, and Lalonde had
nine of his team's goals total.

Yet, despite Taylor, the Patricks, and Lalonde—their his-
trionics notwithstanding—the Millionaires finished the season
down in third place in the National Hockey Association standings, behind the Wanderers and Ottawa. The Wanderers had
won the league race with eleven victories against just one defeat.
The best that Renfrew could manage was eight wins against
three losses. It was the Wanderers who went on to win the
Stanley Cup, not the team that had been bought to do the job.

The failure was a bitter pill for the O'Briens and senior part-

ner Barnett to swallow. It was hardly sweetened by the fact t‍h
they had dropped more than $12,000 in their abortive try for an
instant Stanley Cup.

The players were in somewhat better spirits as there was the
now traditional spring break in New York, where they were
booked for a three-games series against the Wanderers. The stip-
ulation in the $1,500 New York purse offer was that Fred Taylor
would return, this time, of course, with the Millionaires. The
Wanderers were strengthened by the addition of four Ottawa
players, but this didn't alter the usual course of history in these
encounters: the team that had Taylor doing his wildly acclaimed
Little Jeff act again picked up the winner's share of the prize
money.

The interesting development in this particular return to
Gotham was the sudden great to-do over the matter of hockey
players' salaries, and Taylor's in particular. The staid New York
Times dwelt in earnest length on this subject.

"There is the general impression that baseball players in our
big leagues are the highest paid professional athletes in the
world, but this is far from correct. Few Americans know that Canadian professional hockey players receive far more money than
the players of the national game of this country. Yet it is a fact
that the Canadian pros receive sums far in excess of anything
dreamed of by the average American. The actual amount of cash
may not be very large, but they play a very few games over a period of just a few weeks, so that the hockey player gets far more
for his services than the baseball man.

"As in baseball, extra large sums are paid to some players, but
the Canadian average can be rated at around $1,000 for eight to
ten games. As against the average baseball stipend of around
$2,500 for 154 games, the hockey player is much better paid, and
has time to be engaged in another business when not playing
hockey.

"The highest paid player in the Dominion is Fred Taylor, who
receives more than $5,000 a year. This cannot be remotely
approached by any of our top baseball stars over such a short
season span.

"The example involving Renfrew, where salaries are said to average $2,700 a man, is only an instance of what prevails with

other pro hockey teams. Cobalt paid Art Ross at the rate of $10 a
minute in a match against the Haileybury team. Two halves of
30 minutes were played, and Ross received $600. No baseball
player ever received anything like an equivalent sum for a single
game."

These revelations turned the visiting Canadian players into
curios of special interest, and St. Nicholas was jammed to the
rafters as Renfrew swept all three games. Taylor, in his constant
and almost exasperating way of stealing the show, again dominated the headlines.

Summing up the third game under the streamer headline
"Renfrew Easy Winners over Wanderers, 9–4," the sub-head
noted that "Fred Taylor Again Succeeded in Opening Eyes of
Gotham Sport."

"The game was brilliantly played and Cyclone Taylor once
more shone in all his glory. His end-to-end rushes, in which he
eluded the entire opposing team, constantly brought down the
house and fairly swept the fans into a delirium of admiration.
The Wanderers' star, Ernie Johnson, was also magnificent, but
Taylor is the more spectacular and crowd-pleasing of the two."

When the Millionaires returned from their New York safari,
they found that all was not gloom and despair in Renfrew.

Far from it.

The O'Briens and Barnett had dropped a bundle, but they
were not exactly on their uppers. And the Town Council, which
did not have to pick up the bills, was positively elated with
events of the past season, despite the team's failure to win a
championship. So much so that they had decided to tender a lavish civic banquet "to honor the team that over the past year had
caused the town of Renfrew to be advertised in a manner never
before attempted, the leading papers throughout the country and
the United States having reported the doings of the Renfrew
team, thereby making Renfrew known by name and reputation
from the Atlantic to the Pacific . . ."

Banquet or no, the future of the Renfrew Millionaires was to
be just a brief one-year exercise in playing out the string as the
O'Briens prepared to pull up stakes and get on with bigger and
more profitable ventures, such as the construction of a section of

railway track that would become part of the C.N.R. route to the West.

Taylor who headed back to Ottawa for the interim, was willing to wait and go along with the next Renfrew season, but others were not.

The Patrick brothers had their own plans, and right after the Renfrew banquet they caught a westbound train to the family home in Nelson, British Columbia, where the head of the family, Joe Patrick, worked extensive timber properties. And even as Frank and Lester were playing out their first and only season in Renfrew, Joe was selling off some of his rich holdings and preparing for a move farther west, clear to the Pacific Coast. The two oldest brothers in the family of five would certainly have some ideas about that move concerning hockey when the time came.

The ever-restless Newsy Lalonde also decided to fly the coop, and he returned to the Canadiens during the off-season.

Back with his job, his girl friend, his scout troop, and a tentative fling at lacrosse, Taylor summered in Ottawa and admired his swelling bank account. It contained the bulk of the $5,250 that had been banked in his name by Ambrose O'Brien, and he was well on his way to the $10,000 marriage stake he had promised himself.

With the summer over, he again arranged a leave of absence from his government job and went back to the boardinghouse in Renfrew.

The Patricks and Lalonde were no longer there, but two new boys were. They were the brothers from Montreal, Odie and Sprague Cleghorn, a pair of rookies who had just joined Renfrew. This was to be year one in a fifteen year span that would establish this pair as two of the best and toughest forwards in history.

They signed for $1,000 each.

And Fred Taylor, the Cyclone who had blown in from Ottawa via Listowel, Portage la Prairie, and Houghton? Although returning as still without doubt the star of the Renfrew show, he signed without a whimper for $1,800. It was a far cry from the figure his Vancouver schoolteacher friend had negotiated the year before, but Taylor was philosophical about it. Mainly probably because there was no other choice.

"We all knew those big first-year salaries couldn't last. There
was hardly enough coming in at Renfrew to buy the sticks, let
alone pay the salaries. After that first season, we knew that the
O'Briens just wanted to get out, as gracefully as possible."

"As gracefully as possible" was to mean just this one more season, with the schedule enlarged to sixteen games. From this,
Taylor & Co. could salvage no more than eight victories against
eight defeats and a second-place tie with Newsy Lalonde's
Canadiens, behind Ottawa.

Taylor's only consolation in this drab win-loss performance
was a personal one. For the fourth straight season, including his
two with that other league in Ottawa, he was named to the All
Star Team, as a unanimous choice.

He was now twenty-seven years old, getting very thin on top,
and was occasionally referred to in the press as "the old man."
He was hardly that, but he did profit by a significant rules
change initiated in that 1911 season: the switch from two thirty-
minute halves to three period of twenty minutes each, with ten-
minute rest intervals.

This change was a boon to twenty-seven-year-old legs, even
though they seemed as good as ever and still generated the same
old dazzling burst of speed that had marked him as a twenty-
year-old rookie pro down in Houghton, Michigan.

March of 1911 was the end of the line for the Renfrew Millionaires, the ill-fated love-child of Ambrose O'Brien. It was a forlorn
close to what for hockey had been a brief romantic interlude, the
likes of which would not come again.

The demise of the Millionaires, although not yet formally announced, produced a wry twist. Within a week of scoring his
final Renfrew goal in a schedule-closing 7–6 win over the Wanderers, Taylor was New York-bound again—as a specially invited member of the Ottawa Senators. Here he was suddenly
back with the team he had spurned two years before, and that
had turned him a neat-but-not-gaudy black and blue in that
tumultous reception in February 1910.

There was a little Ottawa pride-swallowing involved here. The
Senators coveted the New York trip, but even as the Stanley Cup

champions, the invitation was conditional on their producing Fred Taylor as part of their roster. With this basic condition settled, the trip was on, with the Wanderers back again as the other team.

This fourth Canadian safari into the U.S. was, for the first time, extended beyond New York City to Boston. There, in the New England city, curious thousands flocked to the rink that had just been built across the railroad racks to get their first look at professional hockey. Eager learners, they also picked up some ideas about their own town's hockey future as in B-R-U-I-N-S. This was thinking ahead quite a bit, but there had to be a start, and this was it.

The Ottawas had won the New York series, and proceeded to win the two-game Boston series over the Wanderers, 13–11.

It didn't take long for the Boston headline writers to get into the same old rut—just the first game, to be precise.

CHAMPIONS BEATEN 7 GOALS TO 5
FRED TAYLOR STARS FOR OTTAWA
Taylor's Cyclonic Rushes Electrified Audience
In First Professional Hockey Match
Ever Staged Here

Said the Boston *Globe:* "The first ever pro hockey game in Boston was a smash success. One would have to conclude from the enthusiastic response that the City will demand to see much more of the Canadian game."

Earlier in New York, a *Times* story had reported that "a New York" syndicate has definitely decided to go into professional hockey this winter, three teams being planned for Manhattan and one in Brooklyn. Options are said to have been secured for the services of the following Canadian players: LeSueur, Lake and Smaill of the Ottawas, Johnson and Glass of the Wanderers, and Cyclone Taylor of Renfrew."

This was an interesting story, but there was no truth to it. No options had been secured, and none of the players mentioned had been approached, at least not seriously.

It was just a Manhattan pipe dream, but thanks to the Little Jeff Traveling Road Show, there was no doubt that the seeds of the National Hockey League with its Rangers, Bruins, Black

Hawks, et al., had been well planted, despite a crisis that almost wrecked the Boston series.

Sam Lichtenhein was along on the trip as manager of the Wanderers, and he was very cool toward the star member of the opposition, Fred Taylor. It wasn't that Sam didn't admire Taylor personally, but he was very upset over Taylor's blunt refusal of his "generous" offer to sign with the Wanderers for the next season.

Lichtenhein quietly nursed his pique throughout the stay in New York, but it surfaced suddenly in Boston just before the opening game. Maybe Sam was ruffled because the player who had snubbed him was now rubbing it in further with a brilliant performance that had Ottawa well ahead in the competition, but, for whatever reason, Sam got suddenly belligerent.

Enroute from Montreal to New York he had grumbled about the invitation to Taylor, claiming that the Wanderers owned his rights, but nobody took Sam's grousing too seriously.

Upon arrival in Boston, Sam broached the matter again. He announced that he now refused to recognize Taylor as a member of the Ottawa roster and that if he was not removed, the Wanderers wouldn't play the Boston series. There was a hurried conclave with all parties concerned, but nothing had been resolved by the time the teams left for the arena to dress for the game. Lichtenhein told the Wanderers that unless the matter was resolved to his satisfaction they were not to come out onto the ice.

With the arena jammed and the innocents in the stands unaware of the crisis, the teams sat waiting for the announcer to make the lineup introductions. Ottawa came out first and there was great applause when the announcer shouted out Taylor's name. With all seven Senators on the ice, the announcer then called for "the famous Montreal Wanderers," and out they came, one by one.

Captain Art Ross was later to explain that when they heard Taylor's name called by the announcer they assumed that the problem had been solved, and so out they came to play hockey. But across the rink Lichtenhein was livid as he watched his boys stream onto the ice. He turned and headed for the Boston officials, but Ottawa coach Petie Green raced over and intercepted him. As the two of them stood at rinkside arguing and gesticulating furiously, the referee called out the two centers, dropped the puck, and the game was on.

That was a very smart move on the part of the referee, but that was understandable. This alert chap was none other than the highly regarded ex-captain of the Renfrew Millionaires, Lester Patrick.

Lester had been waiting in Boston when the two teams arrived. He was there on a visit from the latest family homestead in Nelson, B.C., accompanied by his bride of one week. Although Lester didn't bandy it about, he was on hand to check two specific matters of interest: Boston's excellent new artificial ice plant, and the future availability of a player or two for a new league that was being hatched out in the Far West by him and his brother, Frank.

Having been asked to officiate in the Ottawa-Wanderers series, Lester had gladly accepted and refereed both games, after saving the first. For a Patrick, this was as good a way as any to spend a honeymoon.

It was an example of which Taylor took note. Not one too easily upstaged, he would be back in Boston soon with his own bride.

Chapter Six
TO THE COAST

In the late spring of 1911 Taylor left his O'Connor Street boardinghouse and rented a house out on Lyon Street. In the early summer his mother and sister, Elizabeth, moved in with him.

Mother and daughter had gone to live in Toronto two years before, leaving Archie Taylor and the rest of the family to fend for themselves. Taylor insists that there had been no trouble between his parents, explaining that Elizabeth had simply got herself a job clerking in a Toronto department store, and Mary Taylor had gone along to take care of her.

Hearing that his mother hadn't been well, Fred had asked her to Ottawa to live in his newly acquired three-bedroom bungalow. It was there that Mary Taylor got to know Miss Thirza Cook, and the two of them got along famously right from the start.

This pleasant new family life was a welcome island of calm in the sea of controversy that continued to surround Taylor. For the hockey player who apparently couldn't stay out of hot water even if permanently assigned to the polar regions, the summer and fall season of 1911 was just the calm before yet another storm.

What with his prolonged courtship, his Boy Scout Troop, the government job and another season of lacrosse with the Capitals, the months slipped swiftly by, and here it was October with his hockey future once more nicely scrambled. Like a man without a country, Taylor was again a player without a team, although not through any sparsity of claims and offers.

The courtly O'Briens had made their exit from hockey official by disbanding the Renfrew team, and the franchise was transferred to a group in Toronto who were to operate a team named, cleverly enough, the Torontos. This business was tended at the National Hockey Association autumn meeting in Montreal, which also produced legislation to abolish the position of rover in that league, at least on an experimental basis.

Rover, cover-point, wing, center—pick your position, and there would always be a place for Taylor, but the question was with what team? In what country? As usual, Taylor was his own man at a time like this, and he liked to keep his options open.

He and other members of the late-lamented Renfrew Millionaires had been declared league property. Their names were placed in a draw, in what was the equivalent of today's common draft. The Patrick boys, now out on the Pacific Coast and busy with their plans to challenge the East's cozy sole proprietorship of big league hockey, had already heisted three Renfrew stars: Newsy Lalonde, Bert Lindsay, and Bobby Rose, and now the N.H.A. teams dipped into the hat to divide the rest.

The big one, Fred Taylor, was still there, and he was now formally drawn and claimed by the Montreal Wanderers, along with Sprague Cleghorn. Immediately, Ottawa offered to trade their draw, the high-scoring winger Skeenan Ronan, plus $300 for Taylor. This pitch got no more than an amused smile from the Wanderers' president, Sam Lichtenhein. Sam had the man he wanted.

Or had he?

Up to this point, nobody had bothered to ask the principal in this bit of bartering, Frederick Wellington Taylor alias Cyclone, the rebellious one. His unsolicited answer was clear enough: No.

He informed the startled Mr. Lichtenhein that he did not recognize the draft, that he had no intention of playing for the Wanderers, and that he would play only for Ottawa. His job was there, his girl was there, his bank was there, and that's where he'd stay. For this next season anyway.

Two parties who agreed heartily with this mixed bag of reasons were Thirza Cook and the executives of the Ottawa club. The latter concurred so heartily that they not only openly encouraged Taylor's stand but also offered to pay him to stay around while they bargained with the Wanderers.

Ottawa continued to dicker, the Wanderers continued to say no deal, Taylor said no play, and the league said okay, you're suspended. Ottawa then offered Sam their outstanding forward Fred Lake, plus $500 cash. They offered more cash. Lichtenhein politely suggested that they go fly a kite up the Ottawa Valley.

"Taylor," said Sam, "either plays with the Wanderers or he plays nowhere."

The Ottawas were fighting a losing cause as Lichtenhein stayed stubborn, refusing to give up on his man. He admitted that he wanted Taylor badly and was quite frank as to why. A syndicate had promised to build Montreal a new 6,000-seat hockey rink, and it looked as though the deal would now go through. Sam wanted the top draw in the game to help fill those seats.

Also, Sam revealed, there was pressure from people in Boston who were preparing to form a team and hoped to organize an International League that would include the Wanderers, and Taylor. "I want Taylor here, and I think he'll be here," he said, "for three reasons. The Montreal public want him, the Wanderers are prepared to pay him more money than he can get in Ottawa, and he'd be playing international hockey."

Whether or not Lichtenhein's inability to land Taylor influenced the delay or not, the fact was that Boston's grand plan did not materialize in 1912, and that city was still fifteen years away from its first pro hockey team.

Meanwhile, back at the wrangle, it was no business as usual. Lichtenhein dispatched a pair of agents to Ottawa to talk to Taylor. They camped in the Dominion Hotel and called him constantly for three days. Each time, Taylor begged off, citing pressure of business and prior commitments to a Miss Cook for health-giving walks in the country. The agents returned to Montreal without closeting their quarry, so then Lichtenhein got on the phone to see what he could do.

There were headlined stories in the Montreal papers reporting that Sam had talked to Taylor and that Taylor would join the Wanderers. There were headlined stories in the Ottawa papers reporting that no he wouldn't. A Toronto *Journal* report sagely described the situation as "confused." This was the nearest thing to the truth of the matter.

Taylor, under suspension for his refusal to report to the Wanderers, stayed stubborn, and the league schedule started without him. And finished without him.

For the second time since leaving the perils of the Piggery in Listowel fifteen years before, Taylor had been trapped between

the autocratic demands of the system and his own mule stub-
bornness. For the second time, he was doomed to sit out a full
hockey season.

There were some personal compensations. To keep control of
Taylor while they continued throughout the winter trying to
pressure the Wanderers into a deal, the Ottawa club paid him a
full season's salary of $1,200. This was an unheard-of arrange-
ment between management and player.

It was another record for Taylor. Having already been paid
more than any other team athlete for a season's work, he had
now set a new high in salaries for no work at all. In this area of
his trade, at least, he had no other worlds to conquer.

Also, Fred was able to make a few dollars on the side by playing occasional games as a "ringer" with hockey teams in the Ottawa Valley League. Those and other teams asked him back to
do some refereeing for a modest but useful fee, and always with
star billing.

It was not exactly a harsh winter financially or socially, but for
a super player whose life was tuned to winters of exhilarating
competition and the heady roar of the crowd, it was an empty
existence.

Throughout that winter of exile, he had been buoyed by the
news from the Pacific Coast, from where the Patricks—especially
Frank, who was headquartered in Vancouver—kept in touch
through the mails. There was a future there for Taylor anytime
he decided to let it happen, but the time was not yet ripe.

It was just a couple of weeks before the start of the NHA's
1912 season that the Patricks officially launched their new
hockey empire. On December 11, 1911, the hockey world was
rocked by the announcement of the organization of the Pacific
Coast Hockey Association, which was to start play immediately.
The news came from a meeting in the Hotel Vancouver, where
franchises were granted to Vancouver, Victoria, and New Westminster.

If there was not exactly panic in the East over this development, there was certainly concern. It was plain that the Patricks
were going about their enterprise in a very businesslike and aggressive manner, backed by Joe Patrick's ample supply of hard
cash.

Plush Patrick arenas with artificial ice plants had been built in Victoria and Vancouver, and after some shrewd raids on the Eastern circuits, the new P.C.H.A. already had the nucleus of an excellent league roster under contract. The top prize was that talented gadabout, Newsy Lalonde, who had been lured, without great difficulty, from the Canadiens. Newsy was to join Frank Patrick's new team in Vancouver.

So there were the Patricks out there across the Rockies officially in business, offering new horizons for restless twenty-seven-year-old hockey players who found themselves temporarily unemployed, albeit well paid. And the man who once sat with Lester and Frank at those fascinating dinnertime gabfests in a Renfrew boardinghouse was high on their wanted list. This was hardly a secret in Ottawa. There was a major talent war brewing, and a lot of other players were now looking West and listening to the persuasive Patrick pitch. The brothers were in business, and they meant business.

The eastern hockey people had heard all these rumblings, but operating on the tenuous theory that there's none so deaf as those who won't hear, they just pretended it wasn't happening. This represented a gross miscalculation of the mettle of the Patricks as able and ambitious young hockey executives. Taylor himself, ever since those Renfrew boardinghouse sessions with Lester and Frank, was never one to underestimate their style. Now they had built another stage for his talents, and Taylor knew that it was just a matter of time before he got the call to go on.

In the unpublished memoirs he penned many years later, Lester Patrick said of the family move West to build a new hockey empire: "We had Fred Taylor in mind right from the beginning. His acquisition was just a matter of timing." That journal recorded by the oldest of the four Patrick boys outlines the family odyssey that changed the early face of hockey in Canada and left its permanent mark on the game as we know it today.

It was the restless spirit of their father, Joe Patrick, that had opened up the West for the two oldest sons and their dream of expansion there. In 1907, "having been successful locating new timber limits in the Slocan district of British Columbia," Joe bought a new family home in Nelson, B.C., a lovely town of 3,000 on the Kootenay Lake.

Now, with their return to British Columbia, the Patrick boys were able to persuade their father to sell the business and underwrite their daring hockey venture.

"Our family lumber holdings proved attractive and a sale was made in January 1911. The sale sum was $400,000. Immediately after the deal was made Frank and I discussed our futures, and the germ was born to move to the Coast, pioneer artificial rinks in Canada, and introduce pro hockey to the Coast cities. I had just turned twenty-seven, and Frank was twenty-four. We had much to learn as executives, but at this time we were just hockey players with a lot of dreams.

"Our ideas of improving the game were never very much at fault according to the record, but we were just too young to understand that the population and drawing potential on the Coast was limited. We were to realize this later on.

"Had we gone eastward and developed our ideas in the larger population centers, history, in regard to our fortunes, would have been different, certainly more profitable for us."

So it was decided that the family should move to the Coast, lock, stock, and $400,000. The arrangement was that Lester would settle with the family in Victoria and Frank would go to Vancouver. But first, Lester was to go to East and inspect the artificial rinks then operating in the United States while the others prepared to proceed to the Coast to buy properties and get architects to prepare plans. "Originally we had set up a preferred and common stock financial structure, but with the passing of time the finances were taken care of out of the family purse, with help from mortgages."

It was this trip that had brought Lester East to that historic series in Boston then back West through Montreal and Ottawa, on his working honeymoon. Now in the new year of 1912 he was established in Victoria with his bride and his fine new arena.

The Victoria rink, built at a cost of $11,000 and seating 3,500, had been officially opened on Christmas Day with a giant skating party attended by Joe Patrick, Lester, and the rest of the Patrick brood including Frank. Frank, with his own new beauty of a rink just opened in Vancouver, had come over on the C.P.R. ferry for the special occasion.

Here, in Victoria's stylish Oak Bay district, was mute evidence of the imagination and daring of the Patricks in spreading big league hockey to the farthest western reaches of Canada, 3,000 miles from the game's traditional headquarters in Ontario and Quebec. The Patricks had not only brought big-time hockey West, they had brought it West in first-class style, setting it up in this ultramodern rink in Victoria and a larger prototype in Vancouver, both featuring the first artificial ice surfaces in Canada.

Joe Patrick joined the skaters on the ice that Christmas Day in 1911, and the man who had liquidated his timber holdings to make it all possible mingled with the happy mob of over 600 and was indistinguishable from the rest as he skimmed around the boards to the strains of a waltz-time tune.

This rink was to be the home of Lester's Victoria Aristocrats, with brother Frank's Vancouver Millionaires sharing the new Vancouver building with the Coast League's third member, New Westminster. The promised new New Westminster arena was not yet ready, so the Royals were to play their home games in Vancouver.

In both Vancouver and Victoria, the Patrick brothers had multiroles in their respective organizations as president, manager, team captain, and player. They both had ample help from the first-class pool of talent pumped in from the East to launch the precocious Coast enterprise.

In Vancouver, Frank's roster read like a roll call out of both his and Fred Taylor's eastern Canada past. There in the Millionaires colors of maroon and white were old friends, Newsy Lalonde, Tom Phillips, Si Griffis, and Sibby Nichols.

In Victoria, Lester had another collection of former and distinguished eastern contemporaries including three from the Millionaires of Renfrew: Bert Lindsay, Bobby Rose, and Walter Smaill. The indomitable Ernie ("Moose") Johnson was with New Westminster.

Did the Patricks' multiple roles hurt their play on the ice? Well of the brothers' play in that debut season, suffice it to say that they were both unanimous All Stars, and in one game

Fred Taylor on his return from his first trip to Russia in 1958. (*Vancouver Province*)

Prime Minister's Dinner in 1958. Left to right, Taylor, Prime Minister John Diefenbaker, Newsy Lalonde, Lester Patrick. (*Dominion-Wide*)

Taylor turns the sod at the Hockey Hall of Fame in Toronto, 1960. Left to right: Tommy Ivan, Bobby Hull, Fred Taylor, Glenn Hall, Pierre Pilote.

Taylor seated with the Stanley Cup in the new Vancouver Pacific Colosseum before the first NHL game in September, 1970. *(Vancouver Sun)*

Mrs. Thirza Taylor, Fred's wife (on right of picture), as she looked in the late 1950s

Fred Taylor in 1974. *(Vancouver Province)*

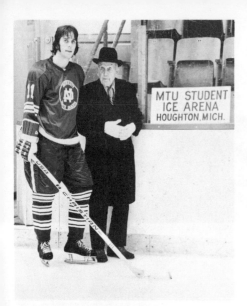

Taylor with eighteen-year-old grandson Mark, on the occasion of his return to Houghton, Michigan (where he played his first professional hockey game), January 1977.

Ken Dryden (All Star goalie) shakes the hand of Cyclone Taylor at the All Star dinner in Vancouver, January 24, 1977. Frank Frederickson is in the middle. *(Vancouver Province)*

against New Westminster, Vancouver's all-everything Frank Patrick scored six goals. Not at all bad for a defenseman.

At season's end, the Victoria Aristrocrats were on top with a record of 9–6, followed by Vancouver 7–8, and Victoria 7–9. The league entrepeneurs had not only picked well, but with a shrewd sense of league balance.

Checking in with his piece of this all-round artistic success as the league gates ranged from good to moderate was the little man, Edouard Newsy Lalonde with a brilliant crop of twenty-seven goals in fifteen games. With Fred Taylor on the shelf back East, Newsy had moved in as the game's most exciting player.

All that Taylor could do back in Ottawa was read about it and burn with frustration. But then late in March there came a reprieve from his self-exile. There was an announcement that an East All Star Team would play a three-game series on the Pacific Coast against a West All Star Team. The Patricks were behind the scheme and had lined up dates in Vancouver and Victoria.

Art Ross was to manage and captain the Easterners, and Art was asked to pick his team. The list Ross sent to Patrick did not include Taylor. Patrick, who wanted Cyclone Taylor's name on the roster to help fill his big new rink, told Ross that Taylor had to be part of the deal. With the trip in jeopardy, Ross recanted and named Taylor to his squad.

Taylor himself was a little confused by it all. "Art and I were always on very good terms and got along fine, and I don't know why he balked at having me along. Granted, I wasn't in the very best of shape, but I'd kept myself in pretty good condition and I was ready to play. Maybe he just thought I wasn't ready, or had some other reason. I never knew. All I know is that once we got on the train we were as good friends as we'd ever been, and he seemed happy to have me along."

Others on the East squad were Skeenan Ronan, Hamby Shore, Jack Darragh, Odie Cleghorn, Paddy Moran, and the battle-scarred roustabout, Bad Joe Hall. Shore was booked to play point with Taylor listed as the rover.

The All Star Team waiting in Vancouver read like a list at a home-coming party. In addition to old-chum Frank Patrick, the team captain, there was Newsy Lalonde, Hughie Lehman, Tom

Dunderdale, Harry Hyland, and Ernie ("Moose") Johnson, all
refugees from the East now prospering in the Patrick's empire.

The first game of the three-game series was in the new Vancouver Arena, with a huge crowd expected, much of which had
been pumped up by the press to look out for "the world's most
sensational hockeyist, Cyclone Taylor." But when the easterners
got into town on April 1, it was announced that Taylor was an
uncertain starter because of a severe hand injury suffered just
before the squad left Ottawa.

He had sustained a badly gashed hand while refereeing a
benefit game for Bruce Ridpath, an Ottawa player who was
seriously ill, and shortly afterward died. As the newspapers reported the incident, Taylor had paid his own way into the
benefit match, took twenty-five of his Boy Scouts along with him
at $.50 a head, refereed the game gratis, and then had to rush to
surgery after a late game collision with one of the players.
Ripped by a skate, Taylor's right hand required a lot of stitching,
and it was heavily bandaged for the trip West.

When the Ross team got into town, reporters were assured
that Taylor would start if at all possible. Said Ross, "He has
played very little all winter and is desperately anxious to get
going again. He says he wants to play even if it kills him."

Taylor did play, and it didn't kill him, nor did it stem the
onslaught that saw the West All Stars win that first game 10–4
before a joyous mob of 8,000. However, Taylor was used only
sparingly because of the injured hand that caused great difficulty
in holding the stick. He must have wondered how far he had
slipped, and how far he might have to come back after the lost
season.

Two nights later, the East lost a 5–1 decision in Victoria, but
Taylor sat out all of that one. He said he was ready to play and
wanted to play, but didn't get the call. He languished on the
bench at the start of the third and final game back in Vancouver,
and was still there when the first period ended with the score 3–1
for the West, and Shore's gang seemingly outclassed.

He didn't get on until midway in the final period, with the
score tied at 3–3 and the East sagging again. Sent in for Hamby
Shore, he immediately turned the tide.

"When Taylor came in with the game tied, the excitement was

intense. Hamby Shore was pulled off by the East, and his replacement was mainly responsible for the East's ultimate victory. Cyclone Taylor came onto the ice just in time to stop a dangerous West rush, stole the puck, and then rushed right through the opposing defense before passing back to Ross for the leading goal. Right after that he made a similar spectacular rush and gave Darragh a similar chance, which he accepted. With a sudden two-goal lead and only ten minutes to play, the East played a defensive game, but there was great excitement when Moose Johnson broke through and scored alone to make it 6–5. However, Taylor's two fine plays were two too many for the West . . ."

And so ended Taylor's brief fling at playing in this elongated season of 1911–12, after the shop had been closed in the East. He had played very little in this first-ever East-West confrontation, but he had played with at least some of the old gusto, and had proved that he was still able to generate that old excitement and light fires on the ice.

Now it was back to Ottawa, with the season long finished and Sam Lichtenhein still grimly holding on, claiming Taylor as the Wanderers' property. Taylor was still suspended; an outcast. And with the season down the drain, the headlines were back humming the old refrain: Would he or would he not play next season; if so, where? Plus all the news on his latest "retirement."

A *Free Press* yarn lamented "The Pathetic Case of Fred Taylor," noting that "last year Taylor was a star of the first magnitude, this year little more than a stick-boy, just hanging around to draw his salary . . . this is the new public image of Fred Taylor alias Cyclone alias the Listowel Thunderbolt . . ."

There was certainly genuine concern in the papers for the man's plight, but also an awareness of his fondness for melodrama and his ability to wring the most out of any dramatic situation. It was observed that his suspension for refusing to compromise his principles had not affected him financially; that he was a "provident man" who didn't smoke, drink, or play poker, and had scraped together what they termed "a formidable little pile."

Still, they willingly gave the devil his due, agreeing that he was one of the most spectacular and exciting players in sport, and that his exile was a matter of great regret to all hockey fans. Oh yes, they were on to Taylor the showman, but gently and with a wry understanding. As in this newspaper passage:

"At every home game, the man with the melancholy face stands at rinkside watching his mates perform. Some people declare that they have seen tears in his eyes, but this is unlikely. Taylor hasn't cried since the Stanley Cup victory banquet here in 1909, when they refused to let him take the trophy home to Listowel to show to his fellow townsmen. But if he did weep now, he'd have good reason."

At his age Taylor could hardly afford the gathering rust of another lost season. Nobody believed his occasional talk of retirement, and come autumn, just to get the game's top gate attraction playing somewhere in the N.H.A., Sam Lichtenhein relinquished his claim on the stubborn holdout.

Sam gave the new Toronto Tecumsehs of the same league permission to deal with Taylor, and the Tecumsehs offered $3,000, double what any other player in the same sport was then earning. Taylor turned the offer down flat. "I don't like the idea of being bought and sold by others. I'm my own man."

He was hardly leaving himself out on a limb, as he now had something else going. He was negotiating with Frank Patrick, who wanted Fred for his Vancouver Millionaires out in the new Coast circuit. Negotiations were coming along well, but with the new season fast approaching Patrick was getting a little anxious. He sent a telegram on November 6 with the message: "Would like to give story of your signing to local papers on Saturday. The information will not get to the East until five days after that as I will not let any wires go through, thus the deal will be completed well before anyone there knows. Our first game is December 7. Wish you could get here by November 25. Will give you equivalent of your salary there for any time lost if you can get here by then. Absolutely depending on you to complete team. —Frank Patrick."

Patrick was hoping to avoid a confrontation with Lichtenhein and other N.H.A. officials in his bid for Taylor, but the papers knew that something was brewing and their pages were jammed with conjecture.

The management of the jilted Toronto Tecumsehs reacted to

rumor by sending a telegram, dated November 20, 1912, with Fred still apparently uncommitted: "If you have definitely decided to leave Ottawa hockey club and go West, can you defer your final move until after the N.H.A. meeting Saturday in Toronto. Tecumsehs will match any Vancouver offer and also look after and guarantee better position in the Immigration Department here. Answer at once. Arena Gardens—W. J. Bellingham."

Little did Mr. Bellingham know that even as he was composing this message, its recipient was closeted in the parlor of a house on Ottawa's Lyon Street, chatting with a visitor. It was like a replay of the scene three years before, when another visitor, a Mr. George Martel of Renfrew, sat with Taylor in another parlor on O'Connor Street, engaged in similar conversation. This time, the visitor was Frank Patrick.

"We were renewing old friendship," recalls Taylor, "and we had a very pleasant discussion. There was no contract. There never was in those days with the Patricks. It was just a verbal agreement, and we shook hands on it. All that was left to do was for Frank to send me my ticket to Vancouver."

The next day's edition of the *Free Press* had the story: "The expected has happened. Fred Taylor, the Ty Cobb of the National Hockey Association and the greatest drawing card in the history of the game has accepted terms to play with Vancouver of the Pacific Coast League and leaves for the West Saturday morning.

"With this signing, the Pacific Coast moguls have scored heavily against the Eastern leaguers. Shouldering liabilities in salaries alone aggregating more than $40,000, the Western club owners have decimated the N.H.A., the major hockey league of the East. They have already stolen eight outstanding Eastern stars and have pushed salaries everywhere sky-high.

"The Pacific Coast's raid of the Eastern stronghold is the biggest in the history of sport, and they have capped it now by taking Taylor, the most sensational hockey player in the World, just as the N.H.A. is preparing to open its season.

"It is a complete route of the N.H.A., and it gives some idea of the way sport is being commercialized in the Dominion."

It was all pretty impassioned stuff, and right up Fred Taylor's alley. He did not let the writers down on Saturday morning.

Taylor arrived at the station to board the westbound train, accompanied by Karl Kendall, another Ottawa player Patrick had signed.

One reporter rhapsodized:

"There were tears in Fred Taylor's eyes as he talked of his friends before boarding his train for the Pacific Coast. He said he was sorry to leave Ottawa and sorry to leave the East. He said that it was not the lure of the West or the jingle of the Patricks' money bags that had made him hie away, but the clanking of the chains of slavery that the Eastern moguls had forged for their hockey players. It was a case of the Coast and liberty or the East and slavery; as much as Freddie loves the East, he loves liberty more. The case is almost as heart-rending as that of the down-trodden woman, as depicted by a famous British suffragette now touring Canada."

One of those left behind in Ottawa that day was Thirza Cook, whom Taylor had just recently cited as one of the reasons for his refusing to leave Ottawa to play for the Montreal Wanderers. Yet here he was puffing off to far more distant parts without his ladylove.

The romance was now five years old, and far from being on the wane, it was now a mutual pact with everything set but the marriage date. Taylor's wedding kitty of $10,000 was getting close to the mark, and he figured that one season on the Coast would do it. Whether or not this burgeoning affluence had any effect on the situation, Amelia Cook had softened considerably toward the pro hockey player and was apparently resigned to the match.

As Fred had arranged for his future bride, he planned to be back East the following spring and summer, and if things worked out well in the West there would be an autumn wedding, followed by a permanent move to Vancouver. It was also arranged that Fred's mother and sister would return to live in Toronto, where Liz would resume her old job in the department store.

As to Taylor's emotional departure, the tears that were said to have welled in his eyes as he boarded the train had nothing to do with the financial aspects of the flight out of town. His one-year pact to play with Frank Patrick's Millionaires was for $1,800, a substantial figure on that year's player market.

Patrick was also working on the other important half of the deal; the transfer of Taylor's Immigration Department job to the Vancouver office. The salary was still only $1,200, but Fred had a great liking for the security of what was turning into the permanent career he had wanted from the start.

As had been the case with his original entry into the Civil Service in the move from Listowel to Ottawa, a little politicking was needed to swing the transfer. Frank Patrick went right to the top in his area with a personal request for assistance from the Premier of British Columbia, Sir Richard McBride.

Sir Richard, who had once seen a hockey game in Ottawa and fancied himself as a fan, got right to work on the project with nothing less than a telephone call to the office of the Prime Minister, Sir Robert Borden. Sir Robert said he'd see what he could do, which was promising. Meanwhile, as the wheels turned on Parliament Hill, Taylor was again on leave of absence from the department.

It was the morning of December 5, 1912, when the train bearing Taylor and his traveling companion puffed into Vancouver after a six-day journey across the Prairies and through the grandeur of the Canadian Rockies that were draped with a new fall of snow.

Waiting on the station platform in a chill gray rain was Frank Patrick and Taylor's friend from the brief Portage la Prairie days, Si Griffis.

"Fred," said Patrick, "I hope you've had a good trip and a nice rest. You two guys are due at the rink for a workout exactly three hours from now. I hope you brought your skates."

To Taylor, it was like a flashback to a very cold January morning in 1905 when he had arrived in Houghton, Michigan, to be greeted by almost the same words. And that time Taylor had forgotten his skates and they'd rushed off to get him a new pair for his first workout with his new teammates.

The difference this time was that Taylor was no frightened rookie far from home and facing his first test as a professional.

"Frank," he said with a grin, "I'm ready when you are."

The two new men were taken straight to their hotel at the corner of Georgia and Burrard, where Patrick pointed to the location of the rink just a few blocks west along Georgia and then left them to unpack.

"Fred," said Griffis on parting, "it's good to see you again. You're going to like it here. You might even stay."

That was as prophetic a suggestion as Si was ever likely to make.

The team workout and a first look at these western Million-aires was scheduled for 2 P.M., and Taylor and Kendall were there. A full assessment of his new teammates would have to wait until a turn or two around the rink and a little knocking at game time, but Taylor's first leisurely inspection of the new Den-man Arena was an eye-opener.

His was an impressive entry into the brave new hockey world of the Patricks, and as he skated out onto the clean, smooth sheet of ice Taylor, even though he had been there before, was over-come by the sheer size of the emporium that sat there in its great, yawning emptiness. It beat anything he had seen in New York, Boston, or Pittsburgh, and was grander than the 7,000-seat building recently opened in Montreal. And that one in Montreal was still back in the old-fashioned natural-ice age.

This structure, built at a cost of $210,000 of Joe Patrick's money, had seats for 10,500. Next to Madison Square Garden, the 12,000 seat arena on New York's Madison Avenue that ca-tered to circus performers and not hockey players, this was the world's largest indoor stadium. Here was the proud domain of the Millionaires' president-coach-player, Frank Patrick, while there across the Straits of Juan de Fuca brother Lester was set-tled into the other fine family establishment with its 4,000-seat capacity.

The artificial ice plants in both buildings were the first in Can-ada, predated only by the pioneer surfaces in New York's St. Nicholas Arena and those in Boston and Pittsburgh, and now a new one in Detroit.

Of the two, the Vancouver project was the more impressive, not so much for its size but for the fact that an arena of this size had been built in such a relatively small and isolated city, with one family's money.

It wasn't exactly the Taj Mahal or the Superdome—as a matter of fact it was a rather homely, barnlike brick triangular structure with more the lines of a warehouse than a sports palace—but there out West it was one of the wonders of the age.

Earlier, during their talks back in Ottawa, Frank had intrigued Taylor with descriptions of the new ice-making machine that would not only produce an ice surface but would also churn out huge supplies of ice for sale to the public storage plants, etc. The profit potential, said Frank, was enormous.

It was a very good idea, but for some reason it never did work out, and Frank's dreams of a smart money-maker vanished with the machine's ability to do more than its basic intent: provide a surface for the rink.

Even the Toronto *News* was impressed with Vancouver's new ice palace, claiming it was "unsurpassed by any other institution of its kind in the world." The story went on to praise the building's construction, the superior lighting system, and the safety features. With fourteen exits, including three fire escapes, "it is estimated that when filled to capacity the building could be emptied in the space of three minutes." The ice surface, covering an area of 85 feet by 210 feet, was reported to be the largest in the world, and the main floor of the arena was eventually to be convertible into a huge swimming pool. It never was.

"There's one thing about the Patricks," said Taylor as he came in from his first wandering cruise around the rink, "they certainly don't think small."

If the arena did have some corporate shortcomings, nobody complained, least of all the hockey fans. Especially in that early December of 1912, with Taylor in town. His old friend and arch-rival, Newsy Lalonde, had enjoyed that first great season of his with the Millionaires, but his restless soul—a mate, in a way, to Taylor's—had taken him East again, back home with the Canadiens.

As a replacement for Lalonde, Taylor was regarded as more than adequate, although he looked a little rusty at that first brisk workout. After a warm-up, Taylor had skated to the post he had patrolled the past several seasons as cover-point, but he was waved away by Patrick.

"You're at center, Fred."

"But I'm a cover-point. Have been for years, you know that, Frank."

"You've been switched. You've got lots of time to get readjusted."

"When's the first game?"

"Tomorrow night. Against New Westminster."

But when tomorrow night rolled around and the New Westminster Royals came out to play, Kendall was at center for Vancouver and Taylor was the rover, stationed just in front of Si Griffis, the cover-point, and Patrick, the point.

A record crowd of 7,000 made it to the league opener, but Taylor almost didn't. On the day of the game, he suffered severe stomach pains and was at times barely able to walk. Patrick told him to stay home and Taylor did, at least until an hour before game time.

Once the skates were on he felt better, although twice during the warm-up Patrick, a worrier, went to him as he winced visibly and told him to go to the bench, but to no avail. The fans had gotten the adrenalin flowing with an ovation when he first appeared on the ice, and for Taylor the roar of the crowd was anesthetic enough.

The best rushes of a night that saw the Millionaires crush New Westminster 7–2 were put together by Taylor, the cover-point Si Griffis, and the point, Patrick. The marked man of the trio was Taylor, a player still trying to shake off the rust of a year's layoff and still looking for his land legs after the long train ride from Ottawa.

The Royals' freely announced intent was to intimidate the new eastern hot-shot right off the bat, and the prime assignment went to that rugged old acquaintance, Ernie ("Moose") Johnson.

On Taylor's first rush, the Moose rattled him exuberantly into the boards, hit him again on the bounce and repeated this maneuver at every opportunity thereafter. The second time this happened, Taylor just bounced, spun, cradled the puck, and sped off down the boards to register the second Vancouver goal of the night and the first of his Coast League career. Still, Johnson continued to stick with his man like a great hulking shadow, and as a result that was Taylor's goal total for the evening. Yet Taylor was still the most dominant figure on the ice.

A cursory scan of the nation's sports pages—and those of New York, Boston, Pittsburgh, and other foreign parts—suggests that there has been no other Canadian athlete who has over a long period provoked so many headlines reflective of so much adulation and mixed controversy.

Disregard this fact and you disregard the unerring black-and-white proof of the man's exceptional ability to excite and incite.

And here, with the first game story of Taylor in the Vancouver papers, it was business as usual—Houghton, Ottawa, Pittsburgh, Renfrew, New York, Boston, etc., revisited. The old master show stealer was back at it again. It was the same old refrain; music by the fans and lyrics by the boys in the press box.

Or, as bannered in the Vancouver Province:

FRED TAYLOR IS A REVELATION
TO PACIFIC COAST FANS:
'Cyclone' Magnificent—Did Everything
But Heave the Puck into the Stands

"Fred Taylor, the sensation of the East for many years, stood head and shoulders above every other player in the Millionaires' victory over New Westminster. There is no question about his ability to 'come back.' As a combination player he is in a class by himself, and the 'Cyclone' more than fills the vacancy caused by Lalonde's departure.

"He scored just one goal but assisted in registering several more while giving a brilliant display on defence. It was no idle boast by Coast League officials when they declared they had secured the top star of Canadian hockey. The 7,000 fans who watched were convinced of that. Times innumerable he engineered a successful Vancouver attack simply through his lightning speed and clever stickhandling. It was Taylor here and Taylor there and Taylor everywhere throughout the entire game. Truly, the new man lived up to his cognomen of 'Cyclone.'"

Carl Kendall, Taylor's roommate, turned in an excellent game at center and was delegated afterward to get his roomie right home to bed. The next day, they co-starred in an unscheduled two-man rush down a fire ladder.

Their hotel caught fire in the early hours of the morning, and with the hall in flames they were trapped in their room. A fire ladder was raised to their window, whereupon with overcoats draped over their flannel pajamas they clambered gratefully down. Kendall, plainly the faster thinker at that time of day, had grabbed his watch and his wallet, but when he got to the street Taylor realized that he had left his wallet behind on the bedside table.

To the fascination of a small but absorbed audience in the street, he began climbing back up again.

He got right to the window ledge before he was intercepted by the fire chief, who brusquely ordered him back down again. There was a brief, animated discussion, but down he came, followed by the chief as smoke billowed out the window. Throughout the years since, Taylor has claimed that he just doesn't know how much money went up in smoke because of that fireman's rude intervention, but the odds are that he does.

With the progress of the Coast League season, the headlines accumulated: "Fred Taylor Idol of Coast Fans" . . . "They Rise and Cheer When Taylor Gets the Puck," etc. and etc. But his story was not all flash and glitter.

There were more sober headings after the second game, noting the severe appendicitis attack had him for a time critically ill and threatened to sideline him for at least several weeks. These were followed by reports of the third game in which he played in defiance of the doctor's orders, and, so it would seem to just ordinary folks, of plain common sense.

"He did pretty fair work for a sick man. He only scored two goals, assisted in three others, and had the New Westminster players skated right off their tubes . . ."

Yet with all the new man's heroics and a strong lineup of top-flight eastern stars that was strengthened more as the season progressed, it was Lester Patrick's Victoria Aristocrats, not Frank's Millionaires, who won the championship. The Aristocrats' Tom Dunderdale took the scoring title with twenty-four goals while Taylor had fourteen in sixteen games.

And again, in that long-gone age when observers were far less impressed by individual statistics than by a player's full, fleshed-out talents, it was no contest as to the league's No. 1 player. Fred Taylor was named to the Pacific Coast Hockey Association All Stars to begin a new unbroken string of All Star selections, just carrying on where he had left off in all his other leagues.

As had been planned, he was back in Ottawa the following summer, but there was to be no wedding this year. First priority went to the business of his final transfer to the Immigration office in Vancouver, which was getting to be a tricky matter.

With the Ottawa hockey club still hopeful of getting him back in the fold, there was a lot of pressure being applied to have the transfer blocked. Ottawa didn't want to see Taylor fly the coop permanently, nor did the other clubs of the new panicky National Hockey Association. The Patricks' talent raids had hurt, and the league badly needed a shot in the prestige that a player of Taylor's stature could supply.

There was a rash of newspaper stories that Taylor would be back with the Senators, and that with him back, others had said they might follow. But that was just window dressing for the back-room action that went on.

Certain lobbyists were pointing out to the Honourable Members of the Liberal Opposition that both Taylor's distinguished B.C. sponsor, Sir Richard McBride and Fred himself were renegade Conservatives. And that Taylor, who had been put into the Government job by the Ottawa club, was a particularly ungrateful one. It reflects well on the morals of the times that the good men and true of the loyal Opposition were not to be corrupted by such vile innuendo, and thus did not intimidate the Immigration Department. Of course, it helped that the Prime Minister was a Tory.

By late autumn, it was arranged that Taylor would have his clerk's desk in the big Immigration Building on the Vancouver waterfront.

When he returned to Vancouver in November, leaving Thirza Cook to wait awhile longer with the promise of a spring wedding, he had not only a new desk but a promotion to the post of Inspector. His duties now took him out of the office and onto the waterfront, checking incoming ships.

Things didn't start too well for Lester Patrick over in Victoria, as Lester broke a leg in training and missed a whole month's play. Frank Nighbor, one of another batch of top eastern stars the Patricks had hi-jacked over the summer, had similar bad luck. After a sensational start with the Millionaires, Nighbor broke his hand, and he too missed a month's play.

But at the finish, as Taylor increased his steadily rising goals total to eighteen behind the repeat scoring champion Tom Dunderdale, it was the Aristocrats repeating as league champions with Vancouver last. Perhaps the strain of running the league as president as well as his multiplayer-executive-owner capacity with the Millionaires was getting a bit much for Frank Patrick. Lester himself, running the whole show in Victoria, had to content himself with a directorship in the league office.

Their tight little island was having financial problems.

The New Westminster club was a disaster at the gate with a net loss of more than $8,000 and a very slim chance of staying afloat for a third season.

These, though, were not Taylor's problems, and within a week of the season's end in that fateful year of 1914, he and the Millionaires were in Ottawa for an exhibition series against the Senators. Taylor himself had a very important personal date with Thirza Cook at the Cook residence on the afternoon of March 14.

Both items were duly noted in the Ottawa *Free Press:*

"The Vancouver team arrived here today to tackle Ottawa in the first game of a special series between the East and West teams.

"His Royal Highness the Duke of Gloucester paid a pretty compliment to the Westerners today. In accepting an invitation to visit Ottawa, he wrote Manager Shaughnessy, stating that he had broken a prior engagement in order that he could be here to help welcome the Vancouver team, of which he had heard splendid reports.

"Fred Taylor will be playing his last game as a bachelor tomorrow. On Wednesday he will be wedded to Miss Thirza Cook, daughter of the late Samuel Cook. Taylor's bride-to-be worked beside him in the Interior Department when he first came to Ottawa in 1907."

It was poetic justice that the *Free Press* man who covered the wedding and penned the report was Malcolm Brice, who, in a way, had started this love match one summer day in 1907 in Listowel.

"Fred Taylor, rover of the Vancouver Hockey Club, was married to Miss Thirza Cook, daughter of the late Samuel Cook of the Interior Department. The ceremony was quietly performed at the home of the bride. Frank Patrick, president of the Coast League and manager of the Vancouver team, acted as best man.

"After the wedding, Mr. and Mrs. Taylor left for New York City, where the bridegroom will take part in a professional hockey series against the Quebec and Wanderers teams. Afterwards, they will go to Vancouver to reside.

"The Ottawa team used the occasion of Patrick's visit here to attempt to purchase Taylor, but the Pacific Coast magnate said he would not trade or sell him at any price.

"The wedding gifts included a magnificent cabinet of silver from the Pacific Coast League, also presents from the members of the Ottawa team and Taylor's many friends everywhere. Dozens of telegrams arrived wishing the happy couple well. One of these telegrams, from Toronto, read: 'All players as well as I wish you and your bride all possible happiness and prosperity in your future wedded life.—Sam Lichtenhein.'"

That was nice of Sam and, in a wry sort of way, much appreciated by the groom. After all, it was good old Sam who had unwittingly sent Taylor west to a new life that would henceforth be shared by the girl from the right side of the Ottawa tracks.

The day after the wedding, the bride and groom were on the train for New York City, accompanied by the best man. Although he was odd-man on this honeymoon journey, Frank Patrick was insurance that the star of the show would be there for the three-team tournament that would begin in the St. Nicholas Arena, with the two winning teams moving on to Boston.

This was the first time that the Manhattan promoters had gone so far afield for a participant, but Vancouver had Taylor and so the Millionaires got their tickets for the 6,000 mile return trip.

The Senators, Wanderers, and Patrick's Millionaires had left Montreal the previous day and the players were gathered ceremoniously in the lobby of their New York hotel when the wedding party arrived. The Wanderers' Art Ross solemnly suggested to Taylor that they all adjourn at once to his room to play a little poker and maybe have a sing-song. The obliging fellow even offered his teammate Harry Hyland as lead tenor. The Taylors thanked Ross for the kind thought, but declined with thanks.

The hotel was a luxury spa—the Waldorf Astoria—located on the 34th Street site later occupied by the Empire State Building. Not even the visiting big league baseball teams that came to town to face the Giants and the Yankees stayed in such toney quarters. As a first-class annual attraction, the Canadians were now getting first-class treatment.

With two days to go before the start of play and before he resumed his role of Little Jeff after a two-year absence, Taylor had time to show Thirza some of the sights and to treat her to a night on the town. Another player—Vancouver goalie Hughie Lehman —had also brought his wife along, so there was a foursome at dinner one night at a nice restaurant on 49th Street. Both Fred and Hughie were quite willing to go all out on a night like this. As Taylor put it: "You could get the finest meal in New York for not much more than a dollar." Fred doesn't recall who picked up the $5.00 check, but does remember that it was a very nice dinner and worth every penny of the splurge.

The dessert had been enlivened by a discussion as to what Broadway show they should take in afterward as a special treat for the ladies.

Hughie, who had received excellent reviews from the other players, was all for a look at *The Ziegfeld Follies of 1914*, starring Ed Wynn and the leggy and luscious Ann Pennington, plus the famous Ziegfeld Girls, who definitely weren't boys. The ladies demurred. Taylor said he was neutral, so Hughie was outvoted two to one. They settled on the new musical *Watch Your Step*, with Vernon and Irene Castle. Even Hughie had to admit that they weren't at all bad.

An interesting and for Taylor a poignant sidelight of the trip was a walk with Thirza to Fifth Avenue on March 17 to watch the traditional New York City St. Patrick's Day parade. As usual, the city cops, known as New York's Finest, led the colorful parade, and in the van with them was one of the great Irish-American heroes of yesterday, John L. Sullivan. Known as the Boston Strongboy when he ruled the world's heavyweight boxers, John L. was now fifty-seven years old, long past the glory days as America's pre-eminent sporting idol.

For Taylor, the sight of the aging folk hero striding past the corner of Fifth Avenue and 42nd Street, with a step a bit less certain that it once was, evoked memories of the boyhood days in Listowel. Many were the times he had heard his father sing the praises of the great John L. He was Archie Taylor's personal idol and would tower to Bunyonesque proportions at times when Archie was slightly in his cups and waxing sentimental.

It was now twenty-five years since the Boston Strongboy had fought and won his epic duel with Jake Kilrain via a knockout in the 75th round in what was the last of the bloody bare-knuckle jousts for the heavyweight championship. It was that long since the great John L. had taken to the theater boards as the star of *Honest Hearts and Willing Hands*, then sailed off on a triumphant world tour—and returned to the humiliation of a 21-round knockout at the hands of James J. Corbett, the San Francisco youth they called "Gentleman Jim."

Taylor remembered that as a sad night in the house in Listowel for it was the end of the line for Sullivan. When a year later a nobody named Jack McCormack knocked him out in the second round, John L. quit the ring. He tried a pathetic, swiftly aborted comeback thirteen years after, when he was forty-seven.

Still, the Irish loyalists known as New York's Finest hadn't forgotten, and here they were, trying to prove the brave claim that Old Soldiers Never Die. But of course they do. Just four years after marching in that St. Patrick's Day parade, John L. Sullivan would pass quietly away in a hospital in the little town of Abingdon, Massachusetts, as a lone Boston reporter stood outside the room, waiting impatiently for the end.

As Taylor walked back to the hotel with his wife to get ready for the night's work in the St. Nicholas Arena, he couldn't help but think of that other ex-heavyweight champion, Tommy Burns, and wonder what he was doing now.

Well, at that time, Tommy, the Noah Brusso of Taylor's youth, was on his uppers, taking on whatever bums he could find in bouts across the Canadian prairies. In his latest appearance, in Calgary in that spring of 1914, he had been knocked out in the second round by somebody named Battling Brant. Burns, too, was heading toward a sad end. It was a strange play of the fates that had Taylor's path constantly crossed by that of fallen champions headed for hard times as his own career continued its full and rewarding course.

In Manhattan that week there was no rewarding course for the Ottawa Senators, who were eliminated in the knockout round and packed for home while the Millionaires and the Wanderers set out for Boston.

There, the two teams were greeted by a swarm of reporters, and a three-quarter page photo of Cyclone Taylor and Frank Patrick standing side-by-side in full hockey gear adorned the sports page of the Boston *Globe*.

There was a $2,500 winner's purse at stake, and it went to the Wanderers, who took the two-game series by a total score of 11–9.

As he had been in New York, Taylor was the most-talked about player on the ice, even in a losing cause, and he came up with a gambit or two apart from his usually brilliant play to keep it that way.

In the first game that went to the Wanderers 4–3, the packed house was treated to the sight of Taylor flying the length of the rink with the puck lying—as if stuck there by glue—on the outstretched blade of his stick. Nobody could get near him to knock it off until he swerved in toward the goal and was met by Odie Cleghorn, who banged it loose with a body check.

In the second game, with the Wanderers on the long end of a 7–6 score, the Wanderers scored a disputed goal, and Hughie Lehman came racing angrily out of the Vancouver net to accost the umpire. Taylor dashed back to join his good friend, and when the other players gathered at the umpire's cage, a wild free-for-all ensued. Taylor became involved in a fist-fight with Sprague Cleghorn, and when the officials finally pried everyone apart, Taylor, Lehman, and Cleghorn were sent off. As this would have left Vancouver without a man in goal, Art Ross generously requested that Lehman's penalty be waived, and Hughie went back into the net.

Just before the end of the game, the folks were up on their feet once more as Taylor and Sprague Cleghorn were at it again, but they were once more parted before any irreparable damage was done. But when the final bell rang, Sprague turned and went right back at Taylor and decked him with a smart right cross. Fred was definitely upset, and so, in her seat up in the stands, was Mrs. Taylor. However, peace-maker Ross hove to and there were no further hostilities.

At the post-game banquet, all was sweetness and light as Frank Patrick answered Art Ross's toast and the Cleghorn brothers took turns regaling Mrs. Taylor with hockey stories, all of them scrupulously clean. And scrupulously dull.

There was a slight problem as the teams boarded the train for home. It was discovered that the Missus Taylor and Lehman had overdone their shopping a little, and had far more than their allowable Customs quota of clothes. The excess was farmed out among the Vancouver players, and Customs officers examining their luggage could have been forgiven for thinking that the entire Millionaires team was traveling in drag.

The return trip itself had a pleasant little diversion for the boys when the train neared the Canadian border and the Customs officers came aboard. Taking a Customs man aside, one of the players pointed out Mrs. Taylor and informed him that the lady had boarded the train at the last station and was chasing after the Vancouver defenseman, Fred Taylor. He said that the tart was making a nuisance of herself and embarrassing poor Fred, and that she should be apprehended and put off.

Glad to oblige, the Customs officer immediately took the lady in charge and was haranguing her as a public nuisance when Fred suddenly came to the rescue and exposed the hoax. "Sure," he recalls, "I was in on it, but I didn't know they'd take it that far. The poor girl was nearly frightened out of her wits."

That trip was Little Jeff's swan song in New York. He would not come back again as a player.

The Taylors' only hint that this year of 1914 might be far different to others had been when the front page of the New York *Times* carried a picture of Kaiser Wilhelm in his already familiar spiked helmet, bristling waxed moustache and beribboned chest. The story beneath the photo had something to do with German outrage and some trouble in the Balkans.

"That man," said Taylor as he eyed the photo, "looks cruel. I hope we never have anything to do with him." If there was similar concern over Kaiser Bill in Vancouver when the Taylors arrived on the morning of April 2, it had certainly not spoiled the buoyant spring mood of the bustling young metropolis.

From the C.P.R. depot, they went straight to quarters Fred had arranged in Florence Court, a pleasant apartment building on the corner of Bute and Georgia. They moved a few weeks later into a house on West 13th. Vancouver would be their home together for the next half century.

Barely fifty years since the roistering adventurer Jack Deighton had rowed across Burrard Inlet with his worldly goods to set up Gassy Jack's Saloon and anoint the primitive waterfront settlement with the name "Gastown," Vancouver was now a thriving city of 150,000. It was in the throes of a spectacular boom, already hailed as Canada's Gateway to the Orient.

In his new duties as a senior Immigration Inspector, Taylor sat at the window of a wide new world that he had hitherto barely realized had existed. From his second-story eyrie in what was fast becoming one of the great ports of North America, his was an exciting panorama, a whole new view of the world that stretched far beyond the boarded confines of a 200-by-85-foot hockey rink.

The port traffic, Taylor's beat, was already immense, with more than forty deep-sea vessels on regular runs to the United Kingdom and Europe via the Orient and the Suez. The Panama Canal was about to open, and the Canadian Pacific Railway's brand new *Empresses of Asia* and *Russia,* the largest liners on the Pacific, had just been put in service to replace the old line of *Empresses.*

There was monthly service around Cape Horn and semi-monthly cargo service to Honolulu and the Antipodes as well as the passenger runs to the Orient. Coast liners departed every five days for San Francisco and Los Angeles; there were a dozen passenger ships in the coast service, and a fleet of deep-sea ships to service the northern halibut fleets. One of Taylor's jobs was to board incoming vessels with the harbor pilot and check the crew and passenger list as they steamed into port to tie up at the dock.

It was with this job and against this harbor backdrop that Taylor, in that spring of 1914, turned again to the spare-time matters of his first love: sport.

So it was that this springtime was graced by headlines hailing the start of a new lacrosse season, with the arch-rival Vancouver and New Westminster teams, regularly among the best in Canada, resuming mortal combat. And there was the ebullient Vancouver promoter Con Jones telling the world that his Vancouver club was the strongest ever, blessed with "increased speed and midfield power."

Prominent in Con's paens of praise for his enterprise was the name of Newsy Lalonde, who despite such imposing western names as the Springs, Turnbulls, Giffords, and Rennies, may have then been the world's finest lacrosse player.

Oh yes, Newsy was still getting round. Having quit Vancouver to go back East to play his hockey with the National Association Canadiens, Lalonde continued to spend his summers playing lacrosse on the West Coast. This was his second summer back with the Vancouver Terminals, and he figured heavily in the team's pending bid for the national title. But when Con Jones spoke of increased speed and talent at midfield, he was talking about somebody else. As the Vancouver Province had it in its headline deck: "Sensational Hockey-lacrosse Expert Will Hold Down Mid-field Position for Vancouver in First Game Ever at Hastings Park." The 'sensational hockey-lacrosse expert was none other than that other well-traveled all-rounder, Fred Taylor.

When Vancouver Mayor Baxter faced off the ball to christen the season at the new Hastings Park, Taylor was off on another regular fling at his summer pastime, for which, in this first season, he was paid $50 a game.

This sum was far less than what Lalonde was paid. But then Taylor had no illusions about Newsy's superlative talent as a lacrosse player.

"Newsy was just a tremendous all-round athlete. As a hockey player, he wasn't lightning fast but he was very quick and agile. He was a very aggressive, supremely confident fellow—cocky is perhaps the word for it—but he could back up anything he said, and he would back down to nobody. But it was as a lacrosse player that Newsy was at his best, and he was a marvelous performer. I believe that Con Jones paid him a salary of $5,000 to play for the Vancouver club, and that was a sum unheard of in lacrosse in those days."

It's also a sum probably unheard of in lacrosse since, but as Con Jones was not one to toss pennies around like confetti at a wedding, Newsy must have been worth every cent of that $5,000. He, with the help of the widely heralded star of the Vancouver Millionaires, Cyclone Taylor, was certainly a major reason why throngs of up to 10,000 flocked to see the games in Vancouver and New Westminster.

Field lacrosse was by nature a tough, brawling game, and Newsy Lalonde was a tough, brawling athlete who did everything with a joyful gusto. Add Taylor's speed, craft, and color, and Con Jones had himself a gilt-edged gate attraction, with some of the ensuing battles with New Westminster long remembered as classics of wide-open, rib-thumping competition.

It was an idyllic springtime for the newly married couple as Taylor settled into learning his job at the waterfront and blew off steam with his weekend lacrosse. But May marked the beginning of an ugly interlude. It was to be Taylor's first test of himself in his Immigration duties, as well as the first drifting shadow cast by the war clouds that already hung heavy over Europe.

It was the affair of the *Komagata Maru,* a brief and bitter saga that is judged in retrospect as the most dramatic and shameful chapter in Canadian waterfront history. Fred Taylor, the hockey-lacrosse player who was now a B.C. District Inspector of Immigration, was deeply involved.

It was two o'clock on the morning of May 24, 1924, when the harsh jangling of the telephone roused Taylor from a deep sleep and launched him into the most disturbing two months of his life. "It was my supervisor, Malcolm Reid, with word that a steamer inbound from the Far East was about to anchor out in Burrard Inlet, and I was to go aboard. This was routine procedure for incoming vessels from abroad, but this situation was a little different. This steamer, a ship of Japanese registry called the *Komagata Maru,* had come from Hong Kong and had 375 East Indians aboard. She had been expected because she had made a stop at the William Head quarantine station the day before, but the early 2 A.M. arrival time was a surprise. The chief was concerned about the development, and I knew why. I could see a pretty touchy situation ahead, but I had no idea how bad it would become." Nor had anyone else.

"I was told to take our department's East Indian interpreter, Bill Hopkinson, aboard with me along with another officer, a fellow named Harry Gwyther. Once on board, I knew what I had to do."

What he had to do was inform the *Komagata Maru* captain that he could not dock until 9 A.M., when the Immigration office opened and more officials were dispatched to check the passengers. That seemingly innocent order was to lead to two months of bloody confrontation out in the harbor, a hunger strike, violent racial riots ashore, and a series of ghastly and macabre murders in two countries over a period of twenty years.

There was a background to Taylor's premonition of trouble as he left for the Immigration wharf in the damp chill of that Victoria Day morning. New Federal laws curbing Chinese, Japanese, and East Indian immigration into Canada had already led to vicious racial rioting in Vancouver, and the recent ban on all East Indian emigrants except those sailing direct from an Indian port was bitterly attacked by the resident East Indians. One, a militant Sikh named Gurdit Singh, decided to test the law. Variously described as a wealthy landowner, a secret agent of the Japanese Government, and a "Punjab agitator," Singh went to Hong Kong, chartered the Japanese freighter *Komagata Maru,* and rounded up 165 fellow Sikhs with the promise of a voyage to British Columbia as landed immigrants. Another 111 Sikhs joined the ship at Shanghai, 86, at Moji, and 14 at Yokohama. With its passenger load of 376 trusting but misled souls, the *Komagata Maru* headed across the Pacific toward Vancouver and a 2 A.M. off-shore rendezvous with Inspector Taylor of Immigration.

"We left the wharf about 4 A.M. in a launch and climbed aboard the *Maru* just as day was breaking. I passed the order along to the ship's captain and to Mr. Singh: They could proceed to the inner harbor, but must drop anchor out in the Narrows until given further information, after the office opened at 9 A.M. I would go with them and stay aboard until relieved.

"I could see that the arrangement didn't sit too well with the passengers, but the ship proceeded as ordered and dropped anchor in the Narrows. It was a long and uncomfortable wait. I could smell trouble. We knew that war in Europe was on the way, and apart from the immigration restriction problem we had been told that there might be enemy agents aboard planted by Germany, perhaps through the Japanese Government. It was all new and a little bewildering to me, but I had my orders. That fellow Gurdit Singh did all the talking for the passengers and seemed more in charge of the ship than the Japanese captain. Singh stayed up all night with me and was pretty edgy, but he was quite friendly. Then at 9 A.M., the Supervisor, Malcolm Reid, came on board and I went home to get some sleep."

A holiday lacrosse date with the Vancouver Terminals was canceled as Taylor had to be on duty again by evening.

Back on the *Komagata Maru,* Reid had allowed thirty-four passengers classified as returning immigrants to go ashore, but told the rest that they must be individually examined and processed. It took three days to complete the examination of the first applicant, who was refused admission.

Hoping for help from Ottawa with this difficult situation, Reid was stalling, and Gurdit Singh and his flock became increasingly restive and sullen as the days dragged on. The ship was getting very short of food and water and the mood aboard changed from sullen to violent as gangs manned the rails and perversely battled patrol boats that came alongside with provisions.

On shore, there were demonstrations by an East Indian community that was stirred into anger by reports of starvation aboard the *Maru*. Still, the examinations continued, until all applicants were rejected.

During all this time, Taylor stood regular shifts aboard the ship on a day-on, day-off basis, and was in the middle of a desperate situation that was getting rapidly out of hand.

"I had no particular station on the ship, but just sort of roamed around seeing to it that nobody came aboard or left without Immigration permission. Every day, swarms of small boats came out with East Indians aboard and circled the ship hour after hour, shouting back and forth in their own language. We didn't understand what was going on, but it certainly kept things stirred up. Things got pretty dicey aboard, and we didn't know what to expect from one minute to another. We were at their mercy."

The Japanese captain was caught in the middle of the mess. He had been refused the charter payment until his human cargo had been landed, and he was desperate to break the siege. On a night in mid-July he attempted to pull anchor and steam out of the harbor. The Sikhs promptly took over the ship, locked the captain in his cabin and threatened to slit the throats of the Japanese stokers if they went to the hold.

The strain aboard increased to near snapping point, but the Immigration shifts continued despite the increasingly belligerent mood of the passengers.

"They'd curse us and press against us and sometimes fought us off as we came aboard, shouting threats and insults, but there was never any physical abuse in my experience. We did get some comfort from the fact that our patrol boats were circling the ship constantly, but I'll admit I'd known more relaxing times in my day."

At one point, the Immigration officers' vigil aboard was suspended in the interests of their safety, and Taylor agrees that he had no urgent quarrel with that decision. But the suspension was soon lifted, as some semblance of control had to be retained and restrictions policed. Attempts to smuggle passengers ashore were thwarted, and two Japanese and two Vancouver Sikhs were caught trying to get aboard.

With the shifts fully restored, an attempt was made to capture an officer and hold him hostage for extra supplies of food and water. He was rescued, and an attempt by other Immigration officers to board the now stinking, festering ship was repelled. Although ordered daily to leave the harbor, the *Komagata Maru* clung defiantly to her anchor chain.

On July 19, the police were called in after a boarding party of Immigration officials had been beaten off. A force of 150 officers plus 50 special police went out in the tug *Sea Lion* in an attempt to board the vessel and provision her for the outward voyage. They were repelled by a hail of coal and lumps of iron and whatever else the screaming Sikhs could lay their hands on. Eleven officers were seriously injured and the force withdrew. Although armed, they had obeyed orders and withheld fire.

Now, the Navy was brought into the fray, and the cruiser *Rainbow* was dispatched from its base in Victoria.

On the morning of July 23 as the newly fitted *Rainbow* steamed into Vancouver harbor and headed toward the *Komagata Maru*, a battalion of Irish Fusiliers manned the Immigration wharf, ready for any eventuality. Thousands of people jammed the tops of buildings and other vantage points in expectation of a bloody sea battle just a few hundred yards from the water's edge. Fred Taylor watched from his office in the Immigration Building, gazing anxiously through the window that looked out over the harbor.

But when the captain of the *Rainbow* came alongside and hailed the *Komagata Maru* from the bridge with his deck guns manned, the hapless mob jammed along the rail turned abjectly away. It was all over.

Those on shore watched in silence as, after two desperate months at anchor, the decrepit freighter swung with the tide and steamed slowly off with its wretched cargo. Alongside steamed the *Rainbow*, which stayed with her until she was well out to sea, bound for Calcutta. "I can tell you," recalls Taylor with that grim long-ago memory forever etched in his mind, "you could hear a sigh of relief go up all over the city. It was a terrible affair, and nobody was proud of it."

On June 29, 1914, the newspapers had carried the story of the assassination of the heir to the Austrian throne, Archduke Ferdinand, and his wife, the Duchess of Sofia, in the far-off Bosnian city of Sarajevo. War was imminent, and as an arm of the Federal Government, the Immigration Department was put on the alert, tightening security on the Vancouver waterfront. Taylor's duties were widened and his hours lengthened.

As now the No. 3 man in the B.C. Department, he carried a heavy responsibility. His weekends in Con Jones Park and at the New Westminster lacrosse field seemed increasingly frivolous as the world teetered on the brink of a mindless catastrophe.

At home, the Taylors knew it was coming, but said little of it.

There were confirmed reports that the German cruisers *Leipzig* and *Nuremberg* were prowling the Pacific just a few miles off the B.C. coast. Bank gold reserves were sent from Vancouver to vaults in Seattle and Winnipeg, and provisions had been made for the burning of all stocks of currency in the event of a raid on the city.

Taylor had to pass through armed guards to get to his office, with the entire harbor now patrolled by the militia. A battery of almost comically inept and ancient defense guns was mounted on concrete emplacements at the entrance to Burrard Inlet. "Nobody," says Taylor, "really knew what to expect, but we prepared for the worst. It was an anxious time."

The anxiety ended at one minute past midnight August 5, just hours after German troops had crossed into Belgium. England was now at war with Germany, and at breakfast, Fred Taylor read out the melancholy words of the British Foreign Minister, Sir Edward Grey, Viscount of Fallendon. "The lamps are going out all over Europe; we shall not see them lit again in our lifetime."

The breakfast was finished in silence, then Taylor kissed his wife and left to catch the usual 8:30 streetcar for the docks. Two weeks later, he went down to the Seaforth Armouries to enlist in the Canadian Army.

"There were a couple of hundred others there, and we were

lined up in ranks in front of a major. We were a pretty nervous, motley bunch. I knew some of them there, and a lot of them knew me. The major went down the rows, calling names, and mine was the fifty-first one called. He barked out the full name— Frederick Wellington—and I took a step forward.

"I was asked if I wished to volunteer for overseas duty, and I said yes. All the others before me had done the same. The fellow on my right was then called out, and he took the step forward, but when asked if he was volunteering for overseas duty he said no, he wasn't.

"Well, that shook me a little. I turned my head toward him and mumbled, 'Why the devil didn't you tell me there was a choice? I just got married a few months ago.'"

The remark was only half in jest, if at all.

Taylor is quite frank about his feelings on enlistment. "I had no illusions about war, and I was not the soldier type. I wasn't anxious to serve overseas, but if they wanted me and needed me, I was willing and ready to go."

As things transpired, the choice was taken out of his hands.

A few days later, Immigration officers were declared exempt from military service as their work was categorized as vital to the national interest. Private F. W. Taylor of the Seaforth Highlanders was given an honorable discharge.

Although there was no great rush to the colors among the hockey fraternity—most of whom were married, with families—a lot of Taylor's contemporaries on the summer and winter playing fields did eventually join up and go overseas. Many were to serve with great distinction before returning. Some would never return.

One Vancouver Millionaire player who did go overseas went in the wrong direction. He was Sibby Nichols, the smart young winger who had come to Vancouver from the Wanderers.

"Sibby was a restless soul who said he'd always wanted to travel and see the world. I told him he should have joined the Navy instead of our hockey club, and when he came to me in the spring and asked if I could get him aboard a ship going off to some interesting foreign parts, I said I'd try.

"I eventually got him a job as a steward aboard the *Empress of Asia*. When I told him the ship's destination was Hong Kong, he was delighted. Unfortunately, the *Empress* first sailed to a port in Siberia, and when it finally docked in Hong Kong, the war had broken out and Sibby was stuck there."

Before the start of the 1915–16 season, Frank Patrick found himself very short of good wingers and remembered Nichols. He sent a cable to Sibby in Hong Kong informing him that he'd pay his passage back to Vancouver, and had booked a berth on the S.S. *Monteagle*, leaving Hong Kong on November 8. However, Patrick's winger was now Seaman Sebastian John Nichols of the Royal Navy Reserve, manning a gun on the foredeck of the *Empress of Asia*, which had been commandeered as a troop ship.

As the *Empress* was about to be returned soon to its owners, Sibby's discharge was imminent, but there were still complications. The *Monteagle* didn't sail, and there was no other passage immediately available.

Poor Sibby didn't make it back to Vancouver until late in the season, by which time he was quite proficient in pidgin Chinese. "He always blamed me for getting him stranded in Hong Kong," says Taylor, "but I told him that it could have been worse. He could have been stranded in Siberia."

With Sibby away and the war on, it was still business as usual when the next hockey season rolled around in December. Frank Patrick continued his presidency of the league, and he had strengthened his Millionaires roster with some new young players.

The New Westminster Royals had drawn poorly, and were moved to Portland. There, they became the Rosebuds, under manager Pete Muldoon. This was the start of a game of musical chairs that was to continue throughout the life of the league, with every club but Vancouver moving at least once.

In the kaleidescope of action that would engulf Taylor throughout his final playing years, this troubled season of 1915–16 was just another hockey campaign, but it did have one memorable highlight: a Stanley Cup triumph that would mark the first time the old mug, once considered the sole property of the East, had come West.

One of the fine new Vancouver players was Mickey Mackay, a speedy forward whom Taylor cites as one of the true all-time greats of the game. He looked it in a debut season that saw him amass a record total of thirty-four goals. Taylor himself was next with twenty-three, one up on another brilliant new teammate and another future Hall of Famer, Frank Nighbor.

A funny thing happened to Victoria's Tom Dunderdale, the previous season's scoring champ, on the way to his new crop of seventeen goals. In the season's opener in Vancouver, Dunderdale surprised Taylor by intercepting one of his passes, and then surprised everyone else in the building by turning the wrong way and firing the puck past his own goalie, Bert Lindsay. That was Vancouver's only goal of the night, but Tom did manage a bit of face-saving as he put one into the right net in the final minutes to salvage a quaint 1–1 tie.

With Taylor again spectacular and lifting Arena fans out of their seats on his nights away from the waterfront, the Millionaires won the league title in a breeze. Then, in the spring of 1915, the Ottawa Senators, champions of the East, came to town to contest the first Stanley Cup series ever played West of Winnipeg.

The star of the Senators was Fred's old adversary, Art Ross, who announced that his top priority was to neutralize the pesky Vancouver rover, Fred Taylor. The Martins and the Coys were back at it once more. When the smoke had cleared, the Millionaires had swept the series in three straight games, and the man Ross was to neutralize had the series high total of seven goals, plus two assists. Even when held occasionally in check, he was a dominant figure throughout.

The game scores were 6–2, 8–3, and 12–5 and, the fans in the Arena went jubilantly berserk.

With both he and Mackay were credited with skating Ross and his Senators all but right out to sea in the opener. Taylor scored twice after Mickey had made a dazzling end-to-end rush to open the slaughter.

In the second game, both Taylor and Nighbor got hat tricks to rout the outclassed easterners, and the finale was a shambles. This time, Shore and friends did manage to blanket Taylor by double and sometimes triple checking, but at the expense of letting his mates loose for that embarrassing flood of a dozen goals. Barney Stanley, another new Vancouver player who Taylor had first met back in the old days in Houghton, Michigan, broke loose for four goals, and Mackay and Nighbor had three each.

Frank Patrick's Millionaires, namesakes of the rich Renfrew team that never quite made it, were the Stanley Cup champions, and the reason seemed quite clear to a Vancouver *World* reporter:

"One can easily see why the Vancouver team has it all over Ottawa. The big reason is Fred Taylor, undoubtedly the best hockey player in the world. His marvellous skating and stickhandling ability completely demoralized the Easterners. Their manager, Frank Shaughnessy, agrees. He said: 'Cyclone Taylor was the best hockey player in the world when he left Ottawa, and, if possible, he is even better now. He is amazing.'"

This was Fred Taylor at age thirty-one, with some of his finest years yet to come. But of that year and of that Vancouver team, he has said: "The Renfrew team had the greatest collection of individual stars, but that Vancouver team of 1914–15 was the finest in my experience, and I am sure one of the best of all time. Every regular on that team that took us to the Stanley Cup series —Si Griffis, Mickey Mackay, Frank Patrick, Barney Stanley, Hughie Lehman, Frank Nighbor, and myself—made the Hockey Hall of Fame. This has never happened to any other team."

The players, incidentally, received $200 each as the winner's share of the series money.

Taylor has also noted that in his memory he has "never been associated with a cleaner-living group of athletes. To my recollection, very few of them smoked, and they were all teetotalers." And that, for a pro hockey team, although Taylor didn't presume to say so, has to be another team record. If there is a moral there somewhere, he doesn't press it.

The steadily mounting list of war casualties provided a morbid backdrop for the sporting life, but for Taylor the months droned by with their long days at the waterfront, summer weekends at lacrosse, and the winter nights at hockey. With whole neighborhoods stripped of their young men who were fighting and dying in France, these were difficult and depressing and sometimes very testy times for those, like Taylor, who remained behind.

He was luckier than most because his days were so full and active, and he could let off steam in the exhilaration and excitement of tough physical competition, trivial though this might be when measured against the real combat overseas.

Then, suddenly, there was a turning back of the clock. It was the Battle of Fred Taylor all over again.

In the October 19 edition of the Montreal *Star* was the headline:

CYCLONE TAYLOR JUST NOW
REAL STORM CENTRE.

The Ottawa *Journal* echoed:

FIGHT FOR STAR LOOMS
WILL TAYLOR COME EAST?

The stories below the headlines related that the transfer of Taylor back to his old job in the Interior Department in Ottawa had made him once again available to the Ottawa Senators, who would sign him as soon as he got back to town.

Exactly what forces had been at work in Ottawa was not known, although the Senators denied charges of tinkering. It had been suddenly ruled that Taylor's transfer to Immigration in Vancouver had been a temporary measure, and he had now been told to return to his Ottawa job in the Civil Service. Taylor admitted that he had been ordered back, but said that he "would resign first and take up some other position in Vancouver."

On October 24, the Vancouver *World* bannered this message:

PACIFIC COAST MAGNATES DECLARE
ALL-OUT WAR ON N.H.A.

The Toronto *Star*, next day:

N.H.A. WILL FIGHT BACK:
Trouble Originated Over Ottawa
Inducement to Taylor
To Return.

Said Frank Patrick, back in Vancouver: "It won't work. If Taylor does go East, he won't play. There is not enough money in the N.H.A. to negotiate his contract."

Said Lester Patrick in his memoirs: "The East had decided that the temporary peace that had prevailed between East and West was at an end. They were after Taylor again, the game's biggest drawing card. All hell broke loose. We decided to hit hard, and we concentrated our raid on the team in Toronto that had won the Stanley Cup in 1914. We succeeded in signing their finest players: Happy Holmes, Cully Wilson, Frank Foyston, Eddie Carpenter, and Jack Walker. There was never another 'war.'

"All of these players went to Seattle as a nucleus for the new team in the Coast League, to be called the Metropolitans. As an indication of the success of our raid, in the team's second year of operation, 1916-17, Seattle won the Coast championship and went on to defeat the invading Montreal Canadiens and become the first U.S. city to win the Stanley Cup."

As to Taylor, the eternal storm-center, his case took off in another cloud of emergency politicking. At the urging of the Patricks, Premier McBride was back in action, this time dickering with Dr. Roche, Minister of the Interior.

The upshot of it all was a smiling photo of Taylor in the Vancouver *World*, with the caption: "Although the N.H.A. moguls would have the Listowel Whirlwind back in the effete East this season, arrangements have now been made for Taylor to retain his Immigration post in Vancouver permanently, and he will again line up with the Millionaires. He has agreed to a new contract."

Following this, a truce was declared and an interleague agreement was signed. Territorial rights for new players were established, and Stanley Cup challenge rules were laid down, with alternate years of home competition—even years in the East, odd in the West. This agreement would prevail until the dissolution of the Coast League eleven years later.

So, out of chaos: order. The catalyst: the aptly named Cyclone of the storm-blown hockey scene, Fred Taylor.

The year that had begun so well for Taylor finished well for him personally as his steadily increasing goals total rose to twenty-two in eighteen games, one behind Seattle's Bernie Morris. But it was Pete Muldoon's Portland Rosebuds who won the championship and challenged for the Stanley Cup. The Rosebuds now had Moose Johnson on their team, but Moose wasn't quite enough as the Montreal Canadiens won the odd game in five to take the cup back East.

"One of the things that makes Fred Taylor such a great player," Lester Patrick once said, "is that he is so inventive and unpredictable—both on the ice and off." So Lester was there wagging his head with the rest of his Victoria Aristocrats just before the final league game of that 1916 season as he scanned the banner headline in the Seattle *Post-Intelligencer*.

That Millionaires-Aristocrats contest had been moved from Victoria to the Seattle rink, and a *P.-I.* reporter had gotten what looked like one of the big stories of the year. It was there in the big black headline:

VANCOUVER HOCKEY STAR PLAYS HIS LAST GAME:
Fred Taylor, Greatest Player Ever
To Wield a Stick Says
This His Last.

There followed three full columns and a quarter-page box of cartoons depicting Taylor's "fabulous career, now at its end." The story even asked Seattle fans to "chip in" for a suitable farewell gift.

As Taylor skated out to start the game, Patrick skated slowly by, prodded him gently with his stick and said, with a sly grin: "Sure sorry to see you go, Cyc."

"I hope so," Taylor dead-panned.

It was a tough, brawling contest, and going into the third period, Lester's Aristocrats were in command 7–3. And then the old guy who was heading for the rest home turned on the back burner and rapped in three goals in a space of five minutes.

The reporter who had penned Taylor's plaint that he was getting tired of it all and was giving it up after thirteen years as a professional now wrote:

"Taylor, who has announced that this would be his last league appearance ever, played like a champion—a young champion.

"He was skating so fast that in a desperate effort to stop him, Victoria's Kerr took a vicious swipe at him as he went by. That stopped Taylor all right but Cyclone was mad and rapped Kerr

across the head with his stick, drawing blood. Taylor wa
off the ice for 10 minutes for this display of temper. He is
clean-cut, high-class man that his rough-house tactics surprised
everyone. His absence cost the Millionaires their last chance to
tie or win."

After the game, Taylor allowed that on thinking it over he
might be back next season, after all. He doesn't recall how much
the Seattle fans chipped in, but he didn't get a farewell gift.
Maybe they were saving it. If so, hopefully, it wasn't perishable.

The end of the road was still a few years ahead. Taylor was
not only getting older, he was getting better. His only concession
to the years up to that point was his retirement from lacrosse.
The pressures of work were too much, and the field getting too
big.

He bowed out and bequeathed the premises to younger legs,
like those of that tough kid, Newsy Lalonde, who was all of
three years Taylor's junior.

The man's secret of seemingly eternal youth in a game—
played at his blistering pace, that can age a man early—may
have been in the fact that few professional athletes have been
anchored to such a well-rounded life. In Vancouver, the scout
work and the church work he had begun in Ottawa continued.
He was now also deeply involved in Y.M.C.A. work, and contrib-
uted inspirational messages to the Y.M.C.A. publication *The
Boy*.

The measure of respect and affection in which he was held by
young people was reflected in the reaction to reports that Scoutmaster Taylor of the Dundas Troop was headed back east to Ottawa. The boys of the troop called a special meeting and
presented their scoutmaster with a fine scarf pin "as a mark of
our respect and esteem."

Taylor, for once, was lost for words. The surprise gift went
nicely with the gold cuff links given him by his Dominion Troop
when he had left the capital city for the Coast in 1912.

Across the straits in Victoria, Lester Patrick was still bearing
up well under his many hats although he was bitterly disap-
pointed over the poor public support given his Aristocrats. He
felt no joy in the next November when the Victoria Aristocrats
suddenly became the Spokane Canaries. It was the third league

shift to a U.S. city, and while Lester was unhappy over drawing poorly and losing money in Victoria, he was to discover that he could draw worse and lose more money in Spokane, where the poor Canaries twittered and died in the chill of the near-empty Spokane Area.

An item of interest that season as the Taylor years in the Coast League rolled by was the arrival of a new young star from the East named Dick Irvin, who joined the Portland Rosebuds. Irvin's remarkable first-year total of thirty-five goals in twenty-four games was the start of that outstanding career that would reach its climax in Montreal, where he would coach the Canadiens of the modern National Hockey League to four Stanley Cup championships.

Irvin was a one of a host of fine players who played in the Coast League during the Taylor years before moving on to superlative life-time careers. Among these, in addition to others who had come early, would be the Fort William boy, Jack Adams, who would star alongside Taylor during Fred's final two years with the Millionaires. It was less than a decade after his Vancouver beginning that Adams turned up in Detroit to begin building the Red Wings into a National Hockey League power.

Jolly Jawn, as he was called in the more sentimental appraisals, eventually took his Wings to five Cup championships first as coach and then as general manager and one of sport's ablest and most colorful executives.

For Taylor, who as a hockey professional aspired to be no more than he was—an exciting player of exceptional skills—he just took the game a season at a time, and he remembers that one of 1916–17 as a season of contrasts.

A year that began well ended suddenly in mid-term when he was rushed to hospital with another severe attack of appendicitis. He had been ignoring the need of an operation for years, and had played in great pain for two games before collapsing right after the twelfth game of the campaign, when he was rushed to hospital. He had the operation and missed the rest of the season as the Seattle Metropolitans took the league title and then went on to whip the Canadiens and become the first U.S.-based team to win the Stanley Cup.

However, the invalid now had another interest he could oversee from his hospital bed. The month before the start of that 1916–17 season, Thirza had given birth to their first child, Frederick, Jr. He was to be the first of five Taylor children, to be followed two years later by John, then Edward, and two daughters, Mary and Joan.

But with the advent of another generation, time was at last beginning to run out for the old guard.

At the start of the next season, Frank Patrick and Si Griffis were missing from the Vancouver lineup. Both had retired, although Frank stayed on as coach and manager of the Millionaires. In Victoria, Lester Patrick had said he had thought of quitting as a player but decided to hang on for another year.

Taylor, thirty-three, and looking a lot older with that bald pate of his until he started to skate, was back at the old stand. And as if to show the world that the old guard was still around and active, he chose a game against Seattle to revive a legend. With the score tied 2–2 in overtime, and Taylor in a pixieish mood, he stole the puck, flew the full length of the rink along the boards, broke across the goal, then whirled suddenly and with his back to the net flipped the puck neatly past the goalie, Norm Fowler.

Just as another crowd had done a decade before when Cyclone was a Millionaire putting on a show for the home folks in Renfrew, the Vancouver fans rose with a thunderous ovation that lasted until he was off the ice and back in the dressing room.

Asked why he did this sort of thing, he says, "Well, I think the fans like a little extra show once in a while, and if I could provide it without jeopardizing our chances of winning, I occasionally did. After all, hockey is a game, and people are supposed to have fun with games."

But lest that particular bit of goal-getting be misconstrued as just a showboat fluke, the veteran with the speed and cunning that never seemed to diminish made a runaway of the league scoring race. For the fourth time, he won the points-scoring title, and his total of thirty-two goals in eighteen games was a dozen more than that of his closest rival, Seattle's Gordon Roberts.

There was a postscript to this wonderful season in which, according to the laws of age and decline in those grueling days of sixty-minute hockey with practically no substitutions, Taylor should have been on the way down. In the victorious play-offs against Seattle and the following unsuccessful Stanley Cup challenge series with Toronto, Taylor led all players with his total of nine goals and five assists in seven games.

The following summertime was spent in an anxious watch on the final convulsive months of fighting in Europe. By mid-July, the newspapers were ablaze with the news of the defeat of the German General von Ludendorff in the Second Battle of the Marne, and it now seemed sure that the awful carnage that had already taken nearly eight million lives was almost over.

As all the world away from Europe knew, there was a helpless, wrenching agony in just sitting safely thousands of miles away and reading about these terrible events. This was especially so in all those far-flung communities like Vancouver that were heavily bereaved. "There was a nagging frustration and feeling of helplessness," says Taylor. "All we could do was wait, hope, and pray."

The Taylors prayed a lot, at their neighborhood Chalmers Church, and they were there with a full thankful congregation on the evening of November 11, right after the newsboys had been out on the street with their extras, shouting the news that the war was over.

Thirza Taylor was pregnant with her second child, John, who was born just seventeen days later.

Then in December came one of the first visible signs that it really was all over when off the train at the C.P.R. depot stepped Captain Art Duncan of the Royal Flying Corps. Art was better known to Cyclone and to Vancouver hockey fans as that very good young winger with the Millionaires of 1916, when he had played alongside Mickey Mackay. Since then, he had been away, and on the chest of his tunic was the simple ribbon representing one of the Allies' highest awards for valor: the Military Cross.

Two weeks later, he switched uniforms and came out in the strip of the Patrick Millionaires for the first game of the new season, against Seattle. A record and festive crowd of more than 10,000 happy fans jammed the Vancouver Arena for that opening game of a new season and a new era. Peace, such as it was, and while it lasted, was wonderful.

Among the various items of history recorded that month was

the fact that the Portland Rosebuds were no more, hockey had fled that Oregon city, and had returned to its Coast League womb in Victoria. Again, for reasons of economics, Lester Patrick had made the switch, and the Aristocrats were once again in business.

The league that had begun as a three-team circuit was back to the original number, enough to serve as a proving ground for the host of innovations that were restructuring the game. The authors of this quiet revolution were of course Lester and Frank Patrick, the deeply contrasting co-chairmen of those absorbing dinnertime seminars years ago in the Renfrew boardinghouse, when Taylor, Lalonde, Bobby Rowe, Bert Lindsay, and the others just sat back and listened.

The oft-told tale of these Patrick refinements that have produced the game as we know it today is deftly capsuled by Lester in his own modest résumé: "Here are a few innovations that come to mind that were originated by the Coast League: the numbering of players' jerseys; the license for goalies to come out of their old static stance and challenge the shot in any way they saw fit; the establishment of the blue-lines, creating a neutral center zone; the legalizing of forward passing in all zones shortly thereafter; legalizing kicking the puck; the substitution of players during play; the substitution of whole forward lines as units, as used for the first time in 1925 against the Canadiens, when Victoria won the Stanley Cup; the double referee system; standardizing nights of play in all cities; and many others that do not come to mind."

"Nobody really knows," Taylor has said, "which ideas were Lester's and which were Frank's. They may not have known themselves. It didn't matter. They had the brains and the imagination to develop new ideas, and they had the power to install them. Whenever they wanted to try something new—like, say the blue lines to open up the passing—they'd just say, 'well, boys, let's try it,' and we did.

"It was their league. Frank ruled as league president, and Lester was the power behind the throne. What they said went, and it was the great good fortune of hockey that this is the way it was. The game had exactly what it needed in those pioneer days on the Coast: a couple of benevolent dictators."

Picking up right where he had left off the year before, Taylor played twenty games of the 1918–19 season, and again won the scoring title with twenty-three goals after a close fight with Seattle's Bernie Morris. The Millionaires won the league championship, but could get no further in their hopes of a showdown with the Canadiens, the Eastern titlists, for the Stanley Cup.

Their hopes of moving on were dashed when Mickey Mackay was sidelined with a broken jaw after a vicious attack by Seattle's Cully Wilson late in the season. Without the brilliant Mackay and his potent scoring threat to help take the heat off Taylor, the Millionaires were unable to survive their two-game total-goals play-off series with the Metropolitans.

The aging Si Griffis was hauled out of mothballs to replace Mickey, but Si's legs just weren't up to it any more. Taylor himself was held scoreless, and Seattle's big Frank Foyston dominated the series as his club went on to face the Canadiens for the Cup.

Taylor watched from the stands in Seattle as the two teams went at it in the usual mixed East-West rules format. With the Coast League still playing seven-man hockey and the East longsince committed to the six-man game, the rules were alternated, with the home team getting the first-game choice.

The first game was a 7–0 rout for Seattle as the easterners just couldn't get on track, and Taylor spent his time checking on faces that took him back a year or two. Despite that horrible beginning, he liked the look of the Canadiens goalie, Georges Vezina. Fred remembered being impressed with the fellow back in his last season at Renfrew, when Vezina broke in with the Canadiens as a rookie.

Taylor recognized that opening night in the nets in Seattle as a rare bad one for a man who would become the most storied goalie in hockey history, with his name engraved on one of sport's most coveted trophies. But there were other faces in the visitor's lineup that were more familiar than his: that of the right-winger, Didier Pitre, and the left-winger, Odie Cleghorn. They were both out of the Renfrew days, Pitre as the shifty little forward of the then rival Canadiens, and Odie as one of the two brothers who came to Renfrew as the bright new rookies of 1911.

Then of course there was the Canadiens' center, who had been converted to cover-point for the western-rules opener. And if Newsy Lalonde had his old friend and adversary Taylor thinking he might be on the skids with that first night debacle, he rudely squelched that idea three nights later.

The second game was a flashback to those marvelous nights with Taylor back in Renfrew as Lalonde fired in all four of the Canadiens' goals in their 4–2 victory.

There was a brief reunion afterward in the visitor's dressing room.

"Newsy," sighed Taylor, "I'm afraid you're slipping. I can remember a time when you scored seven and you were mad because it wasn't a dozen. What's happened to you?"

"I had a late night," grinned Lalonde. "I was out with Bad Joe."

Oh, yes. Bad Joe Hall. That was the other oh-so-familiar face in the Canadiens' lineup, and this one really went back. Clear back to 1905, when hearts were young and the booming copper town of Houghton, Michigan, was the epicenter of young Taylor's bright new world of hockey.

Hall was now nearing thirty-nine, his hair was thin, and his deeply seamed face was marked with the scars of a trade that he plied with rare abandon. Long established as one of hockey's toughest and most intimidating defensemen, Joe was still full value for his reputation. He showed it in the third game when he decked Foyston with a shuddering body check and then just as neatly disposed of Cully Wilson, who had roared to Foyston's defense. The Seattle papers called that game, won 7–2 by Seattle, "one of the most exciting ever played," and Joe had a hand in that.

That night, Joe was still strong and tough and intimidating. Twelve days later, he was dead.

It was the spring of the influenza epidemic, a plague that surfaced in Seattle during the fifth game of the Cup series when the players of both teams succumbed to exhaustion during the overtime period with the game tied 3–3. Cully Wilson stumbled to the ice and was taken off. Joe Hall skated slowly to the boards looking ill, and was taken to the dressing room. Others were flagging noticeably.

Odie Cleghorn won the game for the Canadiens after sixteen minutes of overtime to tie the series at two wins each. The fourth game had ended in a tie. In addition to Hall, five other Montreal players, including Lalonde and the team manager, George Kennedy, were put into the hospital. The series was abandoned.

Joe Hall died on the night of April 5. He was thirty-eight. "He was quarantined and nobody could go to see him," Taylor recalls. "He died all alone, and that for a man like Joe who loved conviviality and loved to have people around him was a particularly sad thing." The body was brought to Vancouver for burial.

That lonely passing was a lifetime away from that rollicking night in February of 1906 when Bad Joe Hall had staged a wild ride through the streets of Pittsburgh to celebrate the victory of fellow-Canadian Tommy Burns, the new world's heavyweight boxing champion.

Still, there were more games to play, and they were at it again in the following December out on the Coast. But now Mickey Mackay was finished, Barney Stanley, another old original from the Houghton days, had played his last game, and the twilight was at last closing in on the Listowel Thunderbolt.

In the first game of the season in Victoria, Taylor was flying down the ice with what looked like all of that old speed when he ran afoul of that other ageless artisan, Moose Johnson. It was a meeting that Taylor remembered well: "It wasn't all that violent, but it was the beginning of the end for me. Moose just came at me and we went down and our legs got tangled as we hit the ice. As we went down, I twisted my groin and was in such pain that I couldn't get up.

"Well, I guess Moose knew it might be sort of serious and he stood there and looked at me, shook his head and just said, 'I'm sorry, Cyc. It wasn't intentional.' I knew it wasn't."

After that, Taylor was used only sparingly, and he rarely played full time again. He got into fourteen games, and scored six goals as Frank Patrick had to practically tie him to the bench between spot shifts. In the final game of the season, a critical contest with Seattle with first place at stake, he came out for a desperation effort with the Millionaires behind 2–0. That night, the incredible wasn't possible as Seattle hung on to win, but the packed arena stood and tendered an ovation for Taylor's tremendous play while in obvious distress.

At home in the Taylor household, there were deliberations

after that season over whether he should contemplate another. "I talked it over with Thirza, and although she'd leave it up to me I knew she wanted me to quit. We had a growing family, and the pressures of my Immigration job were increasing. Yet, hockey had been much of my life, and still was. It was a difficult decision."

The decision was to try another year, but with an increasingly talented number of young rookies arriving to stake out their piece of territory, these were struggling times for the old bulls trying to hang on.

Typical of the new breed was the rookie over there in Victoria, with Lester Patrick's Aristocrats. He was Frank Fredrickson, the twenty-five-year-old from Winnipeg, the superlative center of that city's Falcons, who was hailed on the prairies as the game's brightest star. That assessment was certainly not far off, if off at all, and the fast-thinking Lester Patrick wasted no time putting this reputation to good use at the box office.

The Vancouver-Victoria game scheduled for New Year's Day, 1921, was billed as the Battle of the World's Greatest Professional versus the World's Greatest Amateur. There was no doubt who Lester had in mind as the World's Greatest Professional, and Taylor, although approaching the age of thirty-seven, was not about to renounce the billing. He didn't at all mind the idea of being tested by this precocious and immensely talented son of Icelandic parentage.

Fredrickson himself had no trouble commenting on the match-up at the time, or, for that matter, fifty-five years later. Having, like Art Duncan, spent the war years as an officer in the Royal Flying Corps and then come back to pick up his sensational amateur career in Winnipeg, he relished the test, and had little doubts as to the outcome. In the engagingly loquacious style of his, he recalled that Victoria meeting: "Sure, I'd heard about Cyclone Taylor and how great he was. There is no doubt at all that he was a great player, but I thought it might be time for him to move over. I wasn't overimpressed by the idea of that first meeting. It wasn't my style to be overimpressed. My idea of hockey was simply to play it as well as I could, and then it was up to the other fellow to do the same. Oh yes, I knew all about Taylor's speed, and he was fast all right. But you know, I wasn't what you might call an extremely slow player."

Victoria won the game 3–1 as the World's Greatest Amateur, now a professional, scored two goals. The World's Greatest Professional was held scoreless, which really didn't bother Taylor too much. He'd been there for a long time. This cocky youth from the prairies had a long way to go to come as far and prove as much.

That Patrick-contrived duel was hardly a test of prime versus prime, but Taylor then and now has no compunction in ticketing Fredrickson for what he was: "Frank was about as fine a player as I've ever seen. He was fast, shifty, smart, and had a wonderful shot." Taylor grinned. "His only problem was that he talked so darned much. It got so bad that Lester finally had a system worked out: He allowed Frank thirty minutes a day to talk. He called him into his office for that half hour and told him to go ahead and get everything off his chest. When the thirty minutes were over, Lester would say, 'Okay, Frank, time's up.' It must have worked, for Frank had some wonderful years with Lester in Victoria."

That he did. One of them was a phenomenal 1923 season in which he scored forty-one goals in thirty games, and another in 1925, when he led Victoria to the Stanley Cup championship with a series total of eight goals and six assists against Georges Vezina and the Canadiens.

Another old-timer who may have looked just a little askance at this harsh but brilliant newcomer to Victoria was that old hand Ernie Johnson, who still patrolled the defense for the Aristocrats after moving through a few other Coast cities. "He seemed to have been around for a hundred years by then," says Taylor, but he really hadn't.

At thirty-five, Johnson, was in fact a year younger than Taylor, but like Joe Hall he had been through a thousand little wars. Still playing fine hockey for the Aristocrats, Lester figured the man deserved a tribute, so he staged a Moose Johnson Night in the Victoria Arena, although Moose almost didn't make it.

A few nights before, he had been badly gashed in a stick fight, and although he was nearly blind with the blood that streamed from the cut over his eye he had insisted on going back onto the ice. He had to be bodily restrained by Patrick and two of the Victoria players.

But there he was before the start of the game at Moose Johnson Night, listening to the tributes, and accepting the gifts. One of the presentations at center ice was made by a couple of little local dandies age nine and five, dressed in smart knee-knickers, with velvet jackets over cream shirts. Their names were Lynn and Frederick Murray—later known as just Muzz—Patrick, sons of Lester. They were still a year or two away from checking into Madison Square Garden as prize rookies with their dad's famous Broadway Blues.

Moose Johnson's Night was to be followed by another season in the Coast League, but there were to be no more for Fred Taylor. The game of March 11, 1921, in Victoria, was his last.

He and Thirza had talked about it before the team took the boat to the island city, and they had agreed that this would be it. "It was an easy decision this time, and there would be no second thoughts."

The Millionaires won that game 11–8. The result was of no meaning to the league standings as the Millionaires had the championship wrapped up. Along the way, playing hurt, Taylor had gotten into just six games and scored two goals.

Now, in his farewell game, just three months short of his thirty-eighth birthday, he went out in style.

He beat Hap Holmes three times with picture goals.

As a last hurrah it was in the mold of another farewell game in another sport twenty-three years later in Boston. There, playing the last game of his magnificent career, a baseball player named George Herman Ruth came out of the Braves' dugout on his aging legs and smote three home runs.

In both cases, the last hurrahs were typical of the men who authored them. They both just naturally generated excitement. It was their way.

After that Victoria finale, Lester Patrick said it simply enough: "Fred has always been a champion. He went out like a champion. I expected nothing less of him.

Chapter Eight
THE TWILIGHT YEARS

It was just a few minutes past 2 A.M. when the towering west wall of the arena collapsed with a deafening roar, barely missing the 15 firemen who had been toiling below. Then the north wall came crashing down, and clouds of dust and flame billowed up from the vast tangle of debris. Sheets of flame now roared up through the adjoining auditorium.

Vancouver Fire Chief, Archie McDiarmid, passed the word to his men to pull out, to give up the fight for the arena and concentrate on containing the conflagration. "My God," he cried, "if this wind picks up, the whole damned West End could go!"

Three firemen had been rushed to hospital with serious injuries. Residents in nearby houses had fled from their burning premises, some overcome with smoke and shock. Only the heroics of one of McDiarmid's men had saved one elderly man from the inferno of his back-room workshop.

The Chief shouted at the crowd to move back, and police constables pushed at the fringe of the mob that jammed Georgia Street. There were already more than a thousand of them there, many clad only in pajamas, nightgowns, and robes, aroused from their sleep by the clamor of the engines rushing to the four-alarm blaze that had started just a little over an hour before. There was a quick scattering as a shower of burning embers and sparks spewed out from a tongue of flame that shot high in the air, casting a lurid glow on the eerie night scene.

In the front row of the crowd that had retreated to a safe distance was Fred Taylor. He was dressed in the dark blue suit he always wore to work at the Immigration Building. This was the early morning of August 21, 1936. Taylor was now fifty-two.

A neighbor had phoned to tell him that the arena was on fire, and he had dressed hurriedly, called a cab, and arrived with the blaze at its peak. There with him were the two youngest Patrick brothers, Guy and Stan. Guy was the arena manager and Stan his assistant. Lester and Frank were both in the East, as yet, of course, unaware of the tragedy.

Now, Taylor and the two Patricks could do nothing but watch as the firemen worked to save the neighboring buildings and prevent a disastrous spread of the fire. Just three hours before the first flames had licked at the building following an explosion in an adjacent Coal Harbor boat shed, a big crowd had sat watched ex-World Heavyweight Champion Max Baer clown through three exhibition bouts, tuning up for a hoped-for return bout with Max Schmeling.

The next night—after the morning of the fire—another big house was expected to watch a wrestling card starring Gus Sonnenberg and Sandor Zsabo, and bookings were heavy right through September and into the next hockey season. After struggling through the early years of the Depression, the Patricks could finally see some prosperous days ahead for the family emporium that still stood as the largest in the West.

Lester's son, Lynn, had come to spend that summer working on the place, painting, cleaning, and sprucing it up for the big fall season. Lynn had just finished his rookie year with his dad's New York Rangers, and with him for the summer's work on the arena was Lester's other strapping son, Muzz, who was scheduled to join the Rangers the following season.

The two brothers had been painting in the basement right up until suppertime, and had then gone to their ring-side seats to watch Baer perform. There, Muzz, who two years ago had been the Canadian Amateur Heavyweight Boxing Champion, took a gentle ribbing from some of the fans for not being up in the ring to try Max on for size. The brothers were in a merry mood, as these were good times again for the Patricks. It was just a few hours later when the first crew left the fire hall.

At the fringe of the crowd that pressed in on the scene, Fred Taylor clutched at Guy Patrick's arm. "It's cruel, Guy," he said. "Just damned cruel." And so it was.

Seven years before, in the autumn of 1929, the Patricks' other arena in Victoria had been destroyed by fire, said to have been the work of a pyromaniac. Now, the second of the historic buildings, insured for only 10 per cent of its value, lay in ruins. The

bold little West Coast Empire built from the dreams of Lester
and Frank and nourished by the hard cash of old Joe Patrick's
timber fortune was no more.

For Taylor and for many of those others who watched with
him until past daybreak, a thousand memories lay buried there
in the charred timbers. Taylor could all but hear the roar of the
arena crowd as he streaked down the boards with the puck, but
the sound was a faint and distant echo.

So much had happened since his last game there.

After his retirement, the three-team Coast League circuit, still
plagued by poor attendance, expanded into the prairies. It took
in teams from Saskatoon, Edmonton, and Calgary, and became
the Western Canada Hockey League. This failed to help, and at
the end of 1926, with only Vancouver drawing well, the league
gave up the struggle. The Patricks sold their Vancouver and Victoria players to the East's National Hockey League for $300,000,
and the rest of the players were claimed in an NHL draft. After
a fifteen-year stay, big league hockey had fled the Coast and returned home.

One prime beneficiary of the big move was that young bull
who had come West from Winnipeg to oust the aging Fred
Taylor as No. 1: Frank Fredrickson. Sent by the Patricks to Boston, where he was offered a fat $4,500 contract, Frank received
some interesting advice from Detroit, who wanted him there. He
was informed that as the western league had been dissolved, his
former owners had no legal right to send him anywhere. He was,
glory be, a free agent. Whereupon Fredrickson promptly signed
with Detroit for $6,000.

It was one of the first major discoveries and uses of a free
agent's bargaining power. The first had been made many years
before by Taylor.

There was a whimsical twist to the Fredrickson caper. The
other players on the Detroit team, almost all of them his old Victoria teammates, were so upset over their own paltry contracts
that averaged less than half of Frank's $6,000, that they refused
to pass him the puck. To solve this quaint dilemma, Fredrickson
was traded back to Boston to join the brilliant new defensive
star, Eddie Shore.

These hijinks were viewed with great interest in Vancouver by

Taylor, who would have dearly loved to be young enough to be in on some of that action. From early conversations with the Patricks, Fred knew that some decision like this sale of the Coast League was in the offing, but when it happened it was still a shock.

Then, a year later and with the newly enlarged ten-team National Hockey League off to a solid start, Fred was at the C.P.R. station to see Lester off to his new job as general manager and coach of the New York Rangers. There in Manhattan Lester replaced Conn Smythe, who returned to his native Toronto to live happily ever after.

Frank Patrick was to have taken over the Detroit club, but something went wrong and Art Duncan got the job. Still, it was thought that Frank, the game's acknowledged inventive genius, was being groomed to succeed Frank Calder as league president, but this too never came about. Later, he would be appointed to a subordinate post as the league's managing director, but this term would be short-lived as Frank Patrick began a melancholy drift out of the game that had been his life.

Fred Taylor? At the time of the big fire, he was already well established in his post as Immigration Commissioner for B.C. and the Yukon, the top man in the West. He was also about to return to hockey in a sparetime capacity as president of the new Pacific Coast League, a top-notch minor organization represented in Vancouver by the Lions.

The destruction of the last of the Patrick landmarks and the site of so many marvelous moments was a severe blow to Taylor, but there had been a greater sadness two years before with the passing of his mother at the age of eighty-eight, ten years after the death of Archie Taylor at seventy-eight.

One of the two most powerful influences on her son's life, Mary Taylor had died at her home in Toronto after a brief illness.

Fred booked a flight East to attend the funeral. He never made it. In that relatively primitive age of commercial flight—it was the winter of 1934—eastbound passages from the Canadian West Coast were routed over long, slow, exhausting hauls across the Northern United States.

Forced to change planes at Salt Lake City, Taylor found himself trapped there by a severe snowstorm that grounded all out-bound traffic. He spent three nights in a downtown hotel and then made the bleak return trip home.

There, Thirza Cook presided over her brood of five, with the oldest, Fred, Jr., now nineteen. Of the three Taylor boys, he and John, a year younger, had taken best to the father's first love, hockey, with John the more proficient of the two. In his father's assessment, John, who learned his hockey down on the arena ice with Frank Patrick's son, Joe, was "a pretty good player who probably could have made it with the Toronto Maple Leafs, at least as a spare . . ."

As it was, he helped the University of Toronto team win two intercollegiate championships before rejecting the advice of the Leafs' Conn Smythe, who thought he should try further. Fred Taylor thought differently. "We—Thirza and I—talked him out of playing professional hockey. I didn't think he had any great future in it, and the rewards then weren't worth giving up study for a law degree."

With another war begun, John Taylor got his law degree in 1940, and was with his dad three years later when the Immigration Commissioner for B.C. and the Yukon turned again to his old trade. In, of all places, Hollywood, California. It was to be Fred's first experience with the latest new breed of hockey players.

One of the clan in that March of 1943 was Toronto's gifted and gregarious goalie, Walter ("Turk") Broda. Broda, an elfin mixture of genius on the ice and irascibility off, was one of the game's reigning characters. With Toronto eliminated from the Stanley Cup play-offs in the opening round, Turk, still a civilian, was free and available for a shot at instant stardom in Tinsel-town, California.

"Mr. Broda," said Fred on the phone from Vancouver, "how would you like to come and play some hockey for me in Holly-wood?"

"Mr. Taylor," said Turk, "you can count me in."

The venture had begun when a letter arrived asking Taylor's help in a Red Cross fund-raising project involving an exhibition hockey series. It was pointed out that the project had the official support of both the National Hockey League and the Canadian

Armed Forces. The support of the latter organization was particularly vital as it had a lot of NHL stars under contract.

The Montreal Canadiens had already agreed to make the trip if they were ousted before the final round of the Stanley Cup play-offs. The Boston Bruins, who would meet the Canadiens in the semifinals, agreed to be the standby club. All that was now needed was a second team, and with Fred Taylor in charge of the entire party, he would "be welcomed in California as Canada's Ambassador of Goodwill."

Fred always was a soft touch for a pitch like that, and besides, the proposition had come to the right man at the right time. He badly needed a break from his onerous Immigration duties here in yet another war time, and between him and young John, now a lieutenant in the Canadian Army Service Corp, they had a line on some pretty good talent.

John was attached to the Army camp in Red Deer, Alberta, which had some very good players on the base team. There were several other good ones at the Navy base over in Victoria. John, appointed as his father's aid in the venture, made an excellent start on recruiting in Red Deer, where a couple of brand new privates had just checked in. These were the renowned Bentley brothers from Delisle, Saskatchewan, Doug and Max. They had just left the Chicago Black Hawks after finishing first and third respectively in the NHL scoring race.

The Bentleys were two of a host of top NHL players who were now in the Armed Forces. Many of them were clustered together at Army and Navy bases to serve the egos of commanding officers playing Walter Mitty with their dreams of running a big league hockey team.

A political row was brewing over this stacking of NHL stars on the home front, and Turk Broda would be an innocent victim. Meanwhile, the Bentley brothers and four others had been more or less browbeaten into leaving the late spring snows of exotic Red Deer for the uncertain wilds of Hollywood. With eight others from Victoria already in the bag, tour manager Taylor had his team.

On April 1, 1943, the squad left the Great Northern platform on the 5:50 P.M. headed South. It wasn't exactly the 1908 special out of Montreal—with the young Cyclone Taylor off with the lads to perform his widely acclaimed role of Little Jeff at the St. Nicks Arena—but there were some similarities. Turk Broda, for instance. There was a lot of Moose Johnson in Turk. Not even the irrepressible Moose could have slipped a case of beer aboard a sleeper with greater elan than had Broda. If Taylor noticed, he didn't let on.

The night before, in Montreal, the Canadiens had been beaten by Boston in the Cup semifinals, and they too were rattling toward California. In charge of the Canadiens was a Taylor acquaintance of the old Coast League days, Dick Irvin, the Montreal coach who was bringing such fine players as Elmer Lach, Toe Blake, and Gordie Drillon.

Upon arrival in Los Angeles, the Taylor party was bussed to team quarters in the Mirimar Hotel, an elegant old spa just off the beach at Santa Monica. The temperature was in the 80s, and when the players arrived, sweating heavily in their service uniforms, they were immediately intrigued by the hotel courtyard scene: a large pool fringed by coconut palms, its patio graced at the moment by a bevy of comely young wenches who were obviously resting between trips to the casting office.

Surveying this vista, Broda, resplendent in shirt sleeves and brightly flushed cheeks, turned to the Army boys, heaved a deep sigh of commiseration, and cried: "Holy Mother! Is this what you guys left Red Deer for?"

Two days later, the Canadiens checked in and the series was on. So was the party. Barring time-outs for the games, the revelry continued unabated for the next two weeks. It was all of a very high-class nature, with the very best of California girls and California Bourbon.

"The beer here," mourned one of the visitors, "is very poor."

The series, split between Hollywood and San Diego, was a huge success, both financially and artistically. Remarkably, and it may be dangerous to draw a moral here, the boys had never played better. As one of the Bentleys explained, "We always play better under pressure."

Manager Taylor, comforted by his aide, Lt. Taylor, who had his bride along, admits to having been "a little upset by all the drinking and carousing," but as the players were there and ready to go for the Red Cross when the puck was dropped, he decided to do nothing more than to occasionally view with alarm. With the exception, that is, of that early morning in a San Diego Hotel when the parties in the adjoining rooms threatened to come through the walls. At that time, he had fled to the reception desk, begged for, and got, a room on another floor.

The actual story of the games was of no important record except to note that they produced a profit of more than $10,000 for the Red Cross and made instant celebrities of the visitors. They were in heavy demand for appearances on network radio shows and at Beverly Hills parties. It was Broda, with his cherubic charm, not to mention his remarkable agility between the pipes, who drew most of the attention.

Among the many invitations to movie stars' homes showered on these spirited men from Mars was one issued to Fred Taylor and three of his uniformed brood one day on Hollywood Boulevard.

As Fred recalls it: "This big roadster pulled up and the driver, a young fellow smoking a pipe, leaned out and said, 'Say, aren't you the boys down here from Canada playing hockey?' Well, one of the boys, I think it was young Riley Mullen of the Navy bunch, spoke right up and said we sure were. I guess Riley recognized him right away. It was that young movie chap that sings. Bing something . . . Crosby, that's it. Anyway, he told us he'd show us around, which he did, and he eventually took us to his home for dinner. He was an awfully pleasant young man."

The ex-scoutmaster and current pillar of the Vancouver Ryerson Church would have been even more impressed had he known that Bing at the time was just about to start work on his classic film, *Going My Way*, in which he portrayed a singing priest engaged in doing good works for the poor kids of the East Side.

There was a somewhat livelier anecdote involving that bon vivant and goalie of note, Turk Broda. It came to light thanks to a U. S. Army Military Police Corporal who was a witness.

Turk's easy facility for making friends took him at one late hour after game time into the company of a similarly gregarious American G.I. They both had the same tastes, and proved it with a stop at a tavern, where a firm alliance was forged. Then, at some point deep in the wee hours, the pair found themselves in Billy Berg's Club, a popular niterie just off the corner of Sunset and Vine.

As it happened, this was a favorite late stop for Hoagy Carmichael, the illustrious composer of such evergreen ballads as "Stardust" and "Up a Lazy River." Hoagy was there that night and in a very mellow mood. At some time along the way he had joined forces at a table with Turk and the G.I. They had apparently gotten along smashingly, for when the M.P. corporal hove to around 3:30 A.M. on his duty rounds, there they were, the three of them, up on the otherwise deserted bandstand. The G.I. was sprawled out fast asleep on a chair in what was probably the saxophone section, nursing a music stand. On the piano bench was Turk, huddled earnestly over the keyboard. Sitting beside him was the distinguished figure of Hoagy Carmichael, frozen in what appeared to be a state of thrall as Turk punched out an uncertain one-fingered rendition of something vaguely reminiscent of "Stardust."

The M.P. swore that Turk got through almost an entire chorus of whatever it was before sliding gently off the stool. That night, in the final game of the tour, won 1–0 by the Canadiens, Turk was sensational. "He never caused me any trouble," says Taylor. "The truth is, I didn't see very much of him. Or the others, for that matter."

Fred spent most of his time sharing a state of mutual resignation with Dick Irvin. Between them, they agreed that as long as nobody got killed, the boys played hockey, and the Red Cross got a little money, that was all that could be expected, what with war-time austerity and all. Turk and the boys couldn't have agreed more.

Taylor and Irvin shared a compartment on the return train trip, but there was little sleep that first night out of Los Angeles. The biggest traveling stag party in Southern California rail history was going on in the sleeper car, and at 2:00 A.M. their compartment door was thrust open and the berth-mates were joined in their cramped quarters by a pair of plump and very distraught pigeons.

"What in heaven's name are these?" cried Taylor as the birds fluttered frantically over his bunk.

"These," said Irvin gravely, with the manner of a man who knows, "are pigeons. In fact, I think they are my pigeons. And they may be ruined."

"Oh," said Taylor.

They scrambled up and out into the corridor, followed by their frantic visitors.

The car was full of flying pigeons and pigeon feathers and whatever else it is that such birds dispense when greatly overexcited. At the far end of the sleeper, Fred Taylor's Armed Forces All-Stars and Dick Irvin's Montreal Canadiens stood surveying the scene with high glee, flushed with the joys of travel.

"They did it!" cried Irvin. "They did it! They swiped my pigeons!"

And so they had.

The happy bird fanciers had raided the baggage car and snaffled the crate of prize pigeons that poor Irvin was taking back home to breed a whole new Ontario dynasty.

The grateful pigeons were then let loose in the sleeping car for a little exercise. Irvin, now in full grim pursuit of the creatures, was getting as much as they were. Most of them were eventually recaptured. The others, hopefully, made it safely back to Los Angeles.

There weren't too many players at breakfast the next morning, and the rest of the ride home was relatively uneventful. For all but Turk Broda. He was going straight on through with the Canadiens to Montreal, where he said he planned to enlist in the Army. He didn't quite make it. To Montreal, that is.

During the Hollywood trip, all hell had broken loose over the matter of the stacking of Armed Forces home-front camps with NHL hockey stars, and the breakup had begun. Ottawa M.P.'s were under pressure to crack down on prominent hockey players who were still in civvies, and shortly after Broda's train pulled out of Toronto, R.C.M.P. officers came aboard and took him in custody, without a warrant. They hauled him right off to a recruiting station, and quicker than Turk could say I was just about to join anyway, he was private Walter Broda of the Canadian Army.

That incident caused another uproar, with Ottawa backbenchers lashing the government for this violation of citizen's rights and using the R.C.M.P. to violate the laws of the land. The way poor Turk had it figured, he should never have left the corner of Sunset and Vine.

He subsequently went overseas and served his country well before coming back to resume his superlative hockey career. Lt. John Taylor, eventually a major, also served overseas, as did Fred Taylor, Jr., as a flying-officer navigator in the R.C.A.F.

Four years and four months after that California adventure and another war—the third in his lifetime—was over, Fred, Sr., was to be seen on a wide green lawn in England, eating strawberries and ice-cream and exchanging pleasantries with Sir Frederick Michael Wells, Kt., the Lord Mayor of London.

Standing next to Fred in their best summer finery, conversing with Her Ladyship was Fred's wife, Thirza, and his daughter, Joan, now a lovely girl of twenty. The postmaster back in Listowel would have been proud.

The local boy was a guest at a Buckingham Palace garden party, and he'd just met the King and Queen. He had been introduced to Their Majesties as Frederick Wellington Taylor, Acting Immigration Commissioner in Europe for Canada, on special assignment at Canada House.

There had been the usual brief and perfunctory exchange, but later on the Queen had come over with the then twenty-one-year-old Princess Elizabeth to chat with Joan about school and university life in Canada.

Being an ardent Loyalist, this was one of the high points in Fred Taylor's life, even though not a soul at this royal bash knew him as Cyclone. But on leaving the royal presence in the usual tradition of exiting backward, he was one up on the rest of the guests. He had no trouble at all with that tricky backward maneuver.

That summer assignment, with the Taylors lodged in a pleasant Kensington hotel, was repeated the following year, as was the garden party invitation. Joan, now the Pacific Coast Figure Skating Champion, gave an exhibition in Wembley Arena. That summer, too, Fred had lunch at Lords Cricket Ground with the famous Australian cricketer, Don Bradman.

It was the summer of the Australia-England Test Matches, the last match of which was hailed in the one huge black, mournful headline in the *Evening Standard:* "England Doomed."

Bradman, already a legendary figure and the game's finest batsmen, was pre-eminent in that British disaster that saw The Ashes returned to Australia. Bradman, soon to be knighted, was and still is one of the most fabled names in British sport. He was to cricket what Babe Ruth was to baseball, and in his time, Cyclone Taylor was to hockey.

Fred had been taken to Lords by a friend, Sir Mathew Wilson, and Bradman joined them for lunch in club rooms of the Marylebone Cricket Club, the mecca of world cricket.

Before lunch, Taylor had watched Bradman at work at the wicket, and he was tremendously impressed with the Australian's masterful and aggressive style and flair. "You couldn't miss him. He had the unmistakable stamp of a fine athlete."

Back again in Canada in 1949 there was an epilogue to those parties at Buckingham Palace when a Royal Warrant arrived, making Taylor a Member of the Order of the British Empire. This, the Empire's highest civilian award, was granted for outstanding service to his country and community as an Immigration officer in two wars.

For Taylor, 1949 was a wonderful year, yet the mounting seasons of a man's life inevitably bring saddening reminders of the past. Such a reminder appeared in a Canadian press wire story that same year, carried under a Vancouver Province heading that said: "Tom Longboat Dies at 61." The brief report told of how tuberculosis had claimed the life of the once-famous marathon runner, simply noting that ". . . the immortal Onandaga Indian athlete, a long-time employee of the City Scavenging Department, passed quietly away yesterday at his home in Toronto . . ." Tom Longboat had died penniless and all but forgotten.

Time, in a different manner, was closing in too on Frederick Wellington Taylor, O.B.E., and a year later he cleaned up his desk at the Immigration Building and walked out into retirement. He had been forty-two years on the job, having traveled a long and scenic road since that 1907 ride to Parliament Hill in Mr. Llewellyn Bate's two-horse rig.

In 1952, feeling restive, he took a fling at politics—in fact two flings. He won one and lost one. He was defeated in his bid for a

Conservative seat in the Federal Government, but was an easy winner in the polling for Parks Commissioner in the Vancouver Municipal Elections.

As a member of the Organizing Committee, he was already involved in the recently established Hockey Hall of Fame, and would be one of the charter members.

There was a trip now with Joan to Los Angeles for a visit at the home of Fred's sister, and for a poignant surprise reunion.

"Joan and I had been invited to watch the shooting of a movie at the Columbia Studios, and as we approached the gate a man in the uniform of a studio guard came up to me, grabbed my hand, and said, 'I heard you were coming, Fred. Do you remember me?' I had to admit that I didn't. He smiled and pumped my hand and said, 'That's all right. Baptie. Norval Baptie. Remember me now?' Of course I did. But it had been an awfully long time. He was in his seventies, and he had changed a lot."

It had been in another century when he had last seen Norval Baptie, the flashy young speed-skating champion who had chased backward after Taylor around the Listowel rink, teaching him the special skill that had helped make one of the best and most exciting of all hockey players.

Fred introduced the Columbia Studios guard to his daughter and then "stayed awhile and had a marvelous chat. It was just wonderful to see him and talk to him again."

Norval Baptie was not on duty when the Taylors finished their studio visit. He later learned that Baptie had left his job soon after, ill with the chronic diabetic condition that over the next four years necessitated the removal of both legs. Still, Baptie, seventy-one when Taylor last saw him, went on to live into his eighty-eighth year.

There was yet another reminder of the passing years just up ahead. A frequent visitor to Vancouver now was Tommy Burns, the aging ex-pugilist Taylor first knew as Noah Brusso on the lacrosse fields of Ontario.

Five years after his savage beating in Australia at the hands of Jack Johnson, Burns had tried a comeback as a promoter with an ill-starred match in Calgary between Arthur Pelkey and Luther McCarthy. Johnson was still champion but was in trouble with the U.S. police and was, at this time, a self-exile in Europe. Burns had billed his fight as for "The White Heavyweight Championship of the World."

As prize-fighting was banned in Calgary, the promotion was staged just outside the town. When McCarthy collapsed and died from a brain hemorrhage after a blow to the jaw in the first round, Burns was on the run and through with boxing for good. After unsuccessfully trying his hand as a London pub-keeper, he turned up as the operator of a speakeasy in New York City. That enterprise also failed.

In a 1952 visit with Taylor, Tommy told of the dramatic new turn in his life, and how it had come about. He had begun suffering terribly from arthritis, a legacy from damage sustained in his fighting days. He was in constant agony, and then, as he related it, "One day I got a feeling that I can't explain, and I simply turned to religion. And here I am."

Here he was in Vancouver, preaching at a small church out on Granville Street. Before that he had been on a pulpit tour of California, had married a fellow-evangilist in the town of Coalinga, and had settled there. The business card that he handed Taylor read: "Compliments of Tommy Burns. Former World Heavyweight Boxing Champion. Demonstrator of Universal Love."

Then a pink-cheeked, kindly-looking, old gentleman of seventy-one with the appearance of an elderly cherub, Burns looked little like anyone's conception of an ex-pug, let alone the survivor of one of the most brutal fights in ring history.

In 1952, nearly a half century after that brawl with Jack Johnson, he said, "It was never meant for a person to try and knock the life out of another being—even an animal. As the scriptures say: 'He that killeth an ox is as if he slew a man.' Had I known in my younger days what I know now, I would never have become a fighter, let alone a world champion."

Three years later, shortly after traveling with Taylor to a Sportsmans' Dinner in Toronto, Burns died in Vancouver of a heart attack. A dozen people were at the funeral, and ten were there in Ocean View Cemetery to see yesterday's hero lowered into an unmarked grave.

But that was not the end of the Noah Brusso-Tommy Burns story.

Taylor had not been in town at the time of Burns' death, and on his return he asked where and how his old friend had been buried. He discovered that Burns' wife had died some time ago, and that Tommy himself was penniless. He had gone literally to a pauper's grave, with money for the funeral provided by anonymous donors. Taylor found this a "sad, sad business. Poor Noah never did seem to find much happiness, except perhaps in the last few years, when he turned in desperation to religion."

Fred found three Vancouver residents who had also known the young Brusso long, long ago, and the four of them went out to visit the grave. "We found it with great difficulty. Just a mound of tangled grass, with no marking. Not even a number. We pledged to start a fund to buy a proper memorial tablet."

A few months later there was another pilgrimage to the grave.

A silent gathering of forty people, all of whom had known Burns, listened to a tribute from the Reverend Arthur Turpin and then viewed the bronze tablet that now marked the resting place of the man that Reverend Turpin had called ". . . the lonely warrior . . ."

The plaque read:

NOAH BRUSSO
(Tommy Burns)
Heavyweight Champion of the World
1906–1908
Born June 17, 1881   Died May 10, 1955
Hanover, Ont.   Vancouver, B.C.

The plaque had been donated by a Burnaby sculpting company, and the $300 that had been raised was turned over to the Canadian Olympic Boxing Team Fund.

These times belonged to another generation, and in 1957 Taylor received some measure of retribution for his own election defeat when son John won a Conservative seat in the John Diefenbaker government. This delighted Fred and greatly pleased Diefenbaker. The two dedicated Conservatives had met for the first time many years before while shopping in Eatons Department Store in Toronto, and had been great friends and mutual admirers since.

It was Diefenbaker who the next year hosted a dinner in the

Parliament Buildings honoring the remaining members of the old Renfrew Millionaires of 1909–10–11. Naturally, Taylor was there, enroute with the others who had been invited back to Renfrew to help celebrate the Centennial of the town made famous a year or two before by M. J. O'Brien and his son, Ambrose. There with Taylor were Herb Jordan, now 73; Bert Lindsay, 77; Newsy Lalonde, 70; Lester Patrick and Fred, both 74. Also at dinner with the Prime Minister was an interloper and old Millionaires adversary, Art Ross. Art, retired after his thirty years at the helm of the Boston Bruins, was 72. Frank Patrick had been too ill to make the trip from Vancouver.

It was a pleasant, sociable dinner, but a bit more decorous than the one that followed down in Renfrew, with the old boys installed at the head table. A host of other special guests included NHL president, Clarence Campbell, and Lester's sons, Lynn and Murray. There too was Fred's son, John, the M.P.

Rising after dessert and pointing to the five survivors of the Renfrew Millionaires, Ross said, "They are still setting records. I've never heard as many lies in my life as I have heard tonight."

Later, there was a heated discussion as to whether Lalonde had scored seven or nine goals one night against Ottawa. Newsy himself, gnarled, bandy-legged, cocky as ever, and wonderfully fit for his years, rose to settle the issue.

"Gentlemen," he said, "I must apologize for these fellows up here. They are all getting a little old and their memories aren't as good as they used to be. The true fact is that I scored nine goals that night against Ottawa." He scratched querulously at his bald pate and frowned. "Or was it ten . . . ?"

When the laughter subsided, all the players took turns reminiscing, and Ross, the only non-member of the Renfrew Old Boys in the special head-table group, again rose to say his piece:

"There was never a team quite like this one. That Lalonde when he knocked you down made damned sure you stayed down. Cyclone Taylor was the most wonderful player who ever lived, and there'll never be another like him."

In his turn, Taylor could find little to say. "The memories come crowding in so many and so fast that I find it impossible to find expression for them. The wonder of it all is in just being able to come back to the old haunts and meet the old friends."

Taylor had barely unpacked back in Vancouver after that marvelous Renfrew reunion when he was off again. This time to the USSR. It was this 1958 jaunt with the Kelowna Packers of the Okanagan League that had produced the warning concerning the rise of a foreign hockey power that would one day challenge the NHL. He had paid his own way be along as a fan and observer as the rambunctious Jack O'Reilly's senior amateurs played five games in Moscow, winning two, tying two, and losing one.

The lightly regarded warning to the fat-and-happy Establishment back home had been particularly emboldened by an eye-opening tour of Moscow's thriving junior development leagues, and a meeting with USSR National Coach, Anatoli Tarasov. Tarasov, the man who had so swiftly brought Soviet hockey from nowhere to a place of power in the world amateur ranks, had learned the game by studying its history and its players. And oh yes, he knew all about Cyclone Taylor.

It was no coincidence that when Fred went back to Moscow fourteen years later he would see some of himself in the style of the Soviet players. Nor was it so strange—even though Taylor couldn't quite get over it—that during that first Moscow trip he had found that old photo of himself in Renfrew strip, hanging in the rotunda of Moscow's Lenin Palace of Sport among a gallery of Soviet hockey stars.

Taylor was both flattered and puzzled. "I don't know where they got that picture, and I wasn't sure whether or not they'd just hurriedly stuck me up there when they heard I was coming, and then took it right down again after I'd left."

He was still curious about this when he returned to Moscow in 1972 with Team Canada, but that part of the rotunda was then closed off for repairs. He never did get to know if he was still up there on the wall with Starshinovs, Alexandrovs, and Kharlamovs.

When he returned to Canada in that late autumn of 1958, Taylor had a long talk with Lester Patrick about what he'd seen in Russia. It was their last conversation together. On June 1, 1960, Lester died in his home in Victoria, of a heart attack. He was seventy-seven. Exactly four weeks later, he was followed by

Frank, seventy-five. His death was also attributed to a heart attack.

The passing of the two brothers who had between them done more than anyone else to chart the course of hockey history was mourned by no one more than their long-time friend, Taylor. The matter of Frank's death so soon after Lester's did not surprise him. "The two were always very close. It's my belief that Frank just simply died of a broken heart."

The tragedy of the Patricks' latter years was that while Lester went into comfortable retirement after his twenty distinguished years as boss of the New York Rangers and vice-president of Madison Square Garden, Frank, who had married and had sent a son to Harvard, was on hard times throughout the last years of his life.

While Lester had gone on to earn his sentimental 1948 farewell party in Madison Square Garden, Frank had been unable to find his place in hockey after the Coast League years. Drifting into seclusion, he had tried to console himself with drink. He lived for a while in a shabby little Vancouver hotel room lit by a naked light bulb, trying to work his way back. He developed a revolutionary new kind of hockey stick that he had high hopes of marketing, but nothing ever came of it. Still, the Patricks had bequeathed innovations enough to the game of hockey, and the major share of them had been the result of the quiet genius of the younger brother, who never did reap his true share of the plaudits.

Three years after the deaths of Lester and Frank, Taylor endured and suffered his greatest personal tragedy since the passing of Mary Taylor nineteen years before. On a gray March day in 1963, Thirza Taylor awoke complaining mildly of chest pains. She died suddenly that evening of a heart seizure.

The death of Thirza in her seventy-seventh year ended the romance that had begun on the ice of the Rideau Canal in the cold, crisp, wonderful Ottawa winter of 1908. It had lasted and thrived through forty-nine years of marriage. It was an idyllic lifetime partnership, and it was over.

Some who watched Fred Taylor grieve throughout the following months thought he might find the loss too much to endure. Others, who knew him better, didn't doubt the strength of the toughness and resilience that had been the hallmark of his turbulent youth.

And in the autumn of 1970, as the National Hockey League came to Vancouver with the birth of the NHL Canucks, in a list of Vancouver NHL "Firsts" recorded in *The Sun* was the item: "First and loudest ovation: for Fred ('Cyclone') Taylor, as he came out to drop the puck in the ceremonial face-off."

For Taylor, then eighty-six, history had come full circle.

What he had helped begin in the 10,500-seat Denman Arena fifty-eight years before was now back for another run in the new 15,500-seat Pacific Coliseum. Thereafter, he would watch the action from his seat in Section W, Row 13, Seat 11. Easily recognizable in natty tan raincoat, or dark blue wool coat, his black Homburg clutched in his lap, he quickly became an arena land-landmark.

In 1971, Newsy Lalonde passed away in Montreal. Fred Taylor was now the lone survivor of the days of Ottawa and Renfrew.

Cyclone Taylor approached his ninetieth year with customary style and grace. The speed that inspired his nickname had ebbed, but he still wore it with easy aplomb.

He was completely bald by now, as he was already becoming back in that violent hockey winter of 1908, playing for the Stanley Cup-bound Ottawa Senators. The hooded eyes that had caused countless goaltenders to quail in baleful close-up were still bright and daring, having no need for spectacles, except for reading. And the frame was still sparse, as it was when it checked into the game at five-eight, 165 pounds, rock solid, and labeled superfast.

He resided alone, continuing a life of crusty independence, but with thirteen grandchildren there was no scarcity of young people around his apartment. Joan's two children, Ben and Kathy, practically made the place a second home. They often came over and stayed for most of the late afternoon after school, talking and watching TV. The trio were more like three friends than two kids and their grandfather.

There were always invitations to various reunions in Listowel, Tara, Ottawa, New York, Boston, and Pittsburgh, and he accepted them all. There was, of course, the return to Moscow with Team Canada, and in the spring of 1974 a memorable skate around the Coliseum rink during an NBC-TV telecast of a game between the Vancouver Canucks and Lynn Patrick's St. Louis Blues.

The TV picture of the ninety-year-old ex-hockey great skating around the boards alongside commentator Brian McFarlane while chatting about how things were in hockey seven decades ago had a tremendous impact on the viewers. Letters poured into NBC-TV from all over Canada and the U.S., commenting on the warmth of the episode. Some of the writers called it the most heart-warming thing they had ever seen on TV. Others just called it "inspiring."

The old master showman hadn't lost his touch.

By the autumn of 1976, grandson Mark, son of Fred, Jr., was off on a hockey scholarship to the University of North Dakota, flashing a touch of his grandfather's old speed and craft with the puck. As to Mark's future in hockey, well, the boy has a very tough act to follow. His grandfather doesn't press him.

In that Autumn, with the Russians and the Czechs gone back home after an exciting Canada Cup Tournament that proved the widening European challenge to the NHL was here to stay, Fred settled down for the NHL season in the Vancouver rink.

Then, in November, Joan Franklin, the youngest and closest of his children, was rushed to hospital seriously ill with a heart weakness thought to be the result of too-stringent dieting during her early days as a champion figure-skater. As soon as he was located and told, Fred rushed to the hospital. By the time he arrived, Joan's heart had already stopped beating. Completely distraught, he just stood there for a long while beside her bed, refusing to be moved.

When he finally returned to his apartment, he walked slowly into the kitchen and put the kettle on. He poured the hot water into a cup, sweetened it with a little sugar, and took it to his armchair in the living room.

He just sat there motionless for a moment, his body racked by a light sob as tears streamed down his face. So many had gone before him. So many. Suddenly, he felt very tired—and very old.

He roused himself, drank the water very slowly, then sank back in the chair to rest.

EPILOGUE

This was the night of the Thirtieth National Hockey League All Star Game, and a sellout crowd of 16,000 had jammed Vancouver's Pacific Coliseum to watch the annual mid-term classic. It was just a few minutes before game time, and the players were cruising briskly around the ice, finishing their warm-up.

The Buffalo Sabres' Gil Perreault came gliding along the boards with those long, smooth strides of his, slowed a little as he went by the penalty box, and smiled at the old gentleman sitting alone there on the bench. Perreault knew the man because they had met at the All Star Dinner the night before. Then, on hand to be honored along with his old friend Frank Fredrickson, Taylor had been taken around the dais to meet the forty All Stars, guided by their guardian and advocate, Al Eagleson.

Fred had shaken hands and chatted a moment with each of them. The great mutual respect was obvious to the diners who sat watching the unusual scene. One of these was the craggy old Maple Leafs warrior, King Clancy, who had come onto the hockey scene just as Taylor had been bowing out. At his table the pixieish Clancy was still chuckling over Fred's remark earlier that day in a Bayshore Inn salon.

Waiting to be fitted for the formal outfit he was to wear as head-table guest, Taylor, genuinely appalled by the high rental prices, shook his head in mock dismay. "I shouldn't have to be here," he groused. "I bought a perfectly good tuxedo just sixty years ago, but I can't find it anywhere."

Now, on this Tuesday evening, he sat at the penalty-box gate, awaiting the call to drop the puck for the ceremonial face-off. He was dandied up for the occasion, attired in his black Homburg and navy blue coat. He was impatient, as always, for the warm glow of the spotlight, but there were sights to relish as he waited.

Hung high across the north end of the arena was a huge sign that read: HAIL CYCLONE—OUR FIRST SUPERSTAR! Across the south end was another banner reading: CYC, WE NEED YOU NOW!

This wasn't exactly the old Denman Arena of so many years ago, with its frenetic hometown fans, but it would do.

And what a month this had been!

It was now barely two weeks since his sentimental return visit to Houghton, Michigan, after an absence of seventy years. That had been a terribly exhausting trip, with the 3,500-mile homeward leg plagued by record cold weather and blizzards that swept the Midwest. The bitter weather had dogged him through his airport changes in Grand Forks, North Dakota, and in Chicago, then held him three days in icy Toronto. Oh, he was dog-tired all right when he finally got back to his Vancouver apartment after a long night haul from Toronto, but that marvelous stay in Houghton had been worth it.

Worth it?

As he watched this big, strong new breed of hockey players roam the rink, he was still marveling at the warmth of his reception in the Michigan copper town where he had once arrived as a twenty-year-old to sign his first pro contract. That, come to think of it, was exactly seventy-two years ago this very month of January, 1977. The friendly Houghton people had invited him back a couple of times before as the last surviving member of the Portage Lake team he had helped lead to two straight International League pennants, but he had been unable to get away.

Then, just before Christmas, they had called again and said, "Cyclone, we want you here to help celebrate our seventy-five years in hockey. You and young Mark. Together."

That had been the clincher.

Mark, Fred, Jr.'s boy, now well into his freshman year on his hockey scholarship, was due in Houghton with the University of North Dakota team for a two-game weekend series against Michigan Tech. It would be a great thrill for Mark, they'd said. It would, Taylor had mused, be an even greater thrill for he himself to be there in Houghton with his eighteen-year-old grandson. Yes, this time he'd go.

Upon arrival in Houghton there it was all over again: the

crowds, the adulation—and the headlines. Right there in the same *Mining Gazette* that had chronicled his exploits nearly three quarters of a century ago: FRED (CYCLONE) TAYLOR ARRIVES TONIGHT: Returns to Home of First U. S. Hockey When Houghton Won World Championship.

There was the airport reception and then the chill ride through the familiar streets to his room in the Douglass Hotel, the same hostel that had been the scene of the banquet staged to celebrate the Portage Lakers' triumphant return from that Pittsburgh series in March of 1907. The building had been gussied up a bit since then, but there it was.

There, too, right across the street, was the saloon where the boys used to go to hoist a couple and shoot a little pool . . . Newsy Lalonde . . . Riley Hern . . . Hod Stuart . . . Bad Joe Hall . . . and the rest. It was as if they were still around, killing a little time before heading for the rink.

Even the old Amphidrome was still there, although the town's college hockey was now played in the smart new arena that had been built close by. This was where Mark was to play the following evening. But first, on the day of the game, there was a lavish luncheon at the hotel, with Mark at the head table with his grandfather. He was plainly impressed, but then what else?

Mark had seen the newspaper stories and the photographs, and he had watched smiling people stop Fred on the street just to say hello and pump his hand and wish him well. He watched them throng around him at the luncheon, and he witnessed the moving moment when Fred spied a familiar face. Changed, but still familiar.

It was that of Carlos Haig, who had not long ago sold his Houghton jewelry store. He had once been a fair amateur goalie, and he used to hang around the rink with Taylor and the Lakers, just hoping for a chance to play a little in the nets. Sometimes, if Riley Hern said it was okay, he got it. He was now ninety-three, a year older than Taylor. They shook hands, but said little. Their memories said it all.

With the honored guest finally seated in the stands following a thunderous greeting from the packed arena, Michigan Tech had beaten North Dakota in that first game, 4–3. Mark, maybe pressing too hard, failed to score. In the return game the next night he was outstanding, with a goal and three assists, but his grandfather was not there to watch. Exhausted after savoring so much of this fleeting return to long ago, he was on his way home.

Then, back in Vancouver, there had come the call to attend the All Star Dinner, and the game. And here he was, all pumped up and ready to go again.

The red carpet had been rolled out to the center ice circle, the Anthems had been sung, and the announcer was intoning Taylor's introduction. Even before his name was called, the applause began and the fans were on their feet with an ovation that lasted throughout his slow walk out and while he stood waiting for the rival centers. Then Bobby Clarke of the Clarence Campbell Team and Guy LaFleur of the Prince of Wales squad crouched over their sticks, and the puck was dropped. The fans were still applauding as Taylor accepted the puck from Clarke and turned back toward the stands.

He walked back through the penalty-box gate and made the long, steep climb up the aisle steps. Upon entering the deserted rotunda, he paused, uncertain and a little confused, remembering that his usual place was occupied for this game by the wife of his son, John. An usher spied him standing there alone and came scurrying up with the arena manager, Mario Caravetta. Caravetta took him gently by the arm and escorted him to his own choice seat up over the red line.

Down on the ice, the puck had been dropped again, this time by the referee, and Fred Taylor settled back to watch.

Clarke had won the draw, and now teammate Rick McLeish had the puck and was flying full speed down the boards as the crowd roared.

Another game had begun.

DATE DUE

T-3009